To the Partner Companies of Vanderbilt's Center
for Services Marketing: AT&T, Northern Telecom,
the Promus Companies, NationsBank,
Union Planters Bank, and Americare Medical Services.

For information about the Center or to get on the mailing list for the AMA Frontiers in Services Conference, please contact:

Roland T. Rust, Director
Center for Services Marketing
Owen Graduate School of Management
401 21st Avenue South
Vanderbilt University
Nashville, TN 37203
Phone: (615) 343-6732
Fax: (615) 343-7177
E-Mail: RUSTRT@VUCTRVAX

SERVICE QUALITY

New Directions in Theory and Practice

editors

Roland T. Rust
Richard L. Oliver

SAGE Publications
International Educational and Professional Publisher
Thousand Oaks   London   New Delhi

For information address:

SAGE Publications, Inc.
2455 Teller Road
Thousand Oaks, California 91320

SAGE Publications Ltd.
6 Bonhill Street
London EC2A 4PU
United Kingdom

SAGE Publications India Pvt. Ltd.
M-32 Market
Greater Kailash I
New Delhi 110 048 India

Printed in the United States of America

Library of Congress Cataloging-in-Publication Data

Main entry under title:

Service quality: new directions in theory and practice/[editors]
 Roland T. Rust, Richard L. Oliver.
  p. cm.
  Includes bibliographical references and index.
  ISBN 0-8039-4919-7 (cloth).—ISBN 0-8039-4920-0 (pbk.)
  1. Customer service—Quality control. 2. Consumer satisfaction.
 I. Rust, Roland T. II. Oliver, Richard L.
 HF5415.5.S468 1994
 658.8'12—dc20   93-31228
                                                                      CIP

94 95 96 97 98   10 9 8 7 6 5 4 3 2 1

Sage Production Editor: Judith L. Hunter

Contents

Preface

Since the late 1970s, there has been a growing realization of the importance of services in the world economy. This realization is reflected in the increasing number of scholarly articles devoted to such topics as customer satisfaction, service quality, customer service, and services marketing and the number of companies that have reemphasized their relationship with the customer. Service quality and customer satisfaction are now seen as integral parts of total quality management.

In the 1980s, a first wave of researchers defined the frontier in service quality. These pioneers included Christian Grönroos of Finland, who established a research agenda for service quality measurement; Len Berry, A. Parasuraman, and Valarie Zeithaml, who devised an influential service quality rating scale; and Lynn Shostack, who argued successfully that managing services was very different from managing products. Steve Brown established the First Interstate Center for Services Marketing at Arizona State, and some important research resulted, led by such people as Terri Swartz, Larry Crosby, and Mary Jo Bitner. Ray Fisk and Steve Grove pioneered the notion that service could be viewed as a drama. These first wave researchers have had an unusually large impact on management, and several are "household names" in the business community.

In the 1990s we are experiencing a second wave in the investigation of service quality. A new generation of researchers, most of whom are highly trained in quantitative methods, psychology, sociology, or anthropology, is establishing new levels of sophistication and rigor, as well as a surprisingly broad set of approaches. This new group includes quantitative modelers such as Ruth Bolton and Jim Drew at GTE; Claes Fornell, Wayne DeSarbo, and Gene Anderson at Michigan; John Hauser and Birger Wernerfelt at MIT; Rick Staelin and Bill Boulding at Duke; Steve Shugan at Florida; and Donna Hoffman at Vanderbilt. The group also includes behavioral researchers such as Morris Holbrook at Columbia, John Deighton at Chicago, Valerie Folkes at USC, and Aaron Ahuvia at Michigan. This second wave is expanding the field of investigation and building upon the efforts of the first wave, which itself continues to make important contributions.

The advent of the second wave in service quality research has been marked by several important events. Vanderbilt University founded its Center for Services Marketing in 1990, with the mission of being "the focal point for cutting edge thought in the management of service quality." Vanderbilt's Owen Graduate School of Management also instituted an innovative curriculum in customer service and service quality.

Vanderbilt's strong ties to both leading academic researchers and the business community created a new opportunity to expand the scope of research in service quality. A TIMS Conference on Service Quality, Customer Satisfaction, and Services Marketing (cosponsored by Vanderbilt's Center for Services Marketing) was held at Vanderbilt in September 1990, and again in March 1992. This conference established a forum for leading thinkers in service quality to trade ideas and quickly attracted some of the leading researchers in marketing academia, along with some of the most advanced researchers in the business community. The conference drew attendees from many nations, from both business and academia. This conference then merged with the AMA's Services Marketing Conference to form the new AMA Frontiers in Services Conference (again cosponsored by Vanderbilt's Center for Services Marketing), first held at Vanderbilt in September 1992. The new conference retained the international flavor of the TIMS conference and its invigorating mix of academics and business people.

This book features many of the second wave researchers who are currently making cutting edge contributions to service quality, as well as some recent work by first wave researchers. The chapters range from measuring the managerial impact of service quality improvement (Bolton), to new methods of measuring the importance of various elements of service quality (DeSarbo), to philosophizing about the nature of customer value

(Holbrook). Many points of view are represented, revealing the great variety of new ideas currently springing up on this topic.

Too many management books, conferences, and seminars get stuck in the same jargon and war stories. This book should prove an exhilarating (if sometimes demanding) change of pace. Both managers and academics should find plenty of stimulating ideas in these pages. We are happy to be part of it.

CHAPTER ONE

Service Quality

Insights and Managerial Implications
From the Frontier

ROLAND T. RUST

RICHARD L. OLIVER

Owen Graduate School of Management, Vanderbilt University

New ideas in service quality currently center on better understanding how the customer is affected by service quality, how a firm implements and measures service quality improvement, and how key trends are likely to affect service quality management in the coming years. Effectively managing service quality requires a clear understanding of what service quality means to the customer. Thus we must understand the nature of customer satisfaction, service quality, and customer value and how these factors interact. Improving the quality of service then requires managing the service product, the service environment, and the service delivery. All of these issues are likely to be affected strongly by several underlying trends, pointing to how business must change in the coming years. We summarize the key issues that should be addressed by managers and by future research.

One of us (Rust) recently gave a lecture to an alumni gathering at Vanderbilt on the topic of Total Quality Management (TQM) and how it was being misapplied (see Kordupleski, Rust, & Zahorik, 1992). The theme was that managers must link internal process quality to the quality perceived by the customer (see also Bolton & Drew, chap. 8, this volume, for an elaboration of these ideas) and that cost reductions through

1

mass layoffs should not be confused with quality improvement, although cost reduction may often be a side benefit of quality improvement. An attendee, a vice president of a major company, objected strenuously, stating that cost reductions through massive layoffs were the true meaning of TQM. He suggested that the professors addressing the gathering should teach their MBA students no more than what companies tell them and that the appropriate role of a professor was to simply be a reporter for the "best practices" of business.

This incident reveals two things: first, that some business people think that academics do not listen to them, and second, that some business people do not want to listen to academics. In this case, the executive's presumption that the professors were ignorant of the business world was wrong. Through the Owen School Center for Services Marketing, we have established close ties to several leading businesses, including AT&T, which has won more Baldrige Awards than any other firm. But the executive was correct in implying that the academic viewpoint and the managerial viewpoint do not meet often enough and that the two worldviews need to be merged for best results.

In this chapter, we seek to merge the academic view with the managerial view. We start from the premise that managers and academics can and should talk to each other. The best academic research has important implications for managers and reveals new insights for managing service quality more effectively. In fact, some of the best academic research is being done by researchers in industry, as may be seen from the sophisticated yet practical chapter by the authors from GTE (Bolton & Drew, chap. 8).

Service quality is by nature a subjective concept, which means that understanding how the customer thinks about service quality is essential to effective management. Three related concepts are crucial to this understanding: customer satisfaction, service quality, and customer value. Managers often treat these concepts as interchangeable, but the latest thinking is that they are quite distinct (cf. Bitner & Hubbert, chap. 3; Cronin & Taylor, 1992; Holbrook, chap. 2; Oliver, 1993; Zeithaml, 1988), which has important implications for management and measurement.

In brief, customer satisfaction is a summary cognitive and affective reaction to a service incident (or sometimes to a long-term service relationship). Satisfaction (or dissatisfaction) results from experiencing a service quality encounter and comparing that encounter with what was expected (Oliver, 1980). Service quality may be measured on an incident-specific or cumulative basis. Value includes not only quality, but also price. A service may be of excellent quality, but still be rated as a poor value if its price is too high. Additionally, value has meaning much beyond the confines of economic analysis (Holbrook, chap. 2). Effective management of service quality requires a working knowledge of these concepts.

Managing service quality involves three distinct aspects: designing the service product, designing the service environment, and delivering the service. Very different methods are appropriate for the three aspects, and all three are addressed thoughtfully in the coming chapters. In particular, the service product is whatever service "features" are offered. It is designed into the service (Neslin, 1983). The service environment is the setting and props required to administer the service (Bitner, 1992). It is also designed into the service. By contrast, the service delivery is how the service is provided on a specific occasion (Bitner, Booms, & Tetreault, 1990).

These distinctions make it clear that service quality measurement must not only differentiate between satisfaction, quality, and value, but it must also involve the service product, service environment, and service delivery. The coming chapters discuss all of these aspects from a wide variety of viewpoints.

In the remainder of this chapter, we attempt to show how the other chapters fit into our framework and also take the opportunity to share some of our own insights. In the next section, we discuss how the customer perceives and reacts to service quality and service satisfaction. In the third section, we discuss the managerial implementation of service quality and how service quality should be measured, and in the final section, gaps in our knowledge and how current trends are likely to affect service quality management in the coming years.

Service Quality: The Customer's Mind

An understanding of the concepts of satisfaction, quality, and value is necessary for managing service quality effectively. These concepts are subjective and occur in the customer's mind, but they also drive customer retention and future choice.

Customer Satisfaction

As noted in Oliver (1993), the word "satisfaction" is derived from the Latin *satis* (enough) and *facere* (to do or make). A related word is "satiation," which loosely means "enough" or "enough to excess." These terms illustrate the point that satisfaction implies a filling or fulfillment. Thus, consumer satisfaction can be viewed as the consumer's fulfillment response.

Recent interpretations in the consumer domain, however, allow for a greater range of response than mere fulfillment (see Oliver, 1989). Fulfillment implies that a satiation level is known, as in the basic needs of water, food, and shelter. Observers of human behavior, however, understand that each of these need levels can be (and frequently is) exceeded in various ways. Thus, consumer researchers have moved away from the *literal* meaning of fulfillment or satisfaction and now pursue this concept as the consumer experiences and describes it.

Oliver's (1989) framework views satisfaction as a state of fulfillment related to reinforcement and arousal. Low arousal fulfillment is described as "satisfaction-as-contentment," which assumes only that the product/service performs satisfactorily in an ongoing, passive sense. One's refrigerator is a good example of this; one is content as long as the food remains at the proper temperature. In contrast, high arousal satisfaction is defined as "satisfaction-as-surprise," which can be positive (e.g., delight) or negative (e.g., shock). "Satisfaction-as-pleasure" results when positive reinforcement occurs, such as when the product/service adds utility or pleasure to a (nonnegative) resting state. Entertainment is one such example. Last, "satisfaction-as-relief" results from "negative reinforcement," or the removal of an aversive state. Pain relievers provide an example of this mechanism.

Thus, these cases describe satisfaction *states* and are not limited to mere satiation. In this sense, overfulfillment can be satisfying, as in exceedingly high arousal (astonishment) and high pleasure (ecstasy) situations. By broadening the old definition of satisfaction as mere fulfillment, service satisfaction can become more meaningful. Unlike product satisfaction, service delivery can be tailored to greatly exceed expectations on both the surprise and pleasure dimensions.

Satisfaction can also be described as a *process.* Currently, the most widely adopted of the process theories is that of "expectancy disconfirmation," in which satisfaction is viewed as largely based on meeting or exceeding expectations (Erevelles & Leavitt, 1992; Oliver, 1977, 1980, 1981; Oliver & DeSarbo, 1988; Tse, Nicosia, & Wilton, 1990; Yi, 1990).

The operation of expectancy disconfirmation in influencing satisfaction is generally seen as two processes, consisting of forming expectations based on external (Steenkamp & Hoffman, chap. 4) or internal (Folkes, chap. 5; Oliver & Winer, 1987) cues, and a subsequent "disconfirmation" judgment, or comparison of those expectations against the outcome (DeSarbo, Huff, Rolandelli, & Choi, chap. 9; Oliver, 1980; Oliver & DeSarbo, 1988). Sometimes this comparison may be actually calculated, especially in early stages of the process; later stages may be interpreted more subjectively (Oliver & Bearden, 1985; Swan & Trawick, 1981). For example, consumers may calculate their automobile gas mileage and then feel that the resulting number of miles per gallon is much worse (or better) than expected. This latter subjective comparison is thought to be a prime determinant of satisfaction or dissatisfaction.

Research has shown that this paradigm is fairly robust across various contexts, including product experience; interpersonal dealings with, for example, salespeople (Oliver & Swan, 1989); and many services, including restaurant dining (Cadotte, Woodruff, & Jenkins, 1987; Swan & Trawick, 1981), health care (Oliver, 1980; Oliver & Bearden, 1985), security transactions (Oliver & DeSarbo, 1988), and telephone service (Bolton & Drew, 1991). Although subjective disconfirmation frequently emerges as the key determinant of customer satisfaction, direct effects of outcomes and expectations are also frequently observed and help explain satisfaction (Adelman, Ahuvia, & Goodwin, chap. 7; Bolton & Drew, chap. 8; Churchill & Surprenant, 1982; Deighton, chap. 6; Oliver, 1980; Oliver & DeSarbo, 1988; Tse & Wilton, 1988).

Service Quality

In response to a perceived dissimilarity between product and service quality, Parasuraman, Zeithaml, and Berry (1985, 1988; Zeithaml, Parasuraman, & Berry, 1990) created a measure of service quality (SERVQUAL) from data on a number of services. Rather than rely on previous dimensions of goods quality, they began their work with qualitative research, which suggested 10 dimensions of service quality. Later empirical verification reduced the 10 dimensions to 5 (tangibles, reliability, responsiveness, assurance, and empathy).

In their approach, the authors propose that customers entertain expectations of performance on the service dimensions, observe performance, and later form performance perceptions. These two key concepts are then compared through difference scores or "gaps." By examining the wording of the expectations and perceptions scales, the thrust of the SERVQUAL instrument becomes more evident, as does the meaning of service quality. The expectations section of the survey is constructed with reference to an ideal company that delivers *excellent* quality of service. As such, the instrument is framed within the concept of *ideal expectations* (Miller, 1977). Thus, the SERVQUAL instrument illustrates the core of what service quality may mean, namely a *comparison to excellence* in service *by the customer.*

Oliver (1993) notes some distinctions between the meanings of quality and satisfaction. First, he points out that the dimensions underlying quality judgments are rather specific, whether they be cues or attributes (Bolton & Drew, chap. 8; Steenkamp, 1990). Satisfaction judgments, however, can result from any dimension, quality related or not. For example, a high-quality dining experience might include a congenial waitperson, exotic entrees, and a varied wine list. However, (dis)satisfaction could be influenced by parking problems, an inordinately long wait, and an inoperative credit card telesystem—none of which are under the control of the restaurateur and thus would not be considered as "quality" dimensions. Similarly, expectations for quality are based on ideals or "excellence" perceptions, whereas a large number of nonquality issues, including needs (Westbrook & Reilly, 1983) and equity, or "fairness" perceptions (Oliver & Swan, 1989), help form satisfaction judgments (see also Folkes, chap. 5). Further, quality perceptions do not require experience with the service or provider. Many establishments (e.g., five-star restaurants) are perceived as high quality by consumers who have never visited them. Satisfaction, in contrast, is purely experiential. Finally, quality has fewer conceptual antecedents, although personal and impersonal communications play a major role (Zeithaml, Berry, & Parasuraman, 1993). Satisfaction, however, is known to be influenced by a number of cognitive and affective processes including equity, attribution, and emotion.

The perspective to be taken here is that, as found in Cronin and Taylor (1992), satisfaction is superordinate to quality—that quality is one of the service dimensions factored into the consumer's satisfaction judgment. Subsequent to this effect, satisfaction may *reinforce* quality perceptions, but only indirectly (cf. Bitner & Hubbert, chap. 3). Quality is hypothesized as one dimension on which satisfaction is based and satisfaction is one potential influence on future quality perceptions. If one can conceptualize occasions where satisfaction and quality are at variance (satisfaction with low quality, dissatisfaction with high quality), then the concepts are not the same.

Satisfaction with low quality can exist whenever one's expectations in a given situation are low and performance is adequate to the task. Emergency situations fit this scenario well. It matters little if a mechanic uses duct tape to fix a broken-down car if that makes the car operational.

Similarly, dissatisfaction with high quality can ensue when some element of the service delivery is not up to personal expectations. An individual's experience at a high-quality restaurant, for example, might be unsatisfactory on a given occasion because this person's favorite waitperson is unavailable. The quality perception, however, might remain high despite this dissatisfying (to the particular customer) experience.

Thus, we view service quality as affecting service satisfaction at the encounter-specific level. Later, separate encounter experiences can be aggregated into overall perceptions of quality (and satisfaction, Bitner & Hubbert, chap. 3). As can be seen, the aggregation level plays a critical role in researching and understanding the meaning of these two concepts (Anderson & Fornell, chap. 11).

Value

Ultimately it is perceived value (Holbrook, chap. 2) that attracts a customer or lures a customer away from a competitor. In this sense, perceived value and satisfaction vie for attention in managerial strategy. And like both quality and satisfaction, value can be encounter specific or a more enduring global perception. Value may be conceptualized as arising from both quality and price or from what one gets and what one gives (Zeithaml, 1988). Value increases as quality increases and as price decreases. Yet exactly how quality and price combine to form value is not well understood.

Holbrook (chap. 2) discusses customer value in very broad terms. He views value as a personal preference, assumed to be essentially subjective, but susceptible to being altered by objective changes. In other words, individuals' views of value are quite different. Although Holbrook sees quality as a type of value, most managers and economic theorists would instead say that value depends on both quality and price. That is, a movie ticket to see *Aladdin* may be a good value to John Doe at $5.50, but a poor value at $100 (e.g., Garvin, 1984). The managers and economists would argue that the quality of the movie does not change, but the value changes considerably. Holbrook would argue that both quality and value decline.

If we adopt the dual-component approach to value, namely that value is some combination of what is received and what is sacrificed, concepts from finance and economics may help us understand how customers form value from quality and price. As Holbrook points out, value is a preference, and thus value should be defined and calculated in such a way that choice and retention are explained, because choice and retention result directly from preference. Finance theorists might contend that customers would choose from among alternative service providers based on return on investment. That is, the customer makes an investment (price) and experiences an outcome (quality). It can be shown easily that a customer who maximizes the quality-to-price ratio (efficiency) also maximizes the return on investment (Danaher & Rust, 1992). This is consistent with what even the consumer psychologist Holbrook refers to as the efficiency type of value. It is also common in economics to assume that consumers seek to maximize the ratio of quality to price.

An alternative viewpoint, and in our view a more reasonable one, results from the economic assumption that a customer maximizes utility. The economic assumption of utility is very well developed and functions as the basis of most of modern microeconomic theory. In this view, customers derive utility from quality, but suffer disutility from price. Figures 1.1 and 1.2 show typical utility curves that might arise from quality and price. The customer then chooses the service alternative that maximizes the utility from quality, minus the disutility from price. This assumption of utility maximization is central to standard microeconomic theory (Lancaster, 1968).

Note that these utility curves are likely to take on predictable shapes. For example, the utility gained from increasing quality shows diminishing returns. For example, if phone service were available 99.9% of the time, the customer might be reasonably satisfied. If great additional quality improvement increased this to 99.99% of the time, the customer might not even notice. The utility increase would be minimal, even though a startling increase in quality had been implemented.

Likewise, quality must reach a certain threshold before utility begins to grow very much. For example, suppose a car started half the time. That would be almost as bad as having no car. The car would have to increase quality to the point where it started a high percentage of the time before utility would reflect that a reliable car was available (Oliva, Oliver, & MacMillan, 1992).

Also the disutility from increasing price increases at an increasing rate. This is because our available money eventually runs out. This curve will be very different for different people. For example, the average person's disutility to price curve for an *Aladdin* movie ticket is likely to be much steeper than Donald Trump's, because the average person's money would run out more quickly. Ultimately, the disutility curve spikes to infinity as a prohibitive "price threshold" is attained.

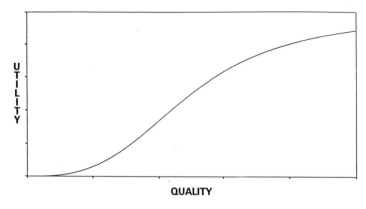

Figure 1.1. Quality and Utility

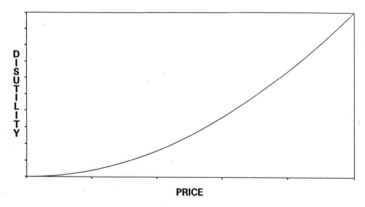

Figure 1.2. Price and Disutility

Let us consider now when it is that these two conceptualizations would yield different results. One scenario is obvious. If Donald Trump and John Doe perceive the quality of an *Aladdin* movie ticket to be the same, then it will have higher value to Donald Trump, even at the same price. Suppose, for example, that *Aladdin* is showing for $100 a ticket, whereas *Dracula* is showing next door for $5. Suppose that both Donald Trump and John Doe agree that *Aladdin* is likely to be twice as good a movie. By the criteria of return on investment and efficiency, both individuals would choose to attend *Dracula*. However, once we realize that the disutility of the $100 price is negligible to Donald Trump (but not to John Doe), we quickly realize that Donald Trump is likely to attend *Aladdin,* whereas John Doe is likely to attend *Dracula.*

For another example, suppose John Doe is buying a car. He is trying to choose between a new Honda and a used Yugo. He knows from reading consumer magazines that the Honda is likely to be about 100 times better. But suppose the Honda costs $15,000, whereas the Yugo is free. According to the quality/price ratio, he will choose the Yugo, because it provides infinite value. Yet the utility gained from the increase in quality (of the Honda over the Yugo) is likely to swamp the disutility of the price disutility, assuming he can afford the $15,000 price tag.

Interestingly, neither the literature nor the present discussion addresses the relationship between value and satisfaction. In a purely speculative sense, we would argue that value, like quality, is an encounter-specific input to satisfaction. Certainly, one can be satisfied with the value received in a service experience. At the aggregate level, we are not so sure, as one can conceive of situations where satisfaction is value (as in a cherished goal) or adds value to a complex service experience (Anderson & Fornell, chap. 11; Bitner & Hubbert, chap. 3; Deighton, chap. 6; Holbrook, chap. 2). Work is needed on this issue.

Summary

We conclude that perceived service quality is a subjective matter, and that service *encounter* satisfaction results from perceived quality, value, performance on nonquality dimensions, relevant prior expectations, and the disconfirmation of those relevant expectations. Value is formed from perceived quality in combination with price. We argue that value is equal to the utility of quality minus the disutility of price and that the relationships of quality and price to utility are likely to be nonlinear and to vary across individuals. Summary judgments of quality, value, and satisfaction follow the same pattern after repeated service exposures.

Service Quality: Managerial Implementation

In this section, we consider the three main elements of service quality that may be targeted for improvement efforts and discuss how to measure and monitor the quality improvement process. Figure 1.3 shows these key elements of service quality. At the center of the diagram is the core product, which may be present (in product industries) or absent (in pure

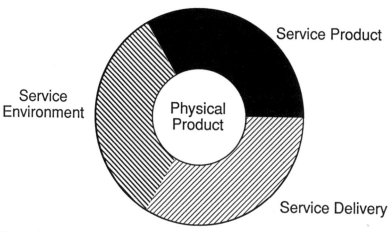

Figure 1.3. Components of Quality

service industries). Whether or not we are talking about a service industry application or a product industry application, the three elements of service quality are always present. They are the service product, the service environment, and the service delivery. Note that we conceptualize all business transactions and relationships as services, which may or may not involve a physical product (see Adelman et al., chap. 7; Deighton, chap. 6).

The Service Product

The service product is the service as it is designed to be delivered. Often this involves specific features. For example, a term insurance policy with an associated payoff and annual premium payment is a service product. The service product also involves service specifications and targets. For example, a bank may set a specification that any customer will wait in line for no more than 5 minutes. The bank may or may not actually accomplish this level of service, but it is a goal that shapes the service offering.

The key managerial decision in the service product is identification of relevant features or specifications to offer. Because of this, designing the service product is somewhat different conceptually from designing the core physical product. Conventional techniques such as conjoint analysis (Green & Rao, 1971; Neslin, 1983) may be applied to this problem in a standard way. DeSarbo et al. (see chap. 9) extend this idea by designing the intended service delivery through an emphasis on aspects of service delivery that conjoint experiments have shown to be most important. Additionally Adelman et al. (chap. 7) and Shugan (chap. 10) identify trends that provide qualitative input to this process, and Bitner & Hubbert (chap. 3) demonstrate use of the critical incidents technique toward this same goal.

Another method that has been applied widely is quality function deployment (QFD) (Hauser & Clausing, 1988). That method is used to show how varying product (or service) attribute combinations affect customer perceptions. It must be emphasized that QFD, like conjoint analysis, is best suited to the design phase. That is, deciding how to design a new service product can make extensive use of these traditional product methods, but it is not so clear how they can be used effectively with existing customers to determine what aspects of an ongoing service require improvement.

The Service Environment

The service environment includes numerous dimensions that can be classified into two main themes, that of the internal environment (the service provider) and that of the external environment. Literature on the internal environment has primarily focused on organizational culture and the overriding philosophy brought to service provision by management. The external theme focuses primarily on the physical ambience of the service setting.

The Internal Environment. Steps to assess the prevailing internal environment are best determined by conducting a services marketing audit (Berry, Conant, & Parasuraman, 1991; Webster, 1992). Berry et al. provide a comprehensive list of dimensions and subdimensions to be explored within the firm to ensure that the internal environment is structured to provide quality service. The major dimensions are the firm's marketing orientation; its service organization; new customer generation; current customer retention; and internal marketing, including employee support and reward systems. Webster provides specific methodological strategies with the goal of facilitating this process, whereas Adelman et al. (chap. 7) illustrate the use of conceptual logic in a growing service industry. Generally, inattention to any of these key areas will hamper the service quality delivery process.

The External Environment. Bitner (1992) recently summarized current knowledge regarding the effect of "atmospherics" on customer *and* employee beliefs, attitudes, and performance. According to her thesis, a number of environmental dimensions, including ambience, space and function, and symbolic elements, combine to form a holistic environment or "servicescape." This has obvious effects on the approach-avoidance and interactive dispositions of employee and customer. Ward, Bitner, and Barnes (1992) illustrate with specific examples a methodology for measuring the relevant imagery consumers perceive in service environments. Mangold and Babakus (1991) discuss employee perceptions and how they differ from customer perceptions. This is a critical dimension of service delivery that management should not ignore.

Service Delivery

The service delivery process can be likened to role performances or scripts (Solomon, Surprenant, Czepiel, & Gutman, 1985). Consumers are thought to possess expected sequences of events and provider role expectations within most service encounters (Folkes, chap. 5; Steenkamp & Hoffman, chap. 4). Research into service "performances" (Deighton, chap. 6; Goodwin & Verhage, 1989; Kelley, Donnelly, & Skinner, 1990) shows that violations of these expectations or the nature of the expectation itself can facilitate or impede critical postencounter behaviors such as repatronage and complaining. In fact, Deighton (chap. 6) discusses situations where consumers may respond favorably to script violations and Kelley et al. (1990) discuss situations where the firm may wish to change expectations so that violations are less (or more) likely to occur. This paradox of effects suggests that management needs to study carefully the service delivery process so that role performance expectations of customers (and employees) can be monitored.

Future Directions

Managing service quality more effectively in the future requires developing a better understanding of how service quality works and capitalizing on some fundamental, underlying trends that will create new areas of emphasis. This translates into establishing a research agenda for service quality research (Anderson & Fornell, chap. 11; Bolton & Drew, chap. 8) and recognizing the key trends that will change management (see Shugan, chap. 10).

Research Needs

Conceptual Interrelationships. Perhaps the most intriguing issue facing service marketers today is the interplay between quality, satisfaction, and value. Specifically, which are antecedent, which are mediating, and which are consequent? To date, no definitive answer exists. Literature on the relation between quality and satisfaction is equivocal. Bitner (1990) and Bolton and Drew (1991) provide conceptual arguments for satisfaction as antecedent to quality. Oliver (1993), in contrast, argues that this may occur only if quality is viewed in a global, enduring sense much as one would conceptualize attitude. He provides an encounter-specific model in which quality feature performance is shown to be one input to the encounter-specific satisfaction judgment (see also Bitner & Hubbert, chap. 3). Cronin and Taylor (1992) have recently presented empirical evidence that this quality-causes-satisfaction sequence may be more defensible.

Regarding quality and value, Zeithaml (1988) presents a conceptual model where quality is antecedent to value. This argument stems from the various meanings of value to the consumer. If one views value as the utility sought by the consumer, Zeithaml argues that value exists at a higher order of abstraction and is therefore a superordinate concept to quality. Similarly, if value is perceived as utility (or quality) per dollar (e.g., Hauser & Urban, 1986), value again emerges as a consequent variable. This is consistent with Holbrook's (chap. 2) view that quality is one of the subordinate concepts underlying value. Regarding satisfaction, the role of value vis-à-vis satisfaction appears not to have been addressed in the literature, however, and further work on this relation is clearly needed.

Thus, research is needed on the causal mechanism that relates these three concepts. If satisfaction is viewed as a summary cognitive and affective response to all elements of the transaction as suggested here, this conceptual arrangement must be tested so that management can focus less on immediate judgments of value or quality and focus more on the manner in which value and quality affect satisfaction. Clarification is needed on this issue.

Anderson and Fornell (chap. 11) detail causal and methodological research agendas at three levels of abstraction. In addition to the individual level, which we have discussed at some length, these authors explore analogous relations at the microeconomic (i.e., firm) and macroeconomic (i.e., societal) levels (see Shugan, chap. 10). Critical issues such as aggregation bias and conceptual divergence are addressed as they pertain to the effect of, for example, customer satisfaction on firm revenues and profits and on social welfare. These issues have been largely overlooked and are ripe for analysis.

Components of Quality. Regarding our three components of quality in Figure 1.3, research on the joint contribution of service product, environment, and delivery to service satisfaction requires much additional research. Presently, each of these three contributors to judgments of service provision appear in separate research streams. Although this is a reasonable approach for early stages of a research agenda, the knowledge generated by each program can only be viewed ceteris paribus. Ultimately, management will have to undertake analysis to determine how these service facets *jointly* affect satisfaction, how they interact, and how their relative influences change as the service script unfolds. DeSarbo et al. (chap. 9) provide an interesting methodology in this regard.

Managerial Opportunities

There are several key trends that will have a strong impact on service quality management. These are discussed in considerable detail by Shugan in Chapter 10. Here we briefly list the trends and then consider their impact in more detail.

First, the advanced economies are all moving toward service economies. The result is that all companies, whether service companies or product companies, must reconceptualize their business as being a service and expect their growth to be in the service-oriented aspects of the business. This means increased attention to the service product, the service environment, and service delivery.

Second, there are an increasing number of women in the work force. This means that service products should increasingly emphasize convenience and speed, especially those service products that substitute for women's work in the home. It also means that business-to-business service delivery needs to be sensitive to women. The old locker room style will no longer be acceptable in many industries.

Third, the population of the United States is aging. This means that there should be an increasing emphasis in the U.S. market on service products that cater to older people. Also, the service environment will have to become easier to use: easier for people who don't walk well, can't see well, and can't hear well. Service delivery will have to become more tolerant of slower, less active customers. At the same time, social skills will become increasingly important, because older people demand more social value out of their business transactions.

A fourth key trend is specialization. As Shugan points out, this involves the unbundling of services to permit specialized companies to accept out-sourced business. The result of this trend on the service product is that companies will have to become increasingly focused—specializing in one narrow service that they do better than anyone else. It also means that the typical company should shed the parts of the business in which it lacks a differential advantage. The service environment will likewise need to become more specialized—customized to be maximally comfortable, efficient, and easy to use for one particular market niche.

The fifth key trend is service export growth. This works in two ways. Some countries will have a natural advantage in supplying (and exporting) certain services, and the other countries will then benefit by importing those services rather than performing them domestically. In general, the key determinants of whether a country should be an importer or exporter of a service are costs, technological climate, and the educational level of the work force. Usually the low-cost countries also have a poor technological climate and low educational level. In that scenario, the most advanced services, those that pay the highest wages and provide the most interesting and challenging jobs, will gravitate to the most technologically advanced countries. The least advanced services (e.g., most manufacturing) will gravitate to the poorer countries. This indicates that manufacturing companies in advanced countries either need to move most of their operations to a cheaper country or they need to greatly build up the service component of their offering. Often, building up the service component implies building up the information component of the service, because the move toward a service economy goes hand in hand with the move toward an information economy.

Summary

Service quality is increasingly important, because service is increasingly important. This is true in both the product sector and the service sector. Researchers have made great progress in the last 15 years, disentangling the concepts of service quality, customer satisfaction, and to a lesser extent, customer value. The results of this work have been put to practical use in designing and monitoring services (see, for example, Bolton & Drew, chap. 8; DeSarbo et al., chap. 9). Further work on service quality and its impact on business performance is needed, especially efforts to implement these ideas in practical settings. For many years it was an embarrassing truth that academia was lagging the quality revolution and that all novel ideas came from industry. In the last 10 years, academia has caught up. It is now the case that the most sophisticated business people pay attention to what is happening on the frontier of service quality research. This gives them a competitive advantage on the basis of knowledge and information, a basis on which companies of the future will need to excel in order to survive.

References

Berry, L. L., Conant, J. S., & Parasuraman, A. (1991). A framework for conducting a services marketing audit. *Journal of the Academy of Marketing Science, 19*, 255-268.

Bitner, M. J. (1990). Evaluating service encounters: The effects of physical surroundings and employee responses. *Journal of Marketing, 54*, 69-82.

Bitner, M. J. (1992). Servicescapes: The impact of physical surroundings on customer and employees. *Journal of Marketing, 56*, 57-71.

Bitner, M. J., Booms, B. H., & Tetreault, M. S. (1990). The service encounter: Diagnosing favorable and unfavorable incidents. *Journal of Marketing, 54*, 71-84.

Bolton, R. N., & Drew, J. H. (1991). A multistage model of customers' assessments of service quality and value. *Journal of Consumer Research, 17*, 375-384.

Cadotte, E. R., Woodruff, R. B., & Jenkins, R. L. (1987). Expectations and norms in models of consumer satisfaction. *Journal of Marketing Research, 24*, 305-314.

Churchill, G. A., Jr., & Surprenant, C. (1982). An investigation into the determinants of customer satisfaction. *Journal of Marketing Research, 19*, 491-504.

Cronin, J. J., Jr., & Taylor, S. A. (1992). Measuring service quality: A reexamination and extension. *Journal of Marketing, 56*, 55-68.

Danaher, P. J., & Rust, R. T. (1992). *Determining the optimal level of media spending.* Working paper, Vanderbilt University.

Erevelles, S., & Leavitt, C. (1992). A comparison of current models of consumer satisfaction/dissatisfaction. *Journal of Consumer Satisfaction, Dissatisfaction and Complaining Behavior, 5*, 104-114.

Garvin, D. A. (1984). What does "product quality" really mean? *Sloan Management Review, 26*, 25-43.

Goodwin, C., & Verhage, B. J. (1989). Role perceptions of services: A cross-cultural comparison with behavioral implications. *Journal of Economic Psychology, 10*, 543-558.

Green, P. E., & Rao, V. R. (1971). Conjoint measurement for quantifying judgmental data. *Journal of Marketing Research, 8*, 355-363.

Hauser, J. R., & Clausing, D. (1988). The house of quality. *Harvard Business Review, 66*, 63-73.

Hauser, J. R., & Urban, G. L. (1986). The value priority hypotheses for consumer budget plans. *Journal of Consumer Research, 12,* 446-462.

Kelley, S. W., Donnelly, J. H., Jr., & Skinner, S. J. (1990). Customer participation in service production and delivery. *Journal of Retailing, 66,* 315-335.

Kordupleski, R. E., Rust, R. T., & Zahorik, A. J. (1992). *Why improving quality doesn't improve quality.* Working paper, Vanderbilt University.

Lancaster, K. (1968). *Mathematical economics.* New York: Dover.

Mangold, W. G., & Babakus, E. (1991). Service quality: The front-stage vs. the back-stage perspective. *Journal of Services Marketing, 5,* 59-70.

Miller, J. A. (1977). Studying satisfaction, modifying models, eliciting expectations, posing problems, and making meaningful measurements. In H. K. Hunt (Ed.), *Conceptualization and measurement of consumer satisfaction and dissatisfaction* (pp. 72-91). Cambridge, MA: Marketing Science Institute.

Neslin, S. A. (1983). Designing new outpatient health services: Linking service features to subjective consumer perceptions. *Journal of Health Care Marketing, 3,* 8-21.

Oliva, T. A., Oliver, R. L., & MacMillan, I. C. (1992). A catastrophe model for developing service satisfaction strategies. *Journal of Marketing, 56,* 83-95.

Oliver, R. L. (1977). Effect of expectation and disconfirmation on postexposure product evaluations: An alternative interpretation. *Journal of Applied Psychology, 62,* 480-486.

Oliver, R. L. (1980). A cognitive model of the antecedents and consequences of satisfaction decisions. *Journal of Marketing Research, 17,* 460-469.

Oliver, R. L. (1981). Measurement and evaluation of satisfaction processes in retail settings. *Journal of Retailing, 57,* 25-48.

Oliver, R. L. (1989). Processing of the satisfaction response in consumption: A suggested framework and research propositions. *Journal of Consumer Satisfaction, Dissatisfaction and Complaining Behavior, 2,* 1-16.

Oliver, R. L. (1993). A conceptual model of service quality and service satisfaction: Compatible goals, different concepts. In T. A. Swartz, D. E. Bowen, & S. W. Brown (Eds.), *Advances in services marketing and management: Research and practice,* (Vol. 2, pp. 65-85). Greenwich, CT: JAI.

Oliver, R. L., & Bearden, W. O. (1985). Disconfirmation processes and consumer evaluations in product usage. *Journal of Business Research, 13,* 235-246.

Oliver, R. L., & DeSarbo, W. S. (1988). Response determinants in satisfaction judgments. *Journal of Consumer Research, 14,* 495-507.

Oliver, R. L., & Swan, J. E. (1989). Equity and disconfirmation perceptions as influences on merchant and product satisfaction. *Journal of Consumer Research, 16,* 372-383.

Oliver, R.L., & Winer, R.S. (1987). A framework for the formation and structure of consumer expectations: Review and propositions. *Journal of Economic Psychology, 8,* 469-499.

Parasuraman, A., Zeithaml, V. A., & Berry, L. L. (1985). A conceptual model of service quality and implications for future research. *Journal of Marketing, 49,* 41-50.

Parasuraman, A., Zeithaml, V. A., & Berry, L. L. (1988). SERVQUAL: A multiple item scale for measuring customer perceptions of service quality. *Journal of Retailing, 64,* 12-40.

Solomon, M. R., Surprenant, C., Czepiel, J. A., & Gutman, E. G. (1985). A role theory perspective on dyadic interactions: The service encounter. *Journal of Marketing, 49,* 99-111.

Steenkamp, J.B.E.M. (1990). Conceptual model of the quality perception process. *Journal of Business Research, 21,* 309-333.

Swan, J. E., & Trawick, I. F. (1981). Disconfirmation of expectations and satisfaction with a retail service. *Journal of Retailing, 57,* 49-67.

Tse, D. K., Nicosia, F. M., & Wilton, P. C. (1990). Consumer satisfaction as a process. *Psychology & Marketing, 7,* 177-193.

Tse, D. K., & Wilton, P. C. (1988). Models of consumer satisfaction formation: An extension. *Journal of Marketing Research, 25,* 204-212.

Ward, J. C., Bitner, M. J., & Barnes, J. (1992). Measuring the prototypicality and meaning of retail environments. *Journal of Retailing, 68,* 194-220.

Webster, C. (1992). What kind of marketing culture exists in your service firm? An audit. *Journal of Services Marketing, 6,* 54-67.

Westbrook, R. A., & Reilly, M. D. (1983). Value-percept disparity: An alternative to the disconfirmation of expectations theory of consumer satisfaction. In R. P. Bagozzi & A. M. Tybout (Eds.), *Advances in Consumer Research* (Vol. 10, pp. 256-261). Ann Arbor, MI: Association for Consumer Research.

Yi, Y. (1990). A critical review of consumer satisfaction. In V. A. Zeithaml (Ed.), *Review of Marketing 1990* (pp. 68-123). Chicago: American Marketing Association.

Zeithaml, V. A. (1988). Consumer perceptions of price, quality, and value: A means-end model and synthesis of evidence, *Journal of Marketing, 52,* 2-22.

Zeithaml, V. A., Berry, L. L., & Parasuraman, A. (1993). The nature and determinants of customer expectations of service. *Journal of the Academy of Marketing Science, 21,* 1-12.

Zeithaml, V. A., Parasuraman, A., & Berry, L. L. (1990). *Delivering quality service: Balancing customer perceptions and expectations.* New York: Free Press.

CHAPTER TWO

The Nature of Customer Value

An Axiology of Services in the Consumption Experience

MORRIS B. HOLBROOK

Graduate School of Business, Columbia University

This chapter focuses on the neglected role of value in consumer behavior and service provision. Toward that end, it views all products as performing services that potentially provide value-creating consumption experiences. Drawing on work in axiology, it defines value as an interactive relativistic preference experience and suggests a taxonomy that distinguishes among eight key types of customer value. It concludes with some suggestions about fruitful directions for future research on the nature of value in the consumption experience.

Customer Value as the Fundamental Basis for Marketing

Two decades ago, in their path-breaking attempts to broaden the concept of marketing, Kotler and Levy (1969; Kotler, 1972) regarded the process of exchange as the essence of marketing activity—a view still enthusiastically endorsed by Kotler (1991) today: "Marketing is a social and managerial process by which individuals and groups obtain what they

AUTHOR'S NOTE: The author thanks Russell Belk, Steve Bell, Kim Corfman, Sarah Holbrook, Joel Huber, and Bob Stinerock for their helpful comments on an earlier draft of this chapter. He expresses his appreciation to Donna Hoffman for generously sharing her extensive library and to John O'Shaughnessy for insights and influences too numerous to mention. He also gratefully acknowledges the support of the Columbia Business School Faculty Research Fund.

need and want through creating, offering, and *exchanging* products of *value* [italics added] with others" (p. 4). These authors have defined exchange as a transaction involving two agents in which each agent gives up something of value in return for something of greater value. From this perspective, two implications follow immediately. First, the exchanges in question—and therefore *marketing activities* in general—are *socially justified* because (if we neglect economic externalities involving third parties) everyone is better off after the exchange than before. Second, marketing involves *exchanges;* exchanges depend on *customer value;* therefore, customer value is the *fundamental basis* for all marketing activity.

But despite this obvious importance of customer value to the study of marketing in general and buyer behavior in particular, consumer researchers have thus far devoted surprisingly little attention to central questions concerning the nature of value. Accordingly, this basic issue constitutes the primary focus of the present chapter. I shall argue here that customer value inheres in an interactive relativistic preference experience of which the essence involves a process wherein all consumer products perform services that potentially provide value-creating experiences. Drawing on three key distinctions or dimensions, I shall develop a systematic taxonomy of the major types of customer value. This typology will position quality (excellence) among such related but different types of value as convenience (efficiency), beauty (esthetics), and reputation (esteem). Further, the logic of the argument will suggest some potentially fruitful directions for future research on customer value in the consumption experience.[1]

Some Preliminaries

For the reasons just mentioned—whether one adopts the perspective of a consumerist, a public policy maker, a marketing manager, or a consumer researcher concerned with addressing the needs of these and other interest groups—one soon encounters central questions concerning the nature and meaning of customer value. Consumerists, for example, tend to regard their job as the protection of customers' ability to pursue what they value without interference from deceptive, anticompetitive, or otherwise rapacious business practices (Andreasen, 1991). Those concerned with public policy hold it as their obligation to seek a balance among the potentially conflicting types of value sought by consumers, business managers, labor unions, and other interest groups so as to maximize various criteria of social welfare (Andrews & Withey, 1976; Galbraith, 1956; Power, 1980; Scitovsky, 1976). Marketing managers, as already noted, define their craft with reference to the exchange process between two agents in which each gives up something of value in return for something of greater value obtained from the other (Kotler, 1991). Combining these perspectives, consumer researchers may regard customer value not only as the basis for purchase decision but, perhaps more important, as the principal outcome of consumption experiences (Holbrook & Hirschman, 1982).

Later, I shall draw an important distinction between "value" (singular) and "values" (plural). The focus on values (plural) has occupied a number of consumer researchers who have drawn upon work in sociology (e.g., Rokeach, 1973) and social psychology (e.g., Fishbein & Ajzen, 1975) to consider such phenomena as individual differences in life-styles (Mitchell, 1983; Wells, 1974), the role of instrumental and terminal values in determining the criteria that underlie the formation of attitudes (Boote, 1975; Howard, 1977), or the empirical correlates of social values (Kahle, 1983b; Pitts & Woodside, 1984). Yet, by contrast, the focus of central interest to the present chapter concerning the nature of value (singular) has seldom received systematic attention in consumer research. In short, the role of customer value lacks clear articulation and will remain poorly understood until consumer behavior theorists direct their efforts toward the remedy of its neglect.

The Problematic Status of Quality

This point has appeared especially evident in the burgeoning body of research on the subject of product and service quality (e.g., Garvin, 1988; Guiry, 1989; Jacoby & Olson, 1985; Steenkamp, 1989; Zeithaml, 1988). Recent survey evidence collected by Price Waterhouse suggests that the vast majority (78%) of U.S. businesses regard quality as a top priority (Schlossberg, 1991). All the more reason, one might suppose, that managers would want to find out what quality *is.*

Though I shall *not* attempt a full systematic review of the relevant literature here, I believe it would be fair to say that issues concerning the nature of product and service quality currently wallow in a sea of confusion. Thus, Garvin (1988) admits that "Quality is an unusually slippery concept, easy to visualize yet exasperatingly difficult to define" (p. xi). Similarly, Steenkamp (1989) acknowledges "There is considerable controversy in the literature with respect to the meaning and the content of

the product quality concept" (p. 7). For example, at an influential conference organized by Jacoby and Olson (1985), most participants spoke
freely of "quality," but few provided careful definitions of this elusive
concept. And those who did tended to contradict one another. Indeed,
issues concerning the meaning of "quality" (which overlap with those
concerning "value") appear to pose formidable barriers to clear thinking.

In this, we are reminded of the popular novel entitled *Zen and the Art
of Motorcycle Maintenance* by Robert Pirsig (1974). Pirsig describes the
intellectual odyssey of Phaedrus, whose search for the meaning of quality
makes up the book's central theme:

> She said, "I hope you are teaching Quality to your students." . . . What the
> hell was she talking about? *Quality?* . . . *Quality?* There was something
> irritating, even angering about that question. He thought about it, and then
> thought some more. . . . *Quality?* . . . It wasn't until three o'clock in the morning
> that he wearily confessed to himself that he didn't have a clue as to what Quality
> was, picked up his briefcase and headed home. (pp. 175-177)

Phaedrus grows so intrigued with this question that he gradually aban-
dons all other activities in his quest for an answer. He searches every-
where. Without success, he climbs a mountain in Tibet to consult a guru.
Finally, in desperation, he enrolls in the doctoral program in philosophy
at the University of Chicago. But the frustrations of his unsuccessful
philosophical quest drive Phaedrus insane before he ever finds a satisfactory answer to his perplexing question. We last see him sitting on a
mattress in a pool of his own urine, mumbling to himself and staring at
the wall:

> Before the electrodes were attached to his head. . . . All he had left was his
> one crazy lone dream of Quality . . . for which he had sacrificed everything.
> Then, after the electrodes were attached, he lost that. . . . What's left now is
> just fragments . . . , which can be pieced together but which leave huge
> areas unexplained. (p. 183)

At the aforementioned quality conference, Holbrook and Corfman
(1985) encountered similarly frustrating perplexities in their attempt to
unravel the meaning of quality in consumer behavior. Based on three
dimensions (implicit/explicit, mechanistic/humanistic, and conceptual/
operational), these authors distinguished eight ways of defining "quality,"
each of which has inspired learned discussions in one or another aca-

demic discipline and many of which were represented by various participants at the conference. A similarly diverse set of quality concepts appears in the summary by Garvin (1988), who distinguishes between definitions based on "innate excellence," "quantity of some ingredient or attribute possessed by a product," "consumers' preferences," "conformance to specifications," and "performance or conformance at an acceptable price or cost" (p. 217). In this connection, Steenkamp (1989) suggests "The main cause of the lack of unanimity is that quality can be and has been studied from many different perspectives" (p. 7); these perspectives include metaphysics (innate excellence), production management (conformance to specifications), economics (product differentiation), and consumer perceptions (judgments based on informational cues): "The coexistence of these four approaches is largely responsible for the confusion surrounding the concept of product quality" (p. 7).

Philosophically speaking, unless one wants to adopt a position of extreme relativism, it appears that so many competing concepts of quality cannot all be correct. Hence, one must confront the clear possibility that many or most of the extant definitions of quality might be wrong. Holbrook and Corfman (1985) blame these conceptual difficulties on the prevailing tendency to try to define "quality" in isolation without placing it in its context as just one among many different types of customer value. In other words, problems in resolving the meaning of "quality" have arisen, in part, because of the widespread tendency to consider this concept as a sort of free-floating and vaguely mystical entity without establishing its place within a broader frame of reference concerning the definition and types of value. Holbrook and Corfman note:

> It appears that available definitions fail to answer our basic question concerning the meaning of quality. The problem, in general, is that we find too many contrasting views—none of which is conceptually well enough grounded to provide definitive guidance. More specifically, we find that each attempts to treat quality in isolation without exploring its conceptual relationships to other types of value. This predicament suggests that we cannot adequately comprehend the meaning of quality without relating it to other terms within the broader sphere of normative discourse. We cannot understand quality unless we can specify how it compares with beauty, convenience, fun, and other types of value judgment. (pp. 39-40)

More generally, this viewpoint suggests that we cannot understand value without understanding how the various types of value relate to one another. In this, I follow the general philosophical position that "in order to say what a thing is, we have to say to what genus it belongs, and then to say how it is differentiated from the other kinds of things in that genus" (Hare, 1982, p. 71). Thus, with specific reference to the concept of value, Von Wright (1963) offers the following suggestion:

> Here it is good to remember that the philosopher seldom deals with a single concept only. He moves in a *field* of concepts. This makes him on the whole more interested in logical *distinctions* and *connexions* between parts of the field than in the "definitions" of local spots on it. (p. 6)

Enter Axiology

The present chapter places such issues as the meaning of "quality" within the overall context of the general nature of value. In developing such a conceptualization, I shall draw on the *theory of value,* or *axiology* (Brightman, 1962; Frankena, 1962b, 1967; Frondizi, 1971; Hartman, 1967; Hilliard, 1950; Lewis, 1946; C. Morris, 1964; Olson, 1967; Perry, 1954; Taylor, 1961; Von Wright, 1963).

One suspects that axiology has important lessons to teach marketing and consumer researchers concerned with the nature of customer value. Yet it is a perspective that has been seriously neglected. It therefore requires our careful attention.

I shall begin by proposing a concept of customer value relevant to consumer behavior; this definition emphasizes that products create value by virtue of the services they provide. I shall then develop a typology of value in the consumption experience and shall describe various key types of customer value, including product quality as just one among many different types. Finally, I shall indicate some potentially fruitful directions for future research on the nature of customer value, the different types of value, and their role in the lives of consumers.

The Definition of Customer Value

Concern for the nature of value plunges us, whether we like it or not, into an area of inquiry in which few questions ever receive definitive answers. Nothing is ever settled in the realm of axiology. Those who choose to move in axiological circles must therefore reconcile themselves to struggling for insights with which many will disagree vehemently and few will agree completely. Nevertheless, consumer research needs and deserves some start in this direction. In the terminology of Frankena (1967), my approach to value theory is "metanormative" rather than "normative." That is, it is concerned not with making value judgments but rather with analyzing the nature of value and valuation. Accordingly, I shall begin by offering a general definition of value that will then serve as a basis for further development and substantiation.

Value as an Interactive Relativistic Preference Experience

In the present view, value is *an interactive relativistic preference experience*. Thus, in general, I define value as a *relativistic* (comparative, personal, situational) *preference* characterizing a subject's *experience* of *interacting* with some object. By "object," I mean any "intentional object"—that is, any possible content of consciousness or, as some philosophers have said (rather ungrammatically), "that which consciousness is conscious of." With respect to *customer* value in particular, the "subject" of interest is a *consumer* whereas the relevant "object" may refer to any *product* (i.e., any good, service, person, place, thing, event, or idea—Juran, 1988, p. 8).[2] The object in question therefore corresponds to what others have called "an evaluatum": "Evaluata may be physical objects . . . , persons . . . , acts . . . , events . . . , situations . . . , states of affairs . . . , rules . . . , policies . . . , practices . . . , organizations . . . , physical conditions or states . . . , the states of mind and dispositions of others, and the immediately felt or perceived qualities of our own experience" (Taylor, 1961, p. 23).

This definition of value as an interactive relativistic preference experience corresponds fairly closely (as shown in brackets) to the definition offered by Hilliard (1950): "*Value* is affectivity [a preference] occurring in the relational contexture [relativistic] determined by the reaction [experience] of an organism to a stimulus object [interactive]" (p. 42). Thus, it raises four points that require further elaboration. First, value involves *preference*—broadly interpreted as favorable disposition, general liking, positive affect, judgment as being good, tendency to approach, pro versus con attitude, and so on. Second, value is neither wholly subjective nor entirely objective but rather entails a *subject-object interaction*. Third, value is *relativistic* in at least three senses: (a) it is *comparative* in that it depends on a rating or ranking of one object against another; (b) it is *personal* in that it differs among individuals; and (c) it is *situational* in that it hinges on the context within which an evaluative judgment occurs.

Fourth, value attaches to an *experience* and pertains not to the acquisition of an object but rather to the consumption of its *services* (i.e., its usage or appreciation).[3] Each of these four points has itself been the subject of considerable discussion in axiology. I shall therefore support the definition of value as an interactive relativistic preference experience by addressing each in turn.

Value as Preference

In defining value as a type of preference, I follow C. Morris (1956, 1964), who regards axiology as "the science of preferential behavior" (1956, p. 187) or "the study of preferential behavior" (1964, p. 17). This perspective prompts agreement among sociologists: "A value . . . turns out, upon closer analysis, to represent a definable preference for something to something else . . . and . . . thus seems to be nothing more than a special kind of preference—a preference for one mode of behavior . . . or a preference for one end-state" (Rokeach, 1973, pp. 9-10). It also squares with the traditional microeconomic focus on a preference ordering that guides choice behavior so that "The . . . consumer chooses . . . a consumption . . . which is optimal according to his preferences" (Debreu, 1959, p. 65) and "A person's *value system* is very close to a person's rational preference-ordering" (Brandt, 1967, p. 24): "Valuation is . . . preference in a given situation when we have to choose between alternatives, both of which we want" (Lamont, 1955, p. 189).

Among axiologists, this general position has been encapsulated most influentially by Perry's (1954) so-called "interest theory of value" (adopted, for example, by Alicke, 1983). Note that, by "interest," Perry (1954) means neither "attention" nor "curiosity," but rather "preference": "The clearest instance of a comparison within the range of a single interest is preference" (p. 5). Thus, Perry (1954) formulates his interest-based definition as follows:

> According to the definition of value here proposed, *a thing—any thing—has value, or is valuable, in the original and generic sense when it is the object of an interest—any interest.* . . . The word "interest" points to attitudes of *for* or *against.* . . . "Interest," then is to be taken as a class name for such names as "liking"-"disliking," "loving"-"hating," . . . "desiring"-"avoiding." (pp. 2-7)

Others have embraced this treatment of value as preference. For example, Frankena (1967) views "value" as "the generic noun for all kinds of critical or pro and con predicates" (p. 229). Moore (1957) regards "a value situation as one in which an organism is affectively committed to an object of its experience" (p. 10). Hall (1961) suggests "Our value judgments finally reduce to emotions, to approvals and disapprovals" (p. 164): "Its evaluative dimension lies in its being favorable or unfavorable . . . to its object" (p. 174). And, rather rapturously, Parker (1957) sees "value" as "satisfaction, pleasure, joy" from experience (p. 7): "I am claiming that value is satisfaction . . . a satisfaction of desire" (p. 27).

Such views of value as preference generally entail the notion of evaluative judgment in accord with some set of *standards* (Kahle & Timmer, 1983; Taylor, 1961), *rules* (Arrow, 1967; Taylor, 1961), *criteria* (Baylis, 1958; Pepper, 1958; Rokeach, 1973), *reasons* (Bond, 1983), *norms* and *selective systems* (Pepper, 1958), *goals* (Veroff, 1983), or *ideals* (Abbott, 1955; Cowan, 1964; Hartman, 1967; Pepper, 1958). Taylor (1961) has been especially conscientious about spelling out the hierarchic process whereby value judgments of empirical facts are *verified* against standards or rules, standards or rules are *validated* against value systems, value systems are *vindicated* by ways of life, and ways of life are *self-justified* by rational choice.

Taylor's (1961) careful exposition helps resolve the aforementioned confusion that sometimes occurs between the terms "value" (singular) and "values" (plural). The former refers to a preferential judgment. The latter—as used, for example, by Rokeach (1973)—refers to the "criteria" (p. 4) by which such judgments are made; Taylor (1961) calls this the "substantive" use of "value" in which "a person's values include all the standards and rules which together make up his way of life" (pp. 297-298).[4] In psychology and consumer research, this use of "values" has characterized applications of the so-called "expectancy-value" or multi-attribute attitude model.[5]

Subjectivist, Objectivist, and Interactionist Theories of Value

Axiology has suffered longstanding debates between polarities variously characterized as "cognitivist/noncognitivist" (Frankena, 1967), "realistic/ idealistic" (Osborne, 1933), "naturalistic/non-naturalistic" (Frankena, 1967; Osborne, 1933), "monistic/pluralistic" (Frankena, 1967), "intensive/extensive" (Pepper, 1958), and "objectivist/subjectivist" (Brightman, 1962). Of these polarities, the last mentioned appears the most fundamental. It concerns the question of whether value is an objective aspect of reality, an aspect of subjective consciousness, or some interaction between the two. We may view theories of value as falling along a continuum from extreme subjectivism to extreme objectivism, with interactionist theories somewhere in between. To clarify the interactionist perspective, I shall offer a brief description of this continuum.[6]

Subjectivism. The extreme subjectivist position holds that "Value is entirely dependent on and relative to human experience of it" (Brightman, 1962, p. 33) and entails "the belief that the source of value is *within* . . . the inner world of the agent" (Bond, 1983, p. 138). According to this view, value is fundamentally . . . descriptive of the personal experience of the analyst himself" (Moore, 1957, p. 11) and involves "an emotion" of the form "X is valuable for me" (Osborne, 1933, pp. 43, 27).

Among philosophers, one finds exemplars of pure subjectivism only with difficulty. Lamont (1955) comes close in arguing "There is always a subjective activity involved in . . . value" (p. 4). Parker (1957) comes even closer in pointing to "the seeming existence of values without objects" (p. 40) where "there occurs . . . satisfaction . . . which seems not to be . . . satisfaction . . . over anything" (p. 41). And Frondizi (1971) refers to Perry (1954) as "the first and most astounding subjectivist theory in the field of contemporary American axiology" (p. 51): "R. B. Perry . . . defends a subjectivist position that . . . looks for the origin and basis of value in subjective experience" (pp. 51-52).

For an unalloyed example of subjectivism, however, one might turn to the popular aphorisms contending that "Man is the measure of all things" (Protagoras, quoted by Hare, 1982, p. 5), that "De gustibus non est disputandum" ("There is no arguing in matters of taste," Frondizi, 1971, p. 17), that "Thinking . . . makes it so," or that "Beauty is in the eye of the beholder" (Hume cited by Frondizi, 1971, p. 40; Nozick, 1981, p. 400). This latter viewpoint is, of course, the theory of value implicitly adopted by Levitt (1960) in his original formulation of extreme customer orientation wherein the customer's satisfaction becomes the sole arbiter of marketing success. It corresponds to what Garvin (1988) calls "user-based definitions" (p. 43). One example would be the statement by Wolff (1986), "If the customer says it's good, it's good; if he says it's bad, it's bad" (quoted by Steenkamp, 1989, p. 59).[7]

Objectivism. By contrast, extreme objectivism holds that "Values are logical essences or subsistences, independent of their being known . . . or . . . integral, objective, and active constituents of the metaphysically real" (Brightman, 1962, p. 33); or in other words, "Value is prior to valuation" (Frondizi, 1971, p. 20). This position entails "the theory that value is resident in objects; that it is a quality of them on an equal footing with any other" (Brightman, 1962, p. 31). According to this view, "Values are objective qualities of things, independent . . . of value-bearers" and are expressed by propositions of the form "X is valuable in its own right and is not mind-dependent" (Osborne, 1933, pp. 78, 27).

Among philosophers, one easily finds objectivists (and even more easily, those claiming to be objectivists). For example, Osborne (1933) favors the conclusion that "Value is . . . the property of being an object towards which moral objects *ought* to experience . . . positive mental states" (p. 93). Lee (1957) agrees that "Value may be called objective, because it is the property of an object" (p. 185). Hall (1961) argues that "Our evaluative language . . . is thoroughly objective" (p. 119) in the sense that "Sentences that express emotions have . . . 'factual content'" (p. 144) whose "legitimacy" can be tested against "the evidence" for "the soundness or correctness of their evaluation" (p. 179). Loring (1966) suggests "A wide and familiar range of value statements . . . may properly be regarded as *objective* . . . in the sense that they . . . genuinely make assertions about objects" (p. 17). Hartman (1967) follows G. E. Moore in contending that "Value . . . is a nondescriptive property which depends only on the descriptive properties of a thing" (p. 42).

Objectivism therefore implicates the strong assumption that various types of value (such as quality or beauty) inhere in an object. In this connection, Lewis (1946) suggests that some value is objective or inherent: "Inherent value is an objective property of the thing to which it is attributable" (p. 434). Lewis (1946) argues "As a property of the object, the value in question—like any other objective property—is a certain potentiality for leading to experiences of a specific kind" (p. 519):

> Evaluations are a form of empirical knowledge, not fundamentally different in what determines their truth or falsity, and what determines their validity or justification, from other kinds of empirical knowledge. . . . Evaluations of things, appraisals of their potentialities for good or ill; are . . . true or false; and must be justified as well as confirmed by reference to experience. (p. 365)

Accordingly, Tuchman (1980) "unhesitatingly" opts for the view that "quality is something inherent in a given work" (p. 39), and Osborne (1933) contends that "Beauty . . . is . . . a formal property of [the] beautiful . . . independent of appreciation" (p. 124). Adler (1981) calls this "admirable beauty"—by which he means "excellence or perfection" (p. 113)—and concludes "Admirable beauty . . . is objective, not subjective" (p. 117).

Less extreme, modified objectivist perspectives have characterized the work of Taylor (1961), Von Wright (1963), and Bond (1983). Thus, Taylor (1961) speaks of the empirical verifiability of value judgments in terms of whether the facts of the case meet the relevant standards or rules:

> Knowledge of facts is sufficient for the verification of value judgments and prescriptions. For it is an empirical question whether a given object fulfills or fails to fulfill a given standard, or whether a given act complies with or violates a given rule. It is only when the standard or rule itself is brought into question that we must go beyond empirical verification. (p. 253)

Von Wright (1963) argues "Genuine judgments of instrumental goodness are always objectively true or false judgments" (p. 29). Bond (1983) extends verifiability to the standards or rules themselves in his distinction between "motivating or explaining reasons" and "justifying or grounding reasons" (p. 28) and in his contention that "value" occurs by virtue of grounding reasons that are "in the world as object" (p. 137):

> I am making the . . . strong . . . claim that the existence of grounding reasons (though not of motivating reasons) has no internal or necessary connection with desires of any kind. . . . The grounding reason, *construed objectively,* . . . is tied to what is worth having . . . whether she is aware of it or not. . . . Grounding reasons . . . *become* . . . motivating reasons . . . upon recognition of the value as a value. (pp. 37-41)

In the area of marketing, the objectivist view is represented by what we have come to call the "product orientation." A product-oriented manufacturer claims that an offering has value because it uses certain scarce resources or materials, reflects certain sophisticated technology or advanced engineering, or benefits from certain production efficiencies or other cost advantages (Levitt, 1960). This corresponds to what Garvin (1988) calls "product-based definitions" (p. 42). In effect, product-oriented manufacturers say their offering possesses value as an inherent property because they *put* it there. This viewpoint thereby also resembles the old labor theory of value, which influenced everyone from the classical economists to Marx and which held that the value of a commodity depended on the amount of labor invested in producing it. Thus, as noted by Dickson (1985), "Marxian theory is production oriented because of its focus on the labor content of a good or service" (p. 12).[8]

The Interactionist View. An intermediate position, advocated here, holds that value entails a "dyadic or relational" nexus between subject and object (Osborne, 1933, p. 37). Pepper (1958) speaks of this relation as involving a "conditional object" (p. 402): "This is an existent object that would be valuable on the condition that someone found a value in it. The object is actual, but it is the valuing that is potential" (p. 402).

This interactionist view appears to be closely allied to the definition of value as preference that we have already embraced. Thus, C. Morris (1964) asserts: "Values are . . . properties of objects . . . relative to a 'subject'. . . . Hence, they involve both subjects (agents) and objects" (p. 18). Parker (1957) concurs that "Value is but a specific relation into which things possessing any ontological status whatsoever, whether real or imaginary, may enter with interested subjects" (pp. 34-35). Similarly, Frondizi (1971) sees value as "the result of a tension between the subject and the object" with "a subjective as well as an objective aspect, deceiving those who look only at one side of the coin" (p. 26):

> If we examine the relationship between the valuable object and the subject that valuates it, we will notice clearly . . . that the value can exist only in relation to a subject that valuates it. . . . No matter how deep one may go in the analysis, there is no possibility of disconnecting the object from the subject. . . . value is a relational notion requiring both the presence of the subject and the object. (pp. 146-147)

In sum, if we accept the interactionist view of value as a relation between subject and object, it follows that customer value requires *both* a consumer *and* a product.[9] The logic behind this position was abbreviated nicely in a simile attributed to Alfred Marshall: "Value is, of necessity, both subjective and objective. . . . The subject and the object are as necessary to the act of valuation as the blades of a pair of shears are to the act of cutting" (Fallon, 1971, p. 47). In other words, one scissor—by itself—produces no results; it is like the sound of one hand clapping.[10]

Value as Relativistic

This proposed definition views value as relativistic in at least the three senses mentioned earlier. Specifically, value is: (a) comparative (among objects), (b) personal (among people), and (c) situational (among contexts). I shall discuss each of these aspects separately.

Value as Comparative. The present view subscribes to the illegitimacy of interpersonal utility comparisons (Bass & Wilkie, 1973; G. M. Becker & McClintock, 1967; Luce & Raiffa, 1957) and, therefore, to the dictum that an object's value for Person A can be assessed not in relation to that object's value for Person B but only in comparison with some other object's value for Person A (Holbrook & Ryan, 1982). Thus, one can legitimately make statements of the form "John loves Mary more than he loves Patricia," but not of the form "John loves Mary more than Ronald does." Hence, value is "commensurable" only among objects for a given subject but is "incommensurable" among subjects (Olson, 1967, p. 370).

This point emerges forcefully from Lamont's (1955) treatment of value as an opportunity cost that depends on the foregone consequences of the next best alternative. According to the economist's perspective, "Value . . . always implies scarcity" (p. 23) and therefore entails "a choice between alternatives both of which are thought good" (p. 42). It follows that "Value is always relative or comparative and never absolute; for 'value' means degree of goodness which one thing has in comparison with others" (Lamont, 1955, p. 182). In this light, one might say that going to the dentist is bad (compared, say, to watching a movie) *or* one might say that going to the dentist is good (compared, perhaps, to being audited by the IRS or attending a funeral).

This view appears to command acceptance from a wide variety of perspectives. For example, Laudan (1977) suggests "All evaluations . . . must be made *within a comparative context*" (p. 120). In this connection, Hilliard (1950) notes "The same occurrence may be judged to include high positive value when compared with a negative instance and low positive value when compared with another positive instance, and so on" (p. 57). Along similar lines, Alicke (1983) cites J. O. Urmson to the effect that "Most ethical or evaluative terms are comparative in the sense that to call a thing good, for instance, is to imply that it is better than something else": "A complete perspective on evaluative judgment must include not only the thing judged but also the comparison objects against which the thing is evaluated" (p. 20). In short, value derives "from the comparison of one thing with another" (Hyde, 1983, p. 60); it "depends on what the object is compared with" (Pettit, 1983, p. 32). Thus, comparative value judgments produce "a hierarchy . . . revealed in preference" (Frondizi, 1971, p. 11) in which "some linear order of values can be thus assigned" (Lewis, 1946, p. 543) such that "The concept of preference . . . is, roughly speaking, the same as the notion of *liking* one thing *better* (more) than another" (p. 5).

Value as Personal. With the exception of the most extreme objectivists, widespread agreement exists concerning the interpersonal relativity of value. Frondizi (1971) traces this point back to Hobbes and Hume. Thus, Lewis (1946) suggests "Our likings and dislikings, enjoyments and dissatisfactions, are . . . variable from one person to another" (pp. 421-422): "The very fact of exchange of goods and of the economic mode of valuation, is rooted in the recognition that what has less value or no value to one may have a real or a higher value to another" (p. 527). Von Wright (1963) agrees that "A preference, of any type, is necessarily relative to a subject [and] . . . is always *somebody's* preference" (p. 12): "A thing which for one subject is a wanted thing, may be regarded as unwanted by another subject. . . . The notion of being wanted . . . is thus relative . . . to a subject" (p. 104). Hilliard (1950) makes a similar point rather poetically in noting "In general, every event which occurs in the universe *ought* to occur from the point of view of some organisms and *ought not* from that of others" (p. 168).

The personal nature of value is recognized by economists in "the multiplicity and divergence of individual preference scales" (Arrow, 1967, p. 12): "Different individuals will prefer different activities and this may lead to different preferences" (Maynes, 1975, p. 546). More generally, personal relativity stems from the fact that—as a basis for evaluative judgment or preference formation—different individuals may adopt different standards, rules, or other criteria: "A normative assertion is true . . . only because we have decided to adopt a standard or rule as applicable to what we are making the assertion about" (Taylor, 1961, p. 248). Hence, different value statements, verified by different criteria, may be true for different judges.

According to Osborne (1933), subjectivists are ipso facto committed to personal relativism: "So long as we adhere to the psychological theory about the nature of Value, we can assert value or obligation only for this person or that person and only on the basis of the mental processes of the person for whom they are asserted" (p. 61). For example, Parker (1957) acknowledges the "relativity of values" (pp. 27, 209) and embraces "relativism" in which "the good and the better have no 'absolute' meaning, but have meaning only with relation to an individual's life plan or matrix self" (p. 237).

Though Parker's (1957) views happen to lean toward subjectivism, note that personal relativism is also compatible with all but the most extreme forms of objectivism. Thus, C. Morris (1964) views value as "objectively relative" (p. 18). Bond (1983) explains that although value is "objective" by virtue of its consistency with true "grounding reasons" (in the sense described earlier), it is "personal" (p. 97) by virtue of the fact that different grounding reasons may apply for different people:

> The account of values I wish to give is objective . . . , but . . . What pleases or interests me need not please or interest you. What I find worthwhile, you may find boring or tedious. These are commonplaces foolish and pointless to deny. . . . I shall say that the value a thing has for one person but possibly not for another is objective but not common. . . . Different individuals take delight in . . . different things—different activities, sensations, experiences, and states of affairs. This is an obvious truth and, furthermore, not something to regret in the least. (pp. 56-61, 97)

In sum, value varies among the people who make evaluations. Some people might actually like going to the dentist better than watching a movie. Others might actually prefer a tax audit to dental drilling. I have not met such people; but they might exist. Indeed, intuitive support for this personal relativity of value is found in the familiar adage, "One man's meat is another man's poison" (Lewis, 1946, p. 526).

Value as Situational. Finally, value is relativistic in the sense that it depends on the context in which a value judgment occurs. Thus, Lewis (1946) argues "Value-quality . . . tends to be determined in some part by the relation . . . to the context": "The value found in it depends in some part on the experiential context" (p. 426).

Specifically, the criteria adopted as the basis for an evaluation tend to reflect the circumstances in which that judgment is made: "Standards . . . will vary as different points of view are taken in an evaluation" (Taylor, 1961, p. 11). It follows that value is situation bound, is "relative, not only to a subject but also to a certain moment or occasion or station in the life of a subject" (Von Wright, 1963, p. 13), and is "almost certainly conditioned by such factors as . . . historical circumstances" (Olson, 1967, p. 368). Accordingly, C. Morris (1964) recognizes this situational nature of value as existing "only in relation to specific contexts" (p. 41). Hilliard (1950) notes that such a context might "be relative and be subject to a time reference": "That which is *good for* an organism now, for example, a baby-rattle, will not necessarily be *good for* it ten years hence" (p. 207).

In short, as summarized by Frondizi (1971): "If the name 'situation' is applied to the complex of individual, social, cultural and historical elements and circumstances, then we maintain that values have existence and meaning only within a specific situation" (p. 158). The situational effects on consumer behavior are too well known to need repeating here (Belk, 1975; Kahle & Timmer, 1983). Previous research has applied this perspective to the development of a preference model for radio stations based on situation-specific ideal points (Holbrook, 1984), a situational psychophysics of taste preferences for lemonade (Huber, Holbrook, & Schiffman, 1982), and a test for the effects of situational arousal on listeners' affective responses to different musical tempos (Holbrook & Anand, 1990, 1992. These studies may be viewed as special cases of the conception of value as situationally relativistic.

Value as Experiential

The Consumption Experience. The present position holds that value in consumer behavior does not reside in the object (good or service) purchased but rather pertains directly to the consumption experience derived therefrom (Holbrook & Hirschman, 1982). Support for the locus of value in experience comes from the work of philosophers such as Hilliard (1950), Parker (1957), Baylis (1958), and Mukerjee (1964):

> All knowledge must reduce finally to immediate experience. . . . Axiological knowledge is no exception. (Hilliard, 1950, p. 92)
> Now the primary insight into . . . values is that they belong to activities or experiences. . . . *Things* may be called "good," but only because they contribute something to experiences. (Parker, 1957, p. 6)
> The value of . . . valuable things is realized and becomes actual only when they are experienced. It is derived from the . . . value of the experience of them. (Baylis, 1958, pp. 490-491)
> Values are . . . lived events and experiences in which the resources of the whole mind—impulse, reason, imagination and intuition—. . . are involved. (Mukerjee, 1964, pp. 108-109)

Insofar as we do attribute value to an object, it must stem from the capacity of that object to contribute to an experience as a form of extrinsic value (discussed later). Thus, Lewis (1946) maintains "*The goodness of good objects consists in the possibility of their leading to some realization of directly experienced goodness*" (p. 387):

The goodness of a good *object* is a potentiality for the realization of goodness in experience. . . . *Values ascribable to objects are always extrinsic values,* intrinsic value attaching exclusively to realizations of some possible value-quality in experience itself. (p. 389) What can be said in general of value in objects is only what was said at the outset: any such value is some potentiality of the object for realizations of satisfaction in experience. (p. 539)

All Products Potentially Provide Services. R. T. Morris (1941) appears to have been among the first to anticipate the appropriate conclusion concerning the nature of consumption and its dependence on the experiences to which products contribute. Further, the perspective of R. T. Morris (1941) connects the value-creating experiences directly to the *services* that all products potentially provide:

> The emphasis . . . is upon the *services* of goods, not upon the goods themselves. Wants should be thought of not as desires for goods—but rather for the events which the possession of them makes possible. . . . Goods are wanted because they are capable of performing services—favorable events which occur at a point in time. (pp. 136-137)

In articulating the implications of this view for the economics of consumer behavior, Abbott (1955) also emphasizes the pervasive role of experience-providing product-derived services:

> The thesis . . . may be stated quite simply. What people really desire are not products but satisfying *experiences.* Experiences are attained through activities. In order that activities may be carried out, physical objects or the services of human beings are usually needed. Here lies the connecting link between man's inner world and the outer world of economic activity. People want products because they want the *experience-bringing services* [italics added] which they hope the products will render. (p. 40)

By now, this experiential service-based perspective has gained wide acceptance by economists. Thus, Katona (1972) defines "value" as "the discounted stream of services obtained from the product during its lifetime" (p. 44). In G. S. Becker's (1976) view, goods and time serve as inputs into a household production function via which a family maximizes utility. Suranyi-Unger (1981) concludes that, in economics, "It has become customary to identify the sources of utility as activities, with goods . . . becoming inputs into those activities" (p. 135). Focusing on "quality" (as opposed to value in general), Maynes (1975) defines "the concept of quality" as "the extent to which a specimen possesses the *service* [italics added] characteristics you desire" (p. 542): "It is the *services* [italics added] . . . which consumers really want, not the means which produce them" (p. 549).

In sum, an emphasis on the consumption experience such as that found in the work of Holbrook and Hirschman (1982; Hirschman & Holbrook, 1982; Steenkamp, 1989) is "radical" only in the sense that it hearkens back to the "roots" of axiology, economics, and consumer behavior theory. Consumption activities or usage behaviors are the grounds for value-producing services on which purchasing decisions depend. This dependence is recognized by our definition of value as an interactive relativistic preference experience.

A Typology of Customer Value

The foregoing considerations concerning the definition of customer value confront some key problems in axiology, but tell us little about differences among the key types of value that occur in consumer behavior. I shall address this latter question by constructing a typology of value in the consumption experience. This typology will help to clarify the roles of various kinds of customer value. To develop this taxonomic scheme, I shall proceed by describing three underlying taxonomic dimensions: (a) extrinsic versus intrinsic value, (b) self-oriented versus other-oriented value, and (c) active versus reactive value.[11] I shall discuss each dimension separately before introducing the full typology.[12]

Dimension 1: Extrinsic/Intrinsic Value

The first dimension employs a distinction commonly drawn in axiology between *extrinsic* and *intrinsic* value. This distinction is fundamental to such frequently encountered contrasts as those between means and ends, between instrumental and ludic behavior, between practical and autotelic motivation, or between utilitarian functions and ends in themselves (Holbrook, 1985, 1986, 1987).

Briefly, *extrinsic value* characterizes those judgments that some thing or event (a product or consumption experience) is a means useful in bringing about some further end (a source of services that accomplishes some purpose). This extrinsic aspect of value has been widely acknowledged (Abbott, 1955; Fallon, 1971; Lamont, 1955; Loring, 1966; Perry,

1954). For example, Parsons (1937) suggests "It is precisely in their character . . . as means to . . . ends that goods and services can be treated in terms of this common denominator, utility" (p. 121). Hilliard (1950) defines "utility" as "a character predicable of any object which was, is, or has the potentiality of being for a particular organism an intermediate means" (pp. 45-46). Lamont (1955) regards utility as "the capacity or power of a thing or action to produce something else" (p. 88). Diesing (1962) agrees that "In a technical context, utility is a means to an end" (p. 62). Von Wright (1963) uses "utilitarian" as "advantageous for some purpose" (p. 10). And Bond (1983) defines "utility" as "the recognition that something is an effective means to a desired end" (p. 20). Similarly, Hilliard (1950) regards "instrumental value" as "affectivity arising in the contexture determined by an organism and an object considered as an intermediate means to certain consequences" (p. 120): "An Object 'acquires' *instrumental value* . . . in its character of being an intermediate means— that is, because of its *utility*" (p. 120). And Von Wright (1963) uses "instrumental goodness" to mean "It serves its purpose well" (p. 20).[13] Extrinsic value is therefore utilitarian, instrumental, or practical.

By contrast, *intrinsic value* characterizes the appreciation of some experience for its own sake, apart from any other consequences that may result therefrom. Thus, "intrinsic or sheer liking" entails "pure preference . . . for its own sake" (Von Wright, 1963, p. 5). Intrinsic value is therefore noninstrumental, self-justifying, autotelic, self-motivating, or ludic. It attaches to an experience prized as an end in itself (Holbrook & Hirschman, 1982)—as in the case of hedonic satisfaction or pleasure (Hirschman & Holbrook, 1982; Oliver, 1989). For example, Pepper (1958) provides a drive-based tension-reduction theory that treats pleasure as intrinsic to the consumption experience: "Affective value is intrinsic to the consummatory act" (Pepper, 1958, p. 309). Thus, the nature of "pleasant experiences" as "intrinsically good . . . worth having for their own sakes . . . good in themselves" (Baylis, 1958, p. 491) has been widely recognized (Frankena, 1967, p. 231): "Hedonic good *lies in* the delightful or agreeable character of the . . . experience. . . . Pleasure . . . is inherently good, or good in virtue of its very nature. . . . Hedonic value . . . is recognized in its being experienced. . . . While enjoying something . . . , one *experiences* it as intrinsically worthwhile" (Bond, 1983, pp. 98-108).[14]

Beginning with Aristotle (Olson, 1967, p. 367), the extrinsic/intrinsic distinction has won an unusual consensus on its key role as an underlying axiological dimension. See, variously, Baylis (1958), Brandt (1967), Hilliard (1950), Lewis (1946), Nozick (1981), Rokeach (1973), and Taylor (1961).

Some axiologists (e.g., Baylis, 1958; Lewis, 1946; Olson, 1967; Taylor, 1961) distinguish further among three types of extrinsic value—*instrumental, contributive,* and *inherent:*

> Values which are extrinsic—which include all values resident in objects—we subdivide into those which are to be found in experience of that object itself to which the value is attributed, and are here called inherent values, and those which are realizable in the experience of something else to which the object in question may be instrumental, which are here called instrumental values. (Lewis, 1946, p. 392)
> Anything is instrumentally good insofar as it is a causal factor in the production of something which is good. . . . Contributive goods . . . are necessary parts of a good whole. . . . Inherent goods . . . derive their value from being objects of experiences which are intrinsically good. . . . The value of inherent goods . . . is derived from the value that is realized when they are apprehended in the appropriate manner. (Baylis, 1958, pp. 488-489)

The latter distinctions clarify the point that *only* an *experience* can be appreciated for its own sake so as to attain intrinsic value (Lewis, 1946): "It is values as immediately realized or realizable in experience . . . which are intrinsic and for their own sake; and all values attributable to objects are extrinsic and for the sake of these" (p. 414). Thus, any other kind of object (e.g., a manufactured good or a marketable service) can at best attain *inherent* extrinsic value (e.g., a painting or a rock concert), *contributory* extrinsic value (e.g., blue oil paint in a painting or the stage in a rock concert), or *instrumental* extrinsic value (e.g., money to buy the oil painting or a ticket to the rock concert) (Hilliard, 1950): "If an evaluatum is not a felt or perceived quality of experience, it cannot have intrinsic value. Objects, acts, situations, and persons can have extrinsic value only" (Taylor, 1961, p. 23). This point underlies Abbott's (1955) important distinction between "basic" and "derived" wants:

> Two levels of wants are . . . distinguishable. The more fundamental kind of want—the desire for an experience—will be termed a *basic want;* its derivative—the desire for a product which actually or supposedly provides the means to that experience—a *derived want.* . . . basic wants may be said to indicate the ends of economic activity . . . , while derived wants indicate the provisional choice of means to those ends. (pp. 40-46)

We therefore return by a different route to a point upon which we insisted earlier—namely, that the value of any product (i.e., any good, service, event, or idea) depends upon its role in providing services that create some consumption experience (Holbrook & Hirschman, 1982):

> We always arrive finally at something whose value does not depend on the value of anything else, and this is something (a quality of experience) having intrinsic value. . . . all extrinsic values in actual life are ultimately dependent upon intrinsic value. . . . extrinsic value depends on intrinsic value. (Taylor, 1961, pp. 26-31)

Dimension 2: Self-Oriented/Other-Oriented Value

A second dimension refers to the distinction between value based on a *self-oriented* perspective and that based on an *orientation toward others*— where "others" may include relevant members of society or any other pertinent aspects of the cosmos, such as a universal world order or deity.

Briefly, *self-oriented value* encompasses those preferences that result largely from self-interest—as when I selfishly prize a product or an experience for *my own* sake, on the basis of how *I* react to it, or for the effect that it has on *me*. This perspective includes those self-interested considerations sometimes referred to as "prudential."

Other-oriented value covers preferences that look beyond the self. Here, the "other" in question could refer to other members of society (family members, friends, neighbors, colleagues)—as when I like something for *their sake*, on the basis of how *they* will react to it, or by virtue of the effect it has on *them*. But the "other" could also refer to any larger part of the environment (the country, planet, solar system, or universe; Mother Nature, the Cosmos, or the Deity)—as when I like or dislike something by virtue of its relation to some Larger Force and how that Larger Force will respond to it (e.g., "It's not nice to fool Mother Nature"). Finally, the "other" of interest could actually be located inside one's own body or personality—as in certain Eastern religions or certain psychoanalytic treatments whose project involves getting in touch with one's hidden Spirit or probing one's own Unconscious.

Like the aforementioned distinction between extrinsic and intrinsic value, the contrast between self-orientation and other-orientation (though called by a greater variety of names) has commanded widespread acknowledgment in the literature. See, variously, Brandt (1967), Hyde (1983), Kahle (1983b), Ladd (1967) Parker (1957), Parsons (1937), Pepper (1958), Riesman (1950), and Rokeach (1973).[15]

Some empirical support for the distinction between self- and other-orientation comes from studies by C. Morris (1956, 1964). For example, one might compare his Factor C, for which "the self rather than society is the focus of attention" (1964, p. 25), with Factor A, for which "there is awareness of the larger human and cosmic setting . . . and an acceptance of the restraints which responsibility to this larger whole requires" (p. 24). Such contrasts lead C. Morris (1956) to conclude that "The common line of cleavage seems to be between orientation to the self and orientation to other than self" (p. 38).

Dimension 3: Active/Reactive Value

A third dimension involves a distinction between *active* and *reactive* value. In the present conceptualization, *active value* occurs when one's valuing results from a manipulation of the environment by some effect (generally physical, but conceivably mental) of the subject on an object (a good, service, or event) or on an experience (an activity or idea). Thus, active value could involve a physical manipulation of a tangible thing (playing a video game), a physical manipulation of a mental event (taking psychedelic drugs), a mental manipulation of an idea (daydreaming), or even a mental manipulation of a tangible object (telekinesis). The key point in all such cases is that some sort of active manipulation of an object or experience produces the value in question (Diesing, 1962).

By contrast, *reactive value* occurs when the individual simply apprehends, appreciates, or responds to an object (Hall, 1961)—as when I react to some product (good, service, event, or idea) by letting *it* act upon *me*.[16] The key point is that the object affects the subject—the product changes the customer—rather than the other way around. In other words, the consumer primarily plays the role of viewer, beholder, receiver, audience member, or worshipper. The object of interest is apprehended, admired, appreciated, or adored.

This third distinction has appeared in the literature somewhat less frequently than those embodied by Dimensions 1 and 2. However, a general formulation in support of Dimension 3 appears in the work of Parker (1957):

Satisfaction comes to us *as* an assuagement of desire. . . . the objective of desire is never an object but an activity or passivity, usually with reference to an object. . . . things that we say that we want . . . we want, not as such, but to use; and to use is to be active or passive with reference to them. (p. 92) [See also Hall, 1961; Pepper, 1958; Rokeach, 1973.]

Some empirical support for the active/reactive distinction as a dimension of value again comes from the work of C. Morris (1956, 1964). C. Morris defines his "dominance" dimension as involving "control of objects" in the environment via "appropriate courses of action" (1964, p. 22). In the contrasting "dependence dimension," "the actor must now let the . . . object work upon him" by being "receptive" (1964, p. 22). These hypothesized dimensions appear as Factor B, in which "the stress is upon delight in vigorous action for the overcoming of obstacles" (pp. 24-25), and Factor D, in which "the emphasis is upon receptivity to persons and to nature . . . a stress upon responsiveness and devoted receptivity" (p. 25).

A Typology of Value in the Consumption Experience

Combining the extrinsic/intrinsic, self-oriented/other-oriented, and active/reactive dimensions generates a typology that distinguishes among eight kinds of value in the consumption experience, as shown in Table 2.1. This typology speaks directly to our motivating question concerning the nature of different types of customer value. In what follows, I shall offer a brief description of each cell in hopes of shedding further light on the role of value in consumer behavior.

Types of Customer Value

Efficiency (Output/Input Ratio or Convenience)

Efficiency is the extrinsic value that results from the active manipulation of some means in pursuit of some self-oriented end(s). Efficiency is therefore inseparable from the act of product usage to achieve some selfish purpose. For example, most of the objects that one carries in one's pocket provide services directed toward the satisfaction of self-interested goals: a handkerchief for blowing one's nose, a key for opening one's door, a wallet for carrying one's credit cards, or a dollar for buying one's newspaper.

The extrinsic, self-oriented, active nature of efficiency has been widely recognized (e.g., Lamont, 1955). For example, Bond (1983) manages to capture all three aspects (shown in brackets) in his concise definition: "In

TABLE 2.1 A Typology of Value in the Consumption Experience

		Extrinsic	*Intrinsic*
Self-Oriented	Active	Efficiency (O/I ratio or convenience)	Play (fun)
	Reactive	Excellence (quality)	Esthetics (beauty)
Other Oriented	Active	Politics (success)	Morality (virtue or ethical acts)
	Reactive	Esteem (reputation)	Spirituality (faith or ecstasy)

the case of . . . efficiency, it is a sufficient condition of an act's [active] possessing that value that it be an efficient means [extrinsic] to some desired end [self-oriented]" (p. 42).

One may equate efficiency with the *output/input ratio* of results-to-effort or use-to-exchange value (Dickson, 1985; Hilliard, 1950; Hyde, 1983). This conceptualization coheres with Pepper's (1958) view of "achievement" as "the attainment of the shortest path to an appetitive goal" (p. 312). Similarly, Diesing (1962) defines "technical rationality" as "the efficient achievement of a given end" (p. 9) where "efficiency is the maximum achievement of a given end with given resources" (p. 11), according to a principle of rationality that says "maximize the output/input ratio" (p. 12): "Technical rationality appears in actions [active] which are undertaken for the sake [extrinsic] of achieving a given end [self-oriented]" (p. 9). In consumer behavior where time resources are a key input, for example, one often identifies efficiency with "convenience" (availability or ease of use).[17] This type of "psychotemporal" value characterizes such services as convenience stores, drive-in fast-food restaurants, and automatic teller windows.

Excellence (Quality)

As another type of extrinsic value aimed at the satisfaction of self-oriented goals, *excellence* differs from efficiency in that it involves an inherently reactive response. Excellence is a type of value associated with a distanced apprehension or receptive admiration—as in the case of *quality*. In the words of Tuchman (1980), what one admires in the quality evaluation is "a condition of excellence" (p. 38). Similarly, Zeithaml (1988) suggests that "quality can be defined broadly as superiority or excellence" (p. 3): "Perceived quality is defined . . . as the consumer's judgment about the superiority or excellence of a product" (p. 5). Thus, one *uses* a product efficiently, whereas one *appreciates* its *quality*. Quality entails a reactive response of *admiring* some object (or experience) for its extrinsic *capacity* to *serve* as a *means* to a self-oriented *end*.[18]

The present view of excellence in general and quality in particular jibes (as shown in brackets) with Abbott's (1955) claim that, like efficiency (active), quality (reactive) involves extrinsic self-oriented value: "If . . . quality is to be explained . . . , the varieties of a differentiated product must be regarded [reactive] as variable means [extrinsic] to some end system [self-oriented], not as ends in themselves" (p. 27). This reactive nature of excellence is emphasized by Bond's (1983) definition of "quality" as "the kind of value that commands or merits *respect*" (p. 121).[19]

In his book *Managing Quality,* Garvin (1988) adopts a multidimensional view of this concept as involving various aspects of performance, features, reliability, conformance (to specifications), durability, serviceability, aesthetics, and customer perceptions.[20] Among these dimensions, that concerned with *performance* corresponds most closely to the present definition:

> Performance . . . refers to the primary operating characteristics of a product. . . . superior performance . . . depends entirely on the task to be performed. . . . Users typically have a wide range of interests and needs; each is likely to equate quality with high performance in his or her area of immediate interest. (pp. 50-51)

This performance-based concept of quality has won support among product-testing experts: "*Consumer Reports,* for example, interprets quality strictly in terms of performance" (p. 108).

In his near-definitive monograph on the subject of product quality, Steenkamp (1989) focuses primarily on perceived quality (clearly, a reactive concept) and suggests, "The best known and most widely adopted definition of perceived quality is simply 'perceived quality is fitness for use' or some variant thereof [such as]. . . 'the degree to which a product fulfills its functions,' . . . 'the rated ability of the brand to perform its functions' . . . [or] 'the fitness for certain goals' [clearly aspects of extrinsic value]" (p. 58). From this perspective, Steenkamp (1989) supports the present view of excellence or quality (as shown in brackets): "The perceived [reactive] quality of a product depends on the degree to which it fulfills the subject's [self-oriented] usage goal(s) [extrinsic]" (p. 105). Further, calling this the "teleological approach," Steenkamp cites the following apposite definition: "The teleological quality concept encompasses . . . the subjective usage goal [self-oriented] and the subjective perception and evaluation [reactive] of the fitness of the product to fulfill this usage goal [extrinsic]" (Wimmer, 1975, p. 7, quoted by Steenkamp, 1989, p. 105).

Zeithaml (1988) and her colleagues have adopted a comparable view of quality in general and of service quality in particular (Parasuraman, Zeithaml, & Berry, 1985, 1988). Specifically, Zeithaml (1988) proposes a multidimensional view of quality where the dimensions of interest differ, for example, between such categories as packaged goods, industrial products, durable goods, and services. As a global concept, she views quality as a "higher level abstraction" that corresponds with the present view (as shown in brackets) insofar as "perceived quality can be defined as the consumer's [self-oriented] judgment [reactive]" where "the instrumentality of actions and objects in achieving ends [extrinsic] could be viewed as a foundation for this definition" so that "quality could be viewed [reactive] as instrumentality [extrinsic]" (p. 3). When applied to the case of services by Parasuraman et al. (1985, 1988), this view translates into a multidimensional concept of service quality, as operationalized by a measure called SERVQUAL based on multi-item scores for tangibles, reliability, responsiveness, assurance, and empathy.

Politics (Success)

As used here, *politics* involves the active pursuit of *success* awarded by others. In other words, it entails the use of one's own products or consumption experiences as a means to the other-oriented end of achieving a favorable response from someone else. Thus, "politics" refers not only to the obvious case of political candidates seeking votes but also to all those interrelational, societal, communal, legal, judicial, executive, organizational, and generally other-oriented concerns that arise in the active pursuit of extrinsic purposes viewed as means to more ultimate interpersonal ends (Perry, 1954). In this spirit (as shown in brackets), Nozick (1981) defines "political philosophy" as: "Mainly the theory of what behavior [active] legitimately may be enforced [other-oriented], and of the nature of the institutional structure that stays within and supports these enforceable rights [extrinsic]" (p. 503). Thus, we shall use "politics" in a broad sense covering virtually any type of consumption-related purposive action aimed at *success*.

One should note that much consumption behavior (e.g., attending school to earn an MBA degree) involves political value in these respects. Many services are designed to help one sell oneself more effectively so as to gain some advantage, including beauty shops, barber shops, career counseling, psychotherapy, and cosmetic surgery. A conspicuous example occurs when we choose our clothing with an eye to the impression that we shall make in a job interview—just the right dark suit; a clean, white shirt or blouse; a striking bow or necktie. In other words, "Dress for Success."

Esteem (Reputation)

The reactive counterpart of political value is that based on social *reputation* in the form of *esteem*. Esteem value arises from the reactive contemplation of one's own status or prestige, as reflected in the approbative opinion of others. Hence, goods or services appreciated for their esteem value serve the extrinsic purpose of contributing to one's other-oriented desire for favorable recognition.[21]

Thus, the major satisfaction from having a nice lawn around one's house—which requires hundreds of dollars in mowing and watering fees paid to the neighborhood children—comes from knowing that this enviable expanse of green makes a positive impression on one's neighbors. One thinks these thoughts reactively while one lounges in one's lawn chair on a warm summer day. Similarly, some people doubtless like to own an expensive art collection not so much for the sake of personal enjoyment as for the hope that their friends will admire it and be jealous.

This longing for esteem or reputation has, of course, inspired Veblen's (1899/1967) treatment of "conspicuous consumption" and Duesenberry's (1949) related concept of social interdependence via the "demonstration effect." More to the point (as shown in brackets), we find support for the present view of esteem value as extrinsic, other-oriented, and reactive in the interpretations of Scitovsky (1976) and Bond (1983):

> Status consumption [is] . . . the part of the consumer's purchases motivated by his desire to gain and assert his membership in the society around him [other-oriented]. . . . Status seeking, the wish to belong [reactive], the asserting and cementing of one's membership in the group is a deep-seated and very natural drive. . . . It seems self-evident that a simple way for an individual

to gain acceptance by and membership in a group is to be useful to its members [extrinsic]. (Scitovsky, 1976, pp. 115-120)

Prestige or status . . . is . . . desirable [reactive] . . . only to the extent that it is merited [other-oriented] . . . and is not to be arrived at by a rational person *for its own sake,* no matter how useful it may be as a means [extrinsic]. (Bond, 1983, p. 161)

Play (Fun)

Play involves an active self-oriented experience enjoyed for its own sake. This intrinsic or ludic nature of *fun* is an important characteristic of games and various creative phenomena that has often been noted in the literature on playful and leisure activities:

> By play we are designating . . . whatever is done spontaneously and for its own sake, whether it have or not an ulterior utility. (Santayana 1896, p. 19)
> Play . . . stands outside the immediate satisfaction of wants and appetites, indeed it interrupts the appetitive process. It interpolates itself as a temporary activity satisfying in itself and ending there. (Huizinga, 1938, p. 27)
> Play is disinterested, self-sufficient, an interlude from work. It brings no material gain. (Stephenson, 1967, p. 192)
> We play, not thereby to achieve some further purpose or to fulfil some obligation, but just for what is involved in the activity itself. (Dearden, 1967, p. 84)
> It is repeatedly asserted that playful activities are carried on "for their own sake" or for the sake of "pleasure." They are contrasted with "serious" activities, which deal with readily identifiable bodily needs or external threats or otherwise achieve specifiable practical ends. (Berlyne, 1969, p. 840)

Thus, the essence of playful activities or leisure services is that we pursue them for their own sake. The minute they take on some ulterior motive, they stop being fun and start being work.

The active component of play is attested to by the importance of its performatory aspects. For example, in games an emphasis on succeeding has often been linked to the need for competence (White, 1959), mastery over the environment (Csikszentmihalyi, 1975), "galumphing" (Miller, 1973), or what Pepper (1958) calls the sense of "triumph" in overcoming obstacles "for the sheer fun of it" (p. 163).

In sum, when describing the intrinsic, self-oriented, active nature of the value to be found in play (as shown in brackets), Bond (1983) concludes:

The pursuit of pleasure [active], namely the pursuit of *whatever he or she likes* [self-oriented] *for its own sake* [intrinsic] . . . is . . . all the things that . . . belong on the leisure side of the common distinction between work and leisure. (p. 113) When I am enjoying my game of golf [self-oriented] I am engaging in some activity [active] in the world that . . . is enjoyed for *its own sake* [intrinsic]. (p. 142)

Esthetics (Beauty)

In contrast to the active nature of play and fun, *esthetic* value arises from an essentially reactive appreciation (Hampshire, 1982; Perry, 1954). For example, Von Wright (1963) distinguishes between the "active pleasure" of "doing things" and the "passive pleasure" of "sensations and other so-called states of consciousness" (p. 64): "The pleasure of watching a game is mainly . . . of the form which we have called passive pleasure. Watching a game means the acquisition of experiences which the man . . . finds pleasant. . . . our man is enjoying a sight" (p. 78).

Like play, *beauty* may be regarded as self-oriented in nature (Eisert, 1983). It involves "a first person hedonic judgment" (Von Wright, 1963, p. 73) and "must specify the organism of reference" (Hilliard, 1950, p. 284): "The category of the aesthetic has . . . the self as the point of reference" (C. Morris, 1956, p. 172).

Most important, *beauty* is enjoyed purely for its own sake without regard to any further practical purpose that it might serve (Lee, 1957; Perry, 1954). This view of esthetic experience as involving intrinsic value can be traced back to the work of Shaftesbury in 1709 (Beardsley, 1967), but owes its most influential exposition to Kant's *Critique of Judgment* in 1790: "Kant discovered the essence of beauty in design enjoyed simply for itself" (Rader, 1979, p. 331). Kant's perspective found further support in Bullough's (1912) concept of "psychical distance" and has since commanded a broad consensus among esthetic philosophers:

The esthetic attitude . . . stands in contrast with that commoner concern which takes what is presented as sign of a clue to something further; also it stands in contrast with those evaluations which are determined by reference to the ends of action. Again, it stands in contrast with attention to and any appreciation of the utilities of things. (Lewis, 1946, p. 438)

We ascribe beauty to those objects which occasion us pleasantness "for their own sakes," immediately, and not because of the recognition or supposition of any causal relation to further valuable objects. Beauty is predicated of objects which are last, not intermediate means. . . . The complex object . . . occasions . . . positive affectivity, and it does so "for its own sake," not because of being an intermediate means to some other object. . . , not because it "has" instrumental value; but it provides immediate pleasure, because it "has" terminal value. (Hilliard, 1950, pp. 276-277)

The aesthetic attitude . . . is most commonly opposed to the *practical* attitude, which is concerned only with the utility of the object in question. . . . One must "perceive for perceiving's sake," not for the sake of some ulterior purpose. One must savor the experience of perceiving . . . itself, dwelling on its perceptual details, rather than using the perceptual object as a means to some further end. (Hospers, 1967, p. 36)

The recognized value of aesthetic experience is partly a sense of rest from intention, of not needing to look through this particular object to its possible uses. (Hampshire, 1982, p. 119) Experience of art is by definition an experience in which practical interests . . . are for a time suspended in an unpractical enjoyment of the arrangement of something perceived. Any strong aesthetic experience is necessarily . . . a relaxing of the usual practical stance. (pp. 244-245)

As noted by Budd (1983) "A person can value an object that is a work of art for many different kinds of reason. . . . his reasons . . . may or may not be because he finds the experience of the work of art intrinsically rewarding. Only if he finds the experience of the work of art intrinsically rewarding does he value the work as a work of art" (p. 153). Thus, in short, my esthetic appreciation for a work of art (the intrinsic value of that experience) has nothing to do with any extrinsic purpose that the artwork might serve.

In sum, beauty (esthetics) differs from quality (excellence as a type of economic value) in its intrinsic nature as an end in itself: "The relation between *aesthetics* and *economics* is . . . that between intrinsic and extrinsic value applied to individual things" (Hartman, 1967, p. 114). But beauty resembles quality in that both types of value are self-oriented and reactive. Thus, neither requires doing anything with the good or service in question. Rather, both involve attending to the object, apprehending it, and admiring it for its capacity to serve as a means to some end (quality) or appreciating it for the sake of the experience itself (beauty). Thus, there is an oft-noted sense in which quality parallels beauty in that (as implied by Table 2.1) quality is to convenience as beauty is to fun. That is:

Excellence:Efficiency::Esthetics:Play

Morality (Virtue)

Morality entails active other-oriented value. *Ethical action* involves doing something for the sake of others—with concern for how it will affect them or how they will react to it. In the view of Lewis (1946), the "ethical command" is "to be concerned about the value-experience of others" (p. 546). Similarly, Von Wright (1963) suggests that "other-regarding duties, . . . which require us to respect the good of other beings, are felt to have a peculiar connexion with morality, to be the moral duties *par excellence*" (pp. 182-183). Thus, the pursuit of *virtue* requires behavior in accord with conscience, where "conscience" consists of internalized social sanctions (Parker, 1957; Pepper, 1958):

> The primary values constituting the objective of morality . . . are largely transcendent in the sense that they are not values of myself, but of other selves. (Parker, 1957, p. 243)
> What ought to be done morally is what the social system and other persons require for their maintenance and development. (C. Morris, 1956, p. 171)

Hence, the active pursuit of virtue must conform to a number of other-oriented "Thou shalt's" and "Thou shalt not's," dictating "actions and forbearances" (Lamont, 1955, p. 310) in the form of "behavior in conformity to . . . human responsibility" (Mukerjee, 1964, p. 48). For example, deontological or "deontic" value (Bond, 1983) is associated with feelings of "duty" and "conscience" (Perry, 1954) and therefore refers to "judgments of obligation" (Frankena, 1962a), where "obligation" is rooted in an other-oriented perspective (Pepper, 1958):

> *Duty* . . . is applicable only to social situations of one sort or another. The use of the term implies that certain aspects of the total behavior pattern of an individual are of affective interest to his fellows. (Hilliard, 1950, p. 246)
> The term *obligation* . . . is . . . derived from persistent or recurrent patterns of reciprocal behavior in the complex of human interrelationships. (p. 258)
> *Responsibility* [means] that a man *will* be held to account for his acts by his fellows [or that he] is influenced in his conduct by . . . the affective consequences of his actions upon others. (pp. 258-259)
> Obligation is a complex concept, . . . expressive of a specific desire in response to the desires of other persons. . . . It is inconceivable that I ought to do anything that someone else does not want me to do. (Parker, 1957, pp. 52-53)
> Whether an act is morally good or bad depends upon its character of being beneficial or harmful, *i.e.* depends upon the way in which it affects the good of various beings. (Von Wright, 1963, p. 119)

Further, morality generally implies a propensity toward action (Lewis, 1946; Hampshire, 1982). Thus, Lewis (1946) argues that "'the moral' has its connotation of the attitude which looks toward action" (p. 439): "This moral sense . . . must be preponderantly active. . . . A good life . . . must be expected to reflect the characteristics findable in goods of action" (pp. 482-483). Hampshire (1982) agrees that "the domain of morality is the domain of action" (p. 90).

Morality shares these active and other-oriented aspects with political value. In contrast to politics, however, virtue is intrinsically rather than extrinsically motivated (Brightman, 1962)—"for its own sake" (Bond, 1983; Von Wright, 1963)—as when we engage in ethical actions "as ends in themselves" (Harré & Secord, 1973; Perry, 1954). One values a moral experience of virtue not because it contributes to some further purpose but because it is "right" in and of itself. Thus, philosophers accept the popular saying that "virtue is its own reward" (Parker, 1957, p. 272; Scruton, 1981, p. 118): "One critical difference between legal and ethical commands is that . . . the moral injunction . . . aims to create a wish for the sake of the intrinsic satisfaction that the fulfillment of that wish will bring" (Parker, 1957, p. 79). This is the essence of regarding virtue as "its own reward." Indeed, the moment we stop pursuing some ethical action as an end in itself and begin pursuing it as a means to some ulterior purpose, it stops being ethical and partakes of some other sort of value.

Here, it is helpful to preserve Frankena's (1973) distinction between ethical obligation (a question of duty or deontic judgment) and moral value (a question of virtue or aretaic judgment). With respect to ethical obligation, an ethical egoist (e.g., Epicurus, Hobbes, Nietzsche) pursues a self-oriented perspective that is clearly inconsistent with the present typology. By contrast, the ethical universalist (e.g., a utilitarian) pursues the greatest *general* good and holds that "An act . . . is right if and only if it is . . . conducive to at least as great a balance of good over evil in the universe as a whole as any alternative would be" (pp. 15-16) or that it promotes "the greatest good *of the greatest number*" (p. 42). Clearly, this perspective is active and other-oriented. Ethical utilitarianism says that: "The moral end to be sought in all we do [active] is *the greatest possible balance of good over evil* . . . in the world as a whole [other-oriented]" (p. 34). With respect to moral value (our more specific concern here), Frankena (1973) suggests that the considerations brought to bear on ethical obligation "could also be recast as kinds of ethics of virtue" (p. 63)—e.g., as "aretaic judgments of action" (p. 63). It follows that virtue may be regarded as pursuing the moral end just defined. In response to the question of *why* one would pursue such an end, Frankena (1973) suggests that virtue (like pleasure, beauty, and love) may be regarded as an intrinsic value desired "for their own sakes" (p. 87): "The *experience* of them . . . is good in itself" (p. 89); "What is intrinsically good is the contemplation or experiencing of them" (p. 89); "The experience of acting virtuously . . . may be intrinsically good" (p. 89); "In this sense virtue is its own reward" (p. 94).

Thus, one might defend one's consumption of charity services on the moral grounds that it is "right" to behave generously without offering any further reason or objective. Donating one's money to the United Fund, one's blood to the Red Cross, or one's time to a soup kitchen constitutes an ethically virtuous action if one pursues helping others purely for its own sake. If, by contrast, one were to invoke the aim of benefiting from tax deductions, earning gratitude, or improving the neighborhood by reducing the number of street people, the relevant type of value would become political rather than moral.[22]

In sum, our view of morality and virtue as intrinsic, other-oriented, and active in nature is consistent (as shown in brackets) with the following sorts of summary statements:

The intention of acting [active] is morally good, if and only if, good for somebody [other-oriented] is intended for its own sake [intrinsic] and harm is not foreseen to follow for anybody [other-oriented] from the act [active]. (Von Wright, 1963, p. 128)

The moral principle . . . extracts an obligation to behave in certain ways [active]. . . . The interest . . . is . . . not *my* interest (self-interest), but my neighbor's interest [other-oriented]. It is for the sake of *my neighbor's good* that moral conduct is required of *me*. . . . By love of one's neighbor [other-oriented], we can understand pursuit of one's neighbor's good "for its own sake" [intrinsic] or, as it can also be called, as an "ultimate end" [intrinsic] of action [active]. (Von Wright, 1983, p. 80)

Ethical pull is the term . . . for the moral claim on us exerted by others [other-oriented] so that, in virtue of what they are like [intrinsic], we ought to behave toward them in certain ways and not others [active]. (Nozick, 1981, p. 451)

The history of moral philosophy revolves around questions of duty and obligation . . . the courses of action [active] one pursues in relation to the other members of a social group [other-oriented]. . . . A central question . . . is . . . the intrinsic worth of . . . moral principles [intrinsic]. (Alicke, 1983, pp. 4-5)

Spirituality (Faith or Ecstasy)

Finally, *spirituality* resembles morality in its emphasis on the attainment of intrinsic other-oriented value. *Faith* is oriented toward "demands upon us by whatever we may mean by 'God' or 'the Divine'" (Parker, 1957, p. 20). Similarly, *ecstasy* is often described as a mystical disappearance of the self-other dichotomy in "a class of states vaguely described as 'exaltation' and 'rapture' accompanied by a 'sense of union'" (Perry, 1954, p. 488): "Religious values are realized in ecstasy and desperation, which measure the proximity to or distance from the holy. The specific corresponding reactions are those of faith, worship and adoration" (Frondizi, 1971, p. 118). In this light, the intrinsic value of religious faith (Brightman, 1962) is pursued for its own sake and is recognized as the Ultimate Good, as "supreme value . . . good . . . above all other goods" (Perry, 1954, p. 464), as "self-validating" (Mukerjee, 1964, p. 86), and as "that than which nothing better can be thought" (Hartman, 1967, p. 116): "For a church, faith seems to be its own justification, as if . . . the belief were regarded as terminal and for its own sake" (Pepper, 1958, p. 585).

By contrast with the engagement in good deeds that characterizes moral virtue, however, spiritual ecstasy involves an essentially reactive response to the Deity or to some other Force as part of a devotional experience. One worships a Divine Power; one adores one's God. This difference between spirituality and morality is the essence of the familiar contrast between sincere faith (reactive) and good works (active).

Finally, we should note the parallelism between spiritual and esthetic value—that is, between ecstasy and beauty. Both are intrinsic and reactive in nature. The difference between them hinges on the tendency for esthetic versus spiritual value to show self- as opposed to other-oriented tendencies. Thus, in general:

$$Ecstasy:Morality::Beauty:Play^{23}$$

Parallelisms in Types of Value

By offering numerous citations in support of the present typology of value, I have not intended to convey the false impression that other writers have arrived at the same taxonomic scheme as that proposed here. Indeed, each investigator has tended to divide the subject differently—

often according to only the most haphazard and vaguely specified method of categorization. Nevertheless, one does note a discernible drift toward consensus concerning key differences in the major types of value. First, at least one author (Rokeach, 1973) defines "value" in a manner that implicitly includes distinctions comparable to the three dimensions underlying the present typology. We may gloss the Rokeach definition (where key parallels are shown in brackets) as follows:

A *value* is an enduring belief that a specific mode [extrinsic] of conduct [active] or end-state [intrinsic] of existence [reactive] is personally [self-oriented] or socially [other-oriented] preferable to an opposite or converse mode [extrinsic] of conduct [active] or end-state [intrinsic] of existence [reactive]. (Rokeach, 1973, p. 5)

And second, many of C. Morris's (1956) "Ways to Live" can be clearly classified as embodiments of efficiency or excellence (e.g., "constantly master changing conditions"), politics or esteem (e.g., "act and enjoy life through group participation"), play or esthetics (e.g., "live with wholesome, carefree enjoyment"), and morality or spirituality (e.g., "obey the cosmic purpose"). Additionally, others have constructed sets of values that overlap partially (though never completely) with those proposed here. (Frankena, 1967; Hartman, 1967; Hilliard, 1950; Mukerjee, 1964; Parker, 1957; Pepper, 1958; Taylor, 1961)

The Blurring and Compresence of Different Kinds of Value in the Consumption Experience

These and other efforts toward the compartmentalization of values should not blind us to the following facts: (a) the three dimensions of value are continua admitting large shaded or gray areas rather than providing sharp dichotomous distinctions, and (b) any one consumption experience is likely to involve more than one type of value simultaneously. Thus, regarding (a), Parker (1957) notes that each aspect of value varies "according to its relative dominance in degree" (p. 93); and C. Morris (1956) suggests that one might conceptualize the problem according to "dimensions which define a 'value space'" with each value "defined by a point in that space" (p. 6). And regarding (b), Taylor (1961) argues for the "possible combinations of . . . value" in the same "experience" (p. 24); and Lee (1957) concludes "Any object may have many values according to the various contextures of which it may be a part" (p. 190). Hence, our discussion should not be interpreted as implying that the eight kinds of value occur in isolation or that they are in any sense mutually exclusive in any given situation. Rather, it suggests that many kinds of value—each in a different degree—tend to commingle in any one consumption experience (Eisert, 1983; Hilliard, 1950; Lewis, 1946).

One favorite example of this blurring among compresent values concerns the case of art and architecture. For example, C. Morris (1964) notes that a painting may be evaluated on both esthetic and moral grounds, and Perry (1954) argues that a house may provide both beauty (as art) and utility (as shelter).

Another favorite example concerns the case of organized religion. Both Perry (1954) and Rokeach (1973) point out that in addition to providing intrinsic value (noted earlier), attending worship services may also be used as a means, as when, for example, "a person . . . employs religion in a utilitarian and opportunistic manner to advance his own success and social status" (Rokeach, 1973, p. 111). We may expand this example to consider the full potential implications for value in the experience of going to church or visiting a synagogue. Without leaving one's pew, one can focus on passing the collection plate as speedily as possible (efficiency); on the plush, comfortable properties of the purple upholstery (excellence); on smiling politely at the boss's spouse in the next pew (politics); and on contemplating with satisfaction the program that lists one's name as donor of the flowers on the altar (esteem). Simultaneously, one may invent witty retorts to the minister's sermon (play); one may respond passionately to the majestic tones of the organist's mighty prelude and fugue (esthetics); one may resolve to engage in charitable donations by tithing for the next 12 months (morality); and one may even find some time left over to renew one's profound devotional commitment to the faith (spirituality).

It should be clear, then, that no consumption experience is likely to be interpretable as displaying only one pure type of value. Rather, each instance of consuming behavior tends to engage various kinds of value and thereby to blur the distinctions among them. The distinctions themselves remain useful, however, for they deepen our understanding of the axiological richness implicit in even the most apparently ordinary consumption experience (Olson, 1967).

Directions for Future Research

Having considered a proposed typology of value in the consumption experience, we shall now inquire briefly into its usefulness for suggesting potentially fruitful directions for future research in consumer behavior. I believe that its promise lies primarily in four interrelated areas: (a) calling attention to previously neglected types of customer value, (b) providing a model of competence in linguistic use as opposed to performance in psycholinguistic usage, (c) highlighting the need for consumer research at the macro level across product categories, and (d) helping to demarcate the boundary between marketing intelligence and consumer research.

Neglected Types of Customer Value

Consumer researchers have long recognized the importance of efficiency or excellence and of politics or esteem through their explicit consideration of the instrumental utility and status implications of consumption activities. Moreover, increased attention has recently focused on the hedonic aspects of consumption directed toward the pursuit of playful activities (e.g., Holbrook, Chestnut, Oliva, & Greenleaf, 1984) or esthetic experiences (e.g., Holbrook & Zirlin, 1985). Further, initial studies have begun to explore the boundaries of spiritual value in consumer behavior; here, note a dissertation by Havlena entitled "The Varieties of Consumption Experience" (Havlena & Holbrook, 1986); LaBarbera (1987; Hirschman & LaBarbera, 1987) and Hirschman (1988, 1990) have examined aspects of sacred as opposed to secular consumption; and Belk, Wallendorf, and Sherry (1989) have written on this subject under the title, "Theodicy on the Odyssey."

However, with the exception of some recent work by Smith (1990), relatively little attention has been devoted by consumer researchers to the study of morality in consumption. Yet, in general, the consumption experiences involved in the pursuit of virtue and ethical action appear to make up an important part of consumer behavior that still awaits investigation. For example, much of family life, social relations, and community activity falls into this category. By investing their scarce time resources in moral activities, people do engage in a form of consumption behavior. Isolated studies have begun to look at such ethical consumption as energy conservation, blood donation, and ecology consciousness—or, conversely, what I have called "consumer *mis*behavior." However, the field still awaits a major frontal attack on the problem of consumer morality.

Competence in Linguistic Use Versus
Performance in Psycholinguistic Usage

In developing a typology of value in the consumption experience, I have emulated the emphasis placed on the use of language by post-Wittgensteinian philosophers. In his later writings, Wittgenstein (1953) enunciated the famous dictum, "The meaning of a word is its use in the language" (p. 20e): "Look at the sentence as an instrument, and at its sense as its employment" (p. 126e). Wittgenstein regarded "the grammar of the word" (a somewhat idiosyncratic use of "grammar") as "the way in which it is used" (Gier, 1981, p. 207) in a language "game" played according to certain rules of ordinary discourse (Fann, 1969): "A language is a set of practices defined by certain rules, namely the rules which govern all the various uses of words in the language" (Taylor, 1961, p. 275). A focus on the rules for linguistic use has thus become the credo of the so-called ordinary language philosophers (Chappell, 1964):

> The way to understand the meaning of a word is to study it in the language-game to which it belongs. . . . In general, the meaning of a word is not an object for which it stands, but rather its use as a language. . . . one gives the use of a piece of language by describing its role in a language-game. . . . a language-game is a more or less complicated sharable human activity. (Kenny, 1973, pp. 14, 168)

Thus far, I have dealt primarily with a formal conceptual model of linguistic use in value terminology. This focus has been helpful in permitting us to distinguish clearly among various more and less closely related value terms. Certainly, one need not apologize for this attempt to clarify the prevailing use of language among writers on value concepts. Indeed, Hartman (1967) argues that such "refinement of *language*" (p. 74) underlies all scientific progress. This linguistic project also appears highly consistent with the viewpoint adopted by Harré and Secord (1973):

> The conceptual system embedded in ordinary language should provide the basis for the concepts employed in a study, and should serve as the model for their logical interconnections. Thus, any serious study should begin with a careful conceptual analysis. (p. 134) We have emphasized the importance of making use of ordinary language concepts. . . . A person's use of ordinary language in describing his own and other's actions . . . is vital to a proper behavioural science. . . . problems arise because of the use of different operations in different experiments and because of the failure to conduct a conceptual

analysis of the concept. . . . One important feature of our recommendations is the priority we give to the preliminary analysis of the concepts to be employed in an empirical study, as those concepts are commonly used. Psychologists, we believe, should make allies of the linguistic philosophers, who have made very thorough and subtle analyses of a great number of psychologically interesting concepts. (pp. 298-303)

However, we must also recognize that, in their real everyday verbal behavior, consumers may or may not tend to use value terms according to the rules by which I have defined them conceptually.

This distinction between the idealized and realistic use of language has often been recognized. For example, Ryle (1964, p. 25) notes a difference between what he calls "the ordinary use of language" (i.e., its standard or stock deployment) and "the use of ordinary language" (i.e., how it functions colloquially in the vernacular). The first he equates with "use," the second with "usage" (p. 30). Similarly, C. Morris (1946, p. 219) distinguishes between "semantics" (dealing with "the signification of signs") and "pragmatics" (dealing with "the origin, uses, and effects of signs within . . . behavior"). The former appears to encompass much of Ryle's "use," the latter much of his "usage." Further, within the area of syntax, Chomsky (1965) emphasizes "a fundamental distinction between *competence* (the speaker-hearer's knowledge of his language) and *performance* (the actual use of the language in concrete situations)" (p. 4). In the case of each split, the first member is the proper subject of linguistics whereas the second raises concerns of interest to psycholinguistics. We may therefore summarize this contrast by the phrases *competence in linguistic use* versus *performance in psycholinguistic usage*.

The aforementioned thinkers have clearly recognized that knowledge of use or competence may tell us relatively little about usage or performance because "perfectly mastering a use is not getting to know everything, or even much, about a usage" (Ryle, 1964, p. 32): "Only under . . . idealization . . . is performance a direct reflection of competence. In actual fact, it obviously could not directly reflect competence" (Chomsky, 1965, p. 4). This discrepancy has been acknowledged by the linguistic philosophers (Gendlin, 1973, p. 282). However, much of linguistic analysis rests on the enlightened introspective verbal habits of the philosophers themselves: "Linguistic analysts do not actually go out and observe situations directly. They would not accept an empirical statistical study of the use of a word, because . . . people use words in a sloppy way" (Gendlin, 1973, p. 285). This methodological stance places linguistic philosophers in something of a quandary since they are committed to "understanding . . . the public practice of utterance" (Scruton, 1981, p. 279), yet retain the meditative habits of their profession: "The British analysts of the 'ordinary language' emphasis . . . are apparently caught in the dilemma of trying to deal with . . . ordinary language in a way that is in one sense empirical and in another sense not empirical but 'logical'" (C. Morris, 1964, p. 45). Accordingly, some commentators have raised "certain difficulties" concerning the kinds of conclusions drawn by ordinary language philosophers: "I am mainly interested in the question of how one would go about verifying these statements; insofar as meaning is bound up with verification, this is also a question of their meaning" (Mates, 1964, p. 64).

Such questions have led some philosophers to call for "an empirical investigation of speaking habits" (Carnap, 1966, p. 264). In this spirit, Alicke (1983) urges the need for an empirically based value terminology: "No thorough analysis of evaluative predicates is possible without an understanding of how such terms are used in the specific value-languages of the participants. The meaning of an evaluative term must be referred to the belief and attitude system of the user" (Alicke, 1983, p. 22). Late in his career, C. Morris (1956, 1964) moved strongly in this direction, turning increasingly to laboratory techniques for investigating the usage of words in psycholinguistic performance as a basis for understanding their meaning:

> There is a need for . . . experimental methods in the determination of the signification of value terms which do not depend upon the utilization of the signification of other signs. The . . . studies reported here were in part attempts to devise a method for studying the signification (or significations) of the terms . . . without asking the persons using these signs to say anything whatsoever as to what these terms "meant" to them. . . . In what follows, "the signification of a sign" means the properties something must have for the sign to apply to it. (C. Morris, 1964, p. 164)

In short, C. Morris adopted a strategy of empiricism and strove "to get light on the signification of the term . . . by attempting to find the conditions under which it is applied" (1964, p. 170).

I subscribe to the importance and validity of C. Morris's insistence on investigating performance in psycholinguistic usage. In this connection, I strongly suspect that the present typology of value provides a better model of competence in linguistic use than of performance in psycholinguistic usage. In other words, the typology aspires to indicate how value terms *should* be used for conceptual clarity but may not correspond to the actual usage of those terms by which consumers *do* describe their consumption experiences. Indeed, Holbrook and Corfman's (1985) study of the latter issue suggests that in actual usage by real consumers, terms such as "quality" and "fun" indicate levels of evaluative judgment more global than the partitioned categories suggested by the present taxonomy. This initial study therefore indicates the need for further research on the usage of value terms in psycholinguistic performance by consumers making judgments concerning their consumption experiences.

The Need for Consumer Research at the Macro Level Across Product Categories

In my opinion, the systematic study of consumer value will inevitably require the adoption of a macro-level perspective that cuts across product categories (as opposed to the micro-level view that restricts attention to differences among brands or trade names within a product class). This conclusion stems from the fact that dramatic differences in customer value occur more conspicuously between types of goods or services than between various brands of the same good or providers of the same service. The relatively trivial contrast between Gillette and Schick or between McDonald's and Burger King is dwarfed by the comparatively dramatic difference between shaving and chewing gum or between eating in a fast-food restaurant and going to church. If we want to explore the types of value underlying the consumption experiences of flesh-and-blood consumers, we should prepare to investigate the full scope of their consuming activities across the broad range of experiences among which they allocate their time. In other words, we must agree to neglect minor differences in value among brands at the micro level in order to concentrate on major differences in value among types of consumption experiences at the macro level.

The Boundary Between Marketing Intelligence and Consumer Research

It follows that if consumer researchers wish to explore different types of value in the consumption experience, they must depart from the focus of primary interest to marketing managers. In undertaking marketing research, managers generally seek better to understand the determinants of brand preference or choice within a product category. Thus, marketing intelligence typically focuses on interbrand differences at the micro level of analysis: Gillette versus Schick or McDonald's versus Burger King. By contrast, I have argued that consumer research devoted to the study of customer value must adopt a broader focus on interproduct differences at the macro level of analysis: Chewing gum versus church. In comparison with this prescribed focus, marketing intelligence usually chooses to operate within a parochial, unnecessarily constricted view of the consumer's world. Its insights may contribute lucratively to the firm's bottom line. But in the realm of value, its perspectives and procedures conflict with those appropriate to the study of consumer behavior. I therefore consider it unlikely that managerially oriented marketing research will move far toward better understanding the nature of value in the consumption experience. The lead in this direction must come from intrinsically motivated consumer research that views the topic as a subject of interest for its own sake as an end in itself (Holbrook, 1985, 1986, 1987).

Conclusion

This chapter has introduced a concern for the nature and role of value in consumer behavior. Drawing on work from axiology, I have proposed a definition of customer value as an interactive relativistic preference experience. I have suggested that products contribute to customer value insofar as they provide services that create desired consumption experiences. As an elaboration of this definition, I have developed a typology of customer value and have distinguished among eight primary types of value in the consumption experience. This taxonomy indicates neglected kinds of customer value in need of future investigation (e.g., consumer morality), raises questions concerning possible differences between the use and usage of value terms, points to the advantages of studying value experiences across rather than within categories of goods or services, and thereby anticipates one likely divergence between marketing intelligence and consumer research. I suspect that those willing to abandon narrow managerial concerns and to follow this consumer-oriented thread where it leads them will be rewarded by otherwise unobtainable insights concerning the nature of value in the consumption experience.

Notes

1. In what follows, I shall use the term *products* to refer to goods, services, people, places, things, ideas, or events of all types (Juran, 1988). However, at a more fundamental level of analysis, I shall maintain that *all* products perform *services* by contributing to value-creating *experiences*. Moreover, I shall treat quality as just one type of customer value that potentially results from such services. These latter two points are vital to positioning this chapter within the context of the present volume.

2. Thus, the "object" may be a thing or event, or it may be an experience thereof. In the latter case, somewhat paradoxically, value becomes *an experience of an experience*.

3. As noted earlier, this point is crucial to the positioning of this chapter in the present volume.

4. This general distinction between "value" (preferential judgment) and "values" (standards) parallels the second sense of "perceived value" discussed by Zeithaml (1988), whose respondents "emphasized the benefits they received from the product as the most important components of value." She notes: "This second definition is essentially the same as the economist's definition of utility, that is, a subjective measure of the usefulness or want satisfaction that results from consumption. . . . In these definitions, value encompasses all relevant choice criteria" (p. 13).

5. See, for example, Fishbein and Ajzen (1975). Here, the "value" of each attribute refers to one of the standards used to evaluate some object (i.e., thing or event). The resulting "affect" would correspond more closely to the present concept of "value" as an interactive relativistic preference experience.

6. Note that this issue concerns *not* different *types* of value (discussed later) but rather different *theories* of value (Osborne, 1933; Taylor, 1961). Because my definition commits me to an interactionist perspective, I must discuss this issue briefly. However, we cannot expect to resolve the objectivist-subjectivist debate. Indeed, it may be essentially unresolvable (Lamont, 1955). As Frondizi (1971) puts it, "Are things valuable because we value them or do we value them because they are valuable" (p. ix)?

7. In this spirit, the PIMS studies have attempted to measure quality (one type of value) by asking the following question: "Estimate the percentage of this business's sales volume in this year accounted for by products and services that *from the perspective of the customer* are assessed as 'Superior,' 'Equivalent,' and 'Inferior' to those available from the three leading competitors" (Phillips, Chang, & Buzzell, 1983, p. 32).

8. In the classroom, this labor theory can be effectively disproved by laboriously breaking a piece of chalk into tiny little pieces. The labor invested in the chalk increases dramatically, but its value declines precipitously. Dickson (1985) makes essentially the same point by contrasting the labor theory with the usage theory of value.

9. In this light, recall the old conundrum about whether a tree falling in the forest makes a sound if there is no one there to hear it; the point is that, even if it does make a sound, the fact that no one hears it means that the sound can *not* have any *value*. In Frondizi's (1971) words, "The correct assertion that nothing can be [valued] if there is no subject to appraise it can only lead one to infer legitimately that the subject who appraises cannot be discarded when one examines the nature of value" (p. 55).

10. Interestingly, this interactionist perspective corresponds closely to one of Pirsig's (1974) passing shots at defining "quality": "Quality is not objective. . . . Quality is not subjective. . . . Phaedrus . . . went straight between the horns of the subjectivity-objectivity

dilemma and said Quality is neither a part of mind, nor is it a part of matter. It is . . . the *relationship of the two* with *each other*. It is the point at which subject and object meet" (pp. 231-233). As Holland (1973)—another literary figure—put it: "The problem, then, is not to sort out subjective from objective but to see how the two combine when we have experiences" (p. 2).

11. For a comparable taxonomic approach—based on such contrasts as actual/potential, direct/indirect, positive/indifferent/negative, and instrumental/terminal—see Hilliard (1950).

12. I present these dimensions in the form of simple bipolarities, but it should be clear throughout that these distinctions represent continua with various gradations in between the two extremes.

13. As noted by Loring (1966), this emphasis in axiology is essentially Aristotelian. Aristotle "held that goodness in anything was essentially the property of fulfilling its purpose": "When we say a thing is good we mean that it is . . . suited to perform its proper function" (p. 14).

14. Note that this acknowledgement of hedonic value in no way reduces to that branch of philosophy known as Hedonism. The latter takes "pleasure as the one and only intrinsic value" (Pepper 1958, p. 345). By contrast, like Olson (1967), the present argument views (self-oriented) pleasure as one type of intrinsic value and distinguishes this from other major types of value (discussed later).

15. Indeed, one writer (Mukerjee, 1964) has specialized in providing a virtual compendium of self-other terminology: "egoism/altruism" (p. 10); "self-actualization/self-transcendence" (p. 10); "I/Thou" (p. 13); "isolated, subjective self/self-in relation to cosmos" (p. 14); "autonomy and integrity/social harmony" (p. 20); "autonomy/heteronomy" (p. 21); "individuality/order" (p. 21); "self/environment" (p. 21); "individual/society" (p. 24); "individual/collective" (p. 36); "egoism/communion" (p. 36); "inner/outer" (p. 74); "self/other" (p. 80); "self/world" (p. 108); "man/cosmos" (p. 115); "singleness/wholeness" (p. 133); and "finiteness/universality" (p. 133).

16. I use the term "reactive" instead of "passive" because the type of value in question may still involve much (re)active information processing (via the so-called active model of perception).

17. This concept of efficiency-based convenience as an output/input ratio with time as one key input is the type of value in the present typology that corresponds to Zeithaml's (1988) more general definition of value as "the consumer's overall assessment of the utility of a product based on perceptions of what is received and what is given" where "value represents a tradeoff of the salient give and get components" (p. 14). As Zeithaml suggests, "convenience" is one type of value in which a "pivotal concern" is "saving time" or reducing "time, effort, and search costs."

18. Evidence that customers in general and customers for services in particular can distinguish excellence (quality) from other types of value such as efficiency (convenience) comes from the list of quality/value-added components provided by Ragland (1989, p. 20) for different service-related businesses: Banks (financial stability/easy to understand); coffee shops (cleanliness/hours open); convenience stores (clean/items easy to find); discount stores (well-known brands/easy returns); furniture stores (well-known brands/delivery); gas stations (octane rating/speed of pumps); jewelry stores (custom designing/fast service); pizza restaurants (taste/home delivery); specialty tune-up clinics (fixed right the first time/car ready when promised).

19. This carefully specified concept of quality and its differentiation from other types of value is a key contribution of the present typology. An earlier discussion by Holbrook and

Corfman (1985) distinguished between various competing views of quality. The subsequently proliferating alternative conceptualizations of quality are beyond the scope of the present discussion. Further details appear in work by, among others, Garvin (1988), Steenkamp (1989), and Zeithaml (1988).

20. Somewhat disappointingly, Garvin (1988) never does commit himself to any core definition based on the central meaning of the quality concept. Rather, he contends that "analysis along multiple dimensions . . . provides greater insight into how judgments about quality are formed" (p. 112).

21. This approbation could come from oneself—as in the case of self-esteem, in which the "self" is, in some sense, admired by another part of one's own personality. This kind of inner-dwelling "other" sets up an interesting parallel to certain phenomena noted later under the heading of spiritual value.

22. In this connection, when mothers or fathers kiss their infants, we assume that this virtuous activity is done for the sake of the relationship established with the children. By contrast, when candidates for office kiss babies, we know that the purpose is to win votes; the value in question shifts from morality to politics.

23. At times, however, esthetic consumption experiences can become so powerful that they verge on ecstatic rapture (Hilliard, 1950; Makkreel, 1975; Straus, 1981). For example, in listening to the finale of Beethoven's Ninth Symphony, gazing at the ceiling of the Sistine Chapel, reading Milton's epic poetry, or even watching a dramatic sunset, we sometimes feel almost as if we become part of the object of our admiration. We seem to lose our independent consciousness and to merge with the work of art. At such moments, the self-object dichotomy seems to dissolve. We enter a state of ecstatic experience.

References

Abbott, L. (1955). *Quality and competition.* New York: Columbia University Press.

Adler, M. J. (1981). *Six great ideas.* New York: Macmillan.

Alicke, M. (1983). Philosophical investigations of values. In L. R. Kahle (Ed.), *Social values and social change* (pp. 3-23). New York: Praeger.

Andreasen, A. R. (1991). Consumer behavior research and social policy. In T. S. Robertson & H. H. Kassarjian (Eds.), *Handbook of consumer behavior* (pp. 459-506). Englewood Cliffs, NJ: Prentice-Hall.

Andrews, F. M., & Withey, S. B. (1976). *Social indicators of well-being.* New York: Plenum.

Arrow, K. J. (1967). Public and private values. In S. Hook (Ed.), *Human values and economic policy* (pp. 3-21). New York: New York University Press.

Bass, F. M., & Wilkie, W. L. (1973). A comparative analysis of attitudinal predictions of brand preference. *Journal of Marketing Research, 10,* 262-269.

Baylis, C. A. (1958). Grading, values, and choice. *Mind, 67,* 485-501.

Beardsley, M. C. (1967). History of aesthetics. In P. Edwards (Ed.), *Encyclopedia of philosophy* (Vol. 1, pp. 18-35). New York: Macmillan and Free Press.

Becker, G. M., & McClintock, C. G. (1967). Value: Behavioral decision theory. *Annual Review of Psychology, 18,* 239-286.

Becker, G. S. (1976). *The economic approach to human behavior.* Chicago: University of Chicago Press.

Belk, R. W. (1975). Situational variables and consumer behavior. *Journal of Consumer Research, 2,* 157-164.

Belk, R. W., Wallendorf, M. R., & Sherry, J., Jr. (1989). The sacred and the profane in consumer behavior: Theodicy on the odyssey. *Journal of Consumer Research, 16,* 1-38.

Berlyne, D. E. (1969). Laughter, humor, and play. In G. Lindzey & E. Aronson (Eds.), *The handbook of social psychology* (Vol. 3, pp. 795-852). Reading, MA: Addison-Wesley.

Bond, E. J. (1983). *Reason and value.* Cambridge, UK: Cambridge University Press.

Boote, A. S. (1975). *An exploratory investigation of the roles of needs and personal values in the theory of buyer behavior.* Unpublished doctoral dissertation, Columbia University, Graduate School of Business.

Brandt, R. B. (1967). Personal values and the justification of institutions. In S. Hook (Ed.), *Human values and economic policy* (pp. 22-40). New York: New York University Press.

Brightman, E. S. (1962). Axiology. In D. D. Runes (Ed.), *Dictionary of philosophy* (pp. 32-33). Totowa, NJ: Littlefield, Adams.

Budd, M. (1983). Belief and sincerity in poetry. In E. Schaper (Ed.), *Pleasure, preference and value: Studies in philosophical aesthetics* (pp. 137-157). New York: Cambridge University Press.

Bullough, E. (1912). "Psychical distance" as a factor in art and an aesthetic principle. *British Journal of Psychology, 5,* 87-98.

Carnap, R. (1966). *An introduction to the philosophy of science.* New York: Basic Books.

Chappell, V. C. (1964). Introduction. In V. C. Chappell (Ed.), *Ordinary language* (pp. 1-4). New York: Dover.

Chomsky, N. (1965). *Aspects of the theory of syntax.* Cambridge, MA: MIT Press.

Cowan, A. (1964). *Quality control for the manager.* Oxford, UK: Pergamon.

Csikszentmihalyi, M. (1975). *Beyond boredom and anxiety.* San Francisco: Jossey-Bass.

Dearden, R. F. (1967). The concept of play. In R. S. Peters (Ed.), *The concept of education.* New York: Humanities Press.

Debreu, G. (1959). *Theory of value.* New Haven, CT: Yale University Press.

Dickson, P. R. (1985). *Marketing, Marx and added value.* Working paper, Department of Marketing, Ohio State University.

Diesing, P. (1962). *Reason in society: Five types of decisions and their social conditions.* Urbana: University of Illinois Press.

Duesenberry, J. S. (1949). *Income, saving and the theory of consumer behavior.* Cambridge, MA: Harvard University Press.

Eisert, D. C. (1983). Marriage and parenting. In L. R. Kahle (Ed.), *Social values and social change* (pp. 143-167). New York: Praeger.

Fallon, C. (1971). *Value analysis to improve productivity.* New York: John Wiley.

Fann, K. T. (1969). *Wittgenstein's conception of philosophy.* Berkeley: University of California Press.

Fishbein, M., & Ajzen, I. (1975). *Belief, attitude, intention and behavior.* Reading, MA: Addison-Wesley.

Frankena, W. K. (1962a). Ethics. In D. D. Runes (Ed.), *Dictionary of philosophy* (pp. 98-100). Totowa, NJ: Littlefield, Adams.

Frankena, W. K. (1962b). Value. In D. D. Runes (Ed.), *Dictionary of philosophy* (pp. 330-331). Totowa, NJ: Littlefield, Adams.

Frankena, W. K. (1967). Value and valuation. In P. Edwards (Ed.), *The encyclopedia of philosophy* (Vol. 8, pp. 229-232). New York: Macmillan.

Frankena, W. K. (1973). *Ethics* (2nd ed.). Englewood Cliffs, NJ: Prentice-Hall.

Frondizi, R. (1971). *What is value? An introduction to axiology* (2nd ed.). La Salle, IL: Open Court.

Galbraith, J. K. (1956). *American capitalism: The concept of countervailing power.* Boston: Houghton Mifflin.

Garvin, D. A. (1988). *Managing quality: The strategic and competitive edge.* New York: Free Press.

Gendlin, E. T. (1973). Experiential phenomenology. In M. Natanson (Ed.), *Phenomenology and the social sciences* (Vol. 1, pp. 281-322). Evanston, IL: Northwestern University Press.

Gier, N. F. (1981). *Wittgenstein and phenomenology.* Albany: State University of New York Press.

Guiry, M. (1989). *Quality and customer service: The critical focus for a firm* (Conference Summary, Marketing Science Institute, Report No. 89-117, Cambridge, MA 02138).

Hall, E. W. (1961). *Our knowledge of fact and value.* Chapel Hill: University of North Carolina Press.

Hampshire, S. (1982). *Thought and action* (2nd ed.). Notre Dame, IN: University of Notre Dame Press.

Hare, R. M. (1982). *Plato.* New York: Oxford University Press.

Harré, R., & Secord, P. F. (1973). *The explanation of social behavior.* Totowa, NJ: Littlefield, Adams.

Hartman, R. S. (1967). *The structure of values: Foundations of scientific axiology.* Carbondale, IL: Southern Illinois University Press.

Havlena, W. J., & Holbrook, M. B. (1986). The varieties of consumption experience: Comparing two typologies of emotion in consumer behavior. *Journal of Consumer Research, 13,* 394-404.

Hilliard, A. L. (1950). *The forms of value: The extension of hedonistic axiology.* New York: Columbia University Press.

Hirschman, E. C. (1988). The ideology of consumption: A structural-syntactical analysis of "Dallas" and "Dynasty." *Journal of Consumer Research, 15,* 344-359.

Hirschman, E. C. (1990). Secular immortality and the American ideology of affluence. *Journal of Consumer Research, 17,* 31-42.

Hirschman, E. C., & Holbrook, M. B. (1982). Hedonic consumption: Emerging concepts, methods and propositions. *Journal of Marketing, 46,* 92-101.

Hirschman, E. C., & LaBarbera, P. A. (1987). *Sacred and secular aspects of consumption: The role of possessions in the meaning of life.* Working paper, Department of Marketing, New York University.

Holbrook, M. B. (1984). Situation-specific ideal points and usage of multiple dissimilar brands. *Research in Marketing, 7,* 93-131.

Holbrook, M. B. (1985). Why business is bad for consumer research: The three bears revisited. In E. C. Hirschman & M. B. Holbrook (Eds.), *Advances in consumer research* (Vol. 12, pp. 145-156). Provo, UT: Association for Consumer Research.

Holbrook, M. B. (1986). Whither ACR? Some pastoral reflections on bears, Baltimore, baseball, and resurrecting consumer research. In R. J. Lutz (Ed.), *Advances in consumer research* (Vol. 13, pp. 436-441). Provo, UT: Association for Consumer Research.

Holbrook, M. B. (1987). Some notes on the banausic interrelationships among marketing academics and practitioners. In R. W. Belk & G. Zaltman (Eds.), *Proceedings of the Winter Educators' Conference* (pp. 342-343). Chicago, IL: American Marketing Association.

Holbrook, M. B., & Anand, P. (1990). Effects of tempo and situational arousal on the listener's perceptual and affective responses to music. *Psychology of Music, 18,* 150-162.

Holbrook, M. B., & Anand, P. (1992). The effects of situation, sequence, and features on perceptual and affective responses. *Empirical Studies of the Arts, 10,* 19-31.

Holbrook, M. B., Chestnut, R. W., Oliva, T. A., & Greenleaf, E. A. (1984). Play as a consumption experience: The roles of emotions, performance, and personality in the enjoyment of games. *Journal of Consumer Research, 11,* 728-739.

Holbrook, M. B., & Corfman, K. P. (1985). Quality and value in the consumption experience: Phaedrus rides again. In J. Jacoby & J. C. Olson (Eds.), *Perceived quality: How consumers view stores and merchandise* (pp. 31-57). Lexington, MA: D. C. Heath.

Holbrook, M. B., & Hirschman, E. C. (1982). The experiential aspects of consumption: Consumer fantasies, feelings, and fun. *Journal of Consumer Research, 9,* 132-140.

Holbrook, M. B., & Ryan, M. J. (1982). Modeling decision-specific stress: Some methodological considerations. *Administrative Science Quarterly, 27,* 243-258.

Holbrook, M. B., & Zirlin, R. B. (1985). Artistic creation, artworks, and aesthetic appreciation: Some philosophical contributions to nonprofit marketing. *Advances in Nonprofit Marketing, 1,* 1-54.

Holland, N. N. (1973). *Poems in persons: An introduction to the psychoanalysis of literature.* New York: Norton.

Hospers, J. (1967). Problems of aesthetics. In P. Edwards (Ed.), *The encyclopedia of philosophy* (Vol. 1, pp. 35-56). New York: Macmillan and Free Press.

Howard, J. A. (1977). *Consumer behavior: Application of theory.* New York: McGraw-Hill.

Huber, J., Holbrook, M. B., & Schiffman, S. (1982). Situational psychophysics and the vending-machine problem. *Journal of Retailing, 58,* 82-94.

Huizinga, J. (1938). *Homo ludens.* New York: Harper & Row.

Hyde, L. (1983). *The gift: Imagination and the erotic life of property.* New York: Vintage.

Jacoby, J., & Olson, J. C. (Eds.). (1985). *Perceived quality: How consumers view stores and merchandise.* Lexington, MA: D. C. Heath.

Juran, J. M. (1988). *Juran on planning for quality.* New York: Free Press.

Kahle, L. R. (1983a). Dialectical tensions in the theory of social values. In L. R. Kahle (Ed.), *Social values and social change* (pp. 275-283). New York: Praeger.

Kahle, L. R. (Ed.). (1983b). *Social values and social change.* New York: Praeger.

Kahle, L. R., & Timmer, S. G. (1983). A theory and a method for studying values. In L. R. Kahle (Ed.), *Social values and social change* (pp. 43-69). New York: Praeger.

Katona, G. (1972). Product quality: Economic and psychological considerations. In National Academy of Engineering (Ed.), *Product quality, performance, and cost* (pp. 44-48). Washington, DC: National Academy of Engineering.

Kenny, A. (1973). *Wittgenstein.* Cambridge, MA: Harvard University Press.

Kotler, P. J. (1972). A generic concept of marketing. *Journal of Marketing, 36,* 46-54.

Kotler, P. J. (1991). *Marketing management* (7th ed.). Englewood Cliffs, NJ: Prentice-Hall.

Kotler, P. J., & Levy, S. J. (1969). Broadening the concept of marketing. *Journal of Marketing, 33,* 10-15.

LaBarbera, P. A. (1987). Consumer behavior and born again christianity. *Research in Consumer Behavior, 2,* 193-222.

Ladd, J. (1967). The use of mechanical models for the solution of ethical problems. In S. Hook (Ed.), *Human values and economic policy* (pp. 157-169). New York: New York University Press.

Lamont, W. D. (1955). *The value judgment.* Westport, CT: Greenwood.

Laudan, L. (1977). *Progress and its problems: Towards a theory of scientific growth.* Berkeley: University of California Press.

Lee, H. N. (1957). The meaning of "intrinsic value." In R. Lepley (Ed.), *The language of value* (pp. 178-196). New York: Columbia University Press.

Levitt, T. (1960). Marketing myopia. *Harvard Business Review, 38,* 24-47.

Lewis, C. I. (1946). *An analysis of knowledge and valuation.* La Salle, IL: Open Court.

Loring, L. M. (1966). *Two kinds of values.* New York: Humanities Press.

Luce, R. D., & Raiffa, H. (1957). *Games and decisions.* New York: John Wiley.

Makkreel, R. A. (1975). *Dilthey: Philosopher of the human studies.* Princeton, NJ: Princeton University Press.

Mates, B. (1964). On the verification of statements about ordinary language. In V. C. Chappell (Ed.), *Ordinary language* (pp. 64-74). New York: Dover.

Maynes, E. S. (1975). The concept and measurement of product quality. In N. E. Terleckyj (Ed.), *Household production and consumption* (pp. 529-560). New York: Columbia University Press.

Miller, S. (1973). Ends, means, and galumphing: Some leitmotifs of play. *American Anthropologist, 75,* 87-98.

Mitchell, A. (1983). *The nine American lifestyles.* New York: Warner.

Moore, W. (1957). The language of values. In R. Lepley (Ed.), *The language of value* (pp. 9-28). New York: Columbia University Press.

Morris, C. (1946). *Signs, language, and behavior.* New York: George Braziller.

Morris, C. (1956). *Varieties of human value.* Chicago: University of Chicago Press.

Morris, C. (1964). *Signification and significance.* Cambridge, MA: MIT Press.

Morris, R. T. (1941). *The theory of consumer's demand.* New Haven, CT: Yale University Press.

Mukerjee, R. (1964). *The dimensions of values.* London: George Allen & Unwin.

Nozick, R. (1981). *Philosophical explanation.* Cambridge, MA: Harvard University Press.

Oliver, R. L. (1989). Processing of the satisfaction response in consumption: A suggested framework and research propositions. *Journal of Consumer Satisfaction, Dissatisfaction and Complaining Behavior, 2,* 1-16.

Olson, R. G. (1967). The good. In P. Edwards (Ed.), *The encyclopedia of philosophy* (Vol. 3, pp. 367-370), New York: Macmillan.

Osborne, H. (1933). *Foundations of the philosophy of value.* Cambridge, UK: Cambridge University Press.

Parasuraman, A., Zeithaml, V. A., & Berry, L. L. (1985). A conceptual model of service quality and its implications for future research. *Journal of Marketing, 49,* 41-50.

Parasuraman, A., Zeithaml, V. A., & Berry, L. L. (1988). SERVQUAL: A multiple-item scale for measuring consumer perceptions of service quality. *Journal of Retailing, 64,* 12-40.

Parker, D. H. (1957). *The philosophy of value.* Ann Arbor: University of Michigan Press.

Parsons, T. (1937). *The structure of social action* (Vol. 1). New York: Free Press.

Pepper, S. C. (1958). *The sources of value.* Berkeley: University of California Press.

Perry, R. B. (1954). *Realms of value.* Cambridge, MA: Harvard University Press.

Pettit, P. (1983). The possibility of aesthetic realism. In E. Schaper (Ed.), *Pleasure, prefer-ence and value: Studies in philosophical aesthetics* (pp. 17-38). New York: Cambridge University Press.

Phillips, L. W., Chang, D. R., & Buzzell, R. D. (1983). Product quality, cost position and business performance: A test of some key hypotheses. *Journal of Marketing, 47,* 26-43.

Pirsig, R. M. (1974). *Zen and the art of motorcycle maintenance: An inquiry into values.* New York: Bantam.

Pitts, R. E., Jr., & Woodside, A. G. (Eds.). (1984). *Personal values and consumer psychology.* Lexington, MA: Lexington.

Power, T. M. (1980). *The economic value of the quality of life.* Boulder, CO: Westview.

Rader, M. (Ed.). (1979). *A modern book of esthetics* (5th ed.). New York: Holt, Rinehart & Winston.

Ragland, T. C. (1989). Consumers define cost, value, and quality. *Marketing News, 23,* 20.

Riesman, D. (1950). *The lonely crowd.* New Haven, CT: Yale University Press.

Rokeach, M. (1973). *The nature of human values.* New York: Free Press.

Ryle, G. (1964). Ordinary language. In V. C. Chappell (Ed.), *Ordinary Language* (pp. 24-40). New York: Dover.

Santayana, G. (1896). *The sense of beauty.* New York: Dover.

Schlossberg, H. (1991, Feb. 4). U.S. firms: Quality is the way to satisfy. *Marketing News, 25,* 1, 8.

Scitovsky, T. (1976). *The joyless economy.* New York: Oxford University Press.

Scruton, R. (1981). *From Descartes to Wittgenstein.* New York: Harper Colophon.

Smith, N. C. (1990). *Morality and the market: Consumer pressure for corporate accountabil-ity.* New York: Routledge.

Steenkamp, J.B.E.M. (1989). *Product quality: An investigation into the concept and how it is perceived by consumers.* Assen/Maastricht, The Netherlands: Van Gorcum.

Stephenson, W. (1967). *The play theory of mass communication.* Chicago: University of Chicago Press.

Straus, R. A. (1981). The social-psychology of religious experience: A naturalistic approach. *Sociological Analysis, 42,* 57-67.

Suranyi-Unger, T., Jr. (1981). Consumer behavior and consumer well-being: An economist's digest. *Journal of Consumer Research, 8,* 132-143.

Taylor, P. W. (1961). *Normative discourse.* Englewood Cliffs, NJ: Prentice-Hall.

Tuchman, B. W. (1980, November 2). The decline of quality. *New York Times Magazine,* pp. 38-41, 104.

Veblen, T. (1899/1967). *The theory of the leisure class.* Harmondsworth, UK: Penguin.

Veroff, J. (1983). Introduction. In L. R. Kahle (Ed.), *Social values and social change* (pp. xiii-xviii). New York: Praeger.

Von Wright, G. H. (1963). *The varieties of goodness.* New York: Humanities Press.

Von Wright, G. H. (1983). *Practical reason.* Ithaca, NY: Cornell University Press.

Wells, W. D. (1974). *Lifestyle and psychographics.* Chicago: American Marketing Association.

White, R. W. (1959). Motivation reconsidered: The concept of competence. *Psychological Review, 66,* 297-333.

Wimmer, F. (1975). *Das qualitätsurteil des konsumenten: Theoretische grundlagen und empirische ergebnisse.* Frankfurt: Lang.

Wittgenstein, L. (1953). *Philosophical investigations.* New York: Macmillan.

Wolff, M. F. (1986). Quality/process control: What R and D can do. *Research Management, 29,* 9-11.

Zeithaml, V. A. (1988). Consumer perceptions of price, quality, and value: A means-end model and synthesis of evidence. *Journal of Marketing, 52,* 2-22.

CHAPTER THREE

Encounter Satisfaction Versus Overall Satisfaction Versus Quality

The Customer's Voice

MARY JO BITNER

AMY R. HUBBERT

College of Business, Arizona State University

The purpose of this chapter is to first provide definitions for and then explore three interrelated constructs—service encounter satisfaction, overall satisfaction, and perceived service quality—in an effort to understand whether consumers distinguish among the constructs in meaningful ways. A sample of consumers was asked to relate the details of a service encounter and was later asked to respond to both qualitative and quantitative measures of satisfaction and quality. Results of both confirmatory factor analysis and content analysis of open-ended responses suggest that the three constructs are distinct to consumers, but highly correlated. Of the three constructs, service encounter satisfaction appears to be the most distinguishable; overall satisfaction and perceived service quality are less so.

The drive for quality in products and services is apparent worldwide in the growing number of national quality awards (e.g., Lindstrom, 1992; Peacock, 1992; Reimann, 1992), the attention paid in the business press to quality issues (e.g., "The Quality Imperative," 1991), and the growing number of academic publications (e.g., Garvin, 1991; Parasuraman, Zeithaml, & Berry, 1988). Similarly, there is increasing attention among academics and business practitioners to customer satisfaction as a corporate goal (e.g., Bolton & Drew, 1991; Crosby, 1991; Oliva, Oliver, & MacMillan, 1992; Phillips, Dunkin, Treece, & Hammonds, 1990) in addition to traditional financial measures of success (Webster, 1988). In services, this focus on quality and customer satisfaction logically draws attention to the management of individual service encounters between the ultimate customer and representatives of the firm (Bitner, Booms, & Tetreault, 1990; Czepiel, Solomon, Surprenant, & Gutman, 1985), sometimes referred to as "moments of truth" (Carlzon, 1987). It is in these moments of truth that quality is most immediately evident to final consumers.

Without a doubt, customer satisfaction in each individual service encounter, the customer's overall satisfaction with a particular service provider, and perceptions of service quality are interrelated—in many instances highly correlated. Yet to date, neither academic researchers nor practitioners have developed common definitions or ways of measuring these three types of evaluations. Thus, there is overall confusion over which of the three is the better predictor of customer loyalty (if, indeed, any of them predict loyalty at all), what the causal ordering of the three constructs is, and whether they are even distinguishable concepts from the customer's point of view (e.g., Bitner, 1990; Bolton & Drew, 1991; Cronin & Taylor, 1992). Because of the lack of consensus on definition of the basic terms, it would seem that strong conclusions over the direction of causality among the constructs are premature. However, given that practitioners ask customers to respond to questions and scales that give quantitative assessments of quality and satisfaction, a better understanding of what customers are telling us seems warranted.

One purpose of this chapter, therefore, is to review relevant literature on service encounter satisfaction, overall service satisfaction, and service quality and to propose definitions and suggest relationships among the three constructs. The second purpose is to assess empirically, using both qualitative data and consumer responses to quantitative scale items, whether consumers perceive differences or distinguish among these three constructs.

Literature Review

Service Encounter Satisfaction

The service encounter has been defined as that period of time during which the consumer and service firm interact in person, over the telephone, or through other media (Shostack, 1985). By definition, then, the service encounter is a discrete event occurring over a definable period of time. The service encounter is also termed the moment of truth. Each service encounter provides an opportunity for the firm to reinforce its commitment to customer satisfaction or quality, but the evaluation of each encounter will clearly not be perfectly correlated (or necessarily correlated at all) with the consumer's overall satisfaction with the firm or perceptions of the firm's quality. Over time, however, it is likely that multiple positive (negative) encounters will lead to an overall high (low) level of satisfaction.

There is limited empirical research related to consumers' evaluations of discrete service encounters and the relationship of these evaluations to more global constructs (Bitner, 1990; Bitner, Booms, & Tetreault, 1990; Oliver & Swan, 1989; Surprenant & Solomon, 1987). Bitner (1990) showed in a controlled experiment that service encounter evaluation is highly correlated with a more global measure termed "service quality," which was operationalized as a form of overall attitude toward the service provider. Oliver and Swan (1989) and Surprenant and Solomon (1987) similarly found correlations between satisfaction with different types of personalized encounters and evaluation of the service provider, evaluation of the service, and evaluation of the organization. Encounter satisfaction in these two experimental studies is closely tied to what other researchers have referred to as satisfaction with a specific transaction (e.g., Day, 1984; Oliver, 1981) and can be distinguished from overall service satisfaction, attitude, and quality based on this narrower, more focused definition. Often the distinction between encounter satisfaction and overall satisfaction is missed, however. A goal of this chapter is to draw clear distinctions conceptually between service encounter evaluation and other more global constructs.

Overall Service Satisfaction

As implied in the preceding section, many times researchers do not distinguish between transaction (or encounter) satisfaction and more global measures of satisfaction with the organization's services. Cronin and Taylor (1992), for example, define and measure service satisfaction as a one-item scale that captures the consumers' overall feelings toward the organization. This definition does not acknowledge that satisfaction is likely to be multidimensional, nor are measures of encounter satisfaction included in their model. Other researchers (e.g., Crosby & Stephens,

1987; Oliver & Swan, 1989; Surprenant & Solomon, 1987) recognize that service satisfaction occurs at multiple levels in the organization, including satisfaction with the contact person, satisfaction with the core services experienced by the consumer, satisfaction with the institution overall. Although these different types of satisfaction *may* be highly correlated, they aren't necessarily. Still others have suggested that overall service satisfaction is a "latent construct with multiple indicators at the attribute level" (Oliva et al., 1992, p. 86). The attribute indicators that these authors are referring to reflect satisfaction with a number of types of encounters (encounters with personnel, quotations, ordering, delivery, postorder services) within the same firm. Thus, overall satisfaction is viewed as a function of satisfaction with multiple experiences or encounters with the organization (see also Bolton & Drew, 1991).

Service Quality

Perceived quality is frequently compared to overall attitude, and the two constructs are viewed as similar (Bitner, 1990; Parasuraman et al., 1988; Zeithaml, 1988). The classic definition of attitude is "a learned predisposition to respond to an object in a consistently favorable or unfavorable way" (Allport, 1935). Perceived quality is then viewed as similar to attitude because it represents a general, overall appraisal of a product or service. Perceived quality is a relatively global value judgment that relates to the superiority of the overall product (Holbrook & Corfman, 1985). As with satisfaction, it would appear that perceptions of quality could occur at multiple levels in a service organization setting. For example, the consumer is likely to be able to distinguish between the quality of the interaction with the service provider, the quality of the core service, and the overall quality of the organization.

Service quality has been operationalized most often by assessing service expectations and performance on 22 items believed to represent five key dimensions of service quality (Babakus & Boller, 1992; Cronin & Taylor, 1992; Parasuraman et al., 1988, 1991; Zeithaml, Parasuraman, & Berry, 1990). Despite disagreement over use of both the expectations and performance measures and the dimensionality of the SERVQUAL measurement instrument across different industry settings, there is general agreement that the 22 items are good predictors of overall service quality, with R^2 values ranging from 0.5 to 0.7. Typically the dependent overall quality measure is a one-item statement (e.g., "The quality of XYZ's service is . . . ") measured on a 4-point (Parasuraman, Zeithaml, & Berry, 1985; Babakus & Boller, 1992), 7-point (Cronin & Taylor, 1992), or 10-point (Parasuraman et al., 1991) scale.

Although the SERVQUAL items measured at the level of the firm's services appear to be good predictors of overall perceived quality, it is also possible that the 22 items measured at the *encounter* level may be good predictors of *encounter satisfaction*, and that when measured as a function of *multiple experiences* they may be good predictors of *overall service satisfaction*. Looked at another way, it may be that other variables are also significant predictors of overall service quality, especially if overall service quality is viewed as: "The consumer's judgment of overall excellence or superiority. Perceived quality is (1) different from objective or actual quality, (2) a higher level abstraction rather than a specific attribute of a product, (3) a global assessment that in some cases resembles attitude" (Zeithaml, 1988, pp. 3-4). Viewed in this way, perceived service quality is likely to be influenced by the firm's overall image as a function of advertising and word of mouth, as well as price and perceived value, in addition to the specific attributes measured by SERVQUAL.

Definitions and Conceptual Relationships

The above discussion suggests a number of issues emanating from the various definitions of satisfaction and quality that do not clearly distinguish between transaction satisfaction (or encounter satisfaction), overall satisfaction with the firm's services, and overall service quality (as opposed to the quality of a specific transaction). Based on the above discussion, and in an attempt to maximally distinguish the three constructs, the following definitions are proposed.

Service Encounter Satisfaction: The consumer's dis/satisfaction with a discrete service encounter (e.g., a haircut, an interaction with a dentist, a discussion with a repair person, an experience at a hotel check-in desk).

Service encounter satisfaction reflects the consumer's feelings about a discrete interaction with the firm and will result from the evaluation of the events and behaviors that occur during that definable period of time (Bitner, 1990; Bitner et al., 1990). It is believed that consumers will distinguish their satisfaction with a particular encounter from their overall satisfaction with the firm's services. In some instances (e.g., the first encounter or a particularly important or meaningful encounter), evaluation of the one encounter may be perfectly correlated with measures of overall satisfaction. On the other hand, if a consumer has one bad encounter with a firm after having had 20 good ones, the impact of the one encounter on overall satisfaction is likely to be minimal.

Overall Service Satisfaction: The consumer's overall dis/satisfaction with the organization based on *all* encounters and experiences with that particular organization.

Overall service satisfaction is distinguished from encounter satisfaction in that the overall construct reflects the customer's feelings about multiple encounters or experiences. These multiple encounters may include several interactions with one person as well as experiences with multiple contact persons in the same firm (Oliva et al., 1992). If the consumer has no other exposure to the firm through advertising, other forms of communication, or the experiences of others, then overall satisfaction may be perfectly correlated with overall perceptions of service quality. When consumers have other knowledge of the firm, however, the two will not necessarily be correlated. For example, the consumer may have had several satisfying experiences with the firm and thus rate overall personal satisfaction as high. However, the consumer's perception of overall superiority or quality may be tempered by perceptions of value or by the experiences of others that may not have been as good.

Service Quality: The consumer's overall impression of the relative inferiority/superiority of the organization and its services.

In order to maximally distinguish among the three service evaluation constructs, service quality is viewed as a higher order construct that relates to the overall quality of the organization and its offerings. Service quality is the most abstract of the three constructs and as such it is likely to be influenced by more variables than the other two, such as advertising, PR, and the experiences of others. In addition, overall service quality is likely to include dimensions of the other two constructs. For example, the consumer's evaluation of the firm's overall quality will include his/her assessment of individual service encounters as well as his/her overall satisfaction with all experiences with the firm. The dimensions captured by SERVQUAL are then viewed as good predictors of, but not the only determinants of, service quality. The SERVQUAL dimensions will be good predictors of overall quality, but they may also be highly correlated with overall satisfaction, as defined previously.

The Empirical Study

Propositions

An empirical study was designed to explore whether consumers discriminate among the three constructs, measured as defined, and further, whether consumers distinguish among the constructs when asked to talk about them in their own words. The following propositions summarize our expectations:

P_1: Service encounter satisfaction, overall service satisfaction, and service quality will exhibit significant independence when they are measured as defined above.

P_2: Consumers will express significantly different types of thoughts when asked to discuss service encounter satisfaction, service satisfaction, and service quality.

P_{2a}: When discussing encounter satisfaction, consumers will focus on events and employee behaviors during a specific transaction.

P_{2b}: When discussing service satisfaction, consumers will focus on all past personal experiences with the service firm.

P_{2c}: When discussing quality, consumers will focus on broader topics (such as value, image, the experiences of others, advertising) in addition to mentioning their own experiences.

Procedure

Data was collected at the departure gates of an international airport in a Southwestern city. The frame for this convenience sample consisted of adults seated in departure gate areas presumed to be airline passengers waiting to board their flights. Two hundred forty-two usable questionnaires were collected from passengers waiting for a number of different flights over the course of 2 days. Potential respondents were approached and asked to participate in a study about consumer attitudes. Those who consented were given a self-administered questionnaire, which was collected upon completion. Participants were thanked and the purpose of the study was discussed according to the level of interest expressed by the respondent.

Respondents were first asked to recall a recent, specific incident involving an interaction with a service provider, that is, a service encounter. The instructions on the questionnaire assigned each participant to one of three conditions by asking the respondent to recount a positive incident, a negative incident, or a recent experience with an airline. The valence of the airline encounter was not assigned, allowing respondents to recount any memorable interaction with an airline employee. The incidents were collected across these three conditions (positive, negative, no assigned valence) to ensure that a full range of types of incidents were included. The order in which the questionnaires were distributed was randomized. Thus, half of the sample provided a "critical" incident (positive or negative) involving any type of service provider. The other half of the sample was free to choose the nature of the event reported, but was constrained to an incident that occurred with an airline. Several prompts were included in order to elicit as much detail as possible. (See Bitner et al., 1990.)

The incident elicitation was followed by a set of multi-item scales designed to measure the respondent's satisfaction with the encounter, overall satisfaction with the service provider, and perceived quality of the service provider. These are discussed in the measurement section below.

At three different points in the questionnaire, the respondents were asked to verbally elaborate on their responses. The first verbal response was sought during the description of the service incident. Respondents in the positive and negative conditions were asked to explain what made the experience especially positive (negative). Because the valence of the airline encounters was not assigned, this question was omitted from the questionnaires that assigned the airline condition; respondents were simply asked to describe what happened. The other two verbal responses were in reply to "short-answer," open-ended questions that asked respondents what led them, in particular, to respond to the overall service satisfaction and to the service quality items as they had.

The questionnaire concluded with four demographic questions. Respondents were asked to provide their age, gender, educational background, and occupation.

Sample Profile

Two hundred and forty-two airline travelers participated. Almost half of the respondents were between the ages of 25 and 44 (45.6%); a third were between the ages of 45 and 64. Ten percent were age 65 or older.

Half of the respondents were women (50.6%). Thirty percent of the participants had graduated from college, and over one fourth had obtained an advanced degree (26.9%). Seven respondents had not completed high school (3.1%). A wide range of occupations were represented, including managerial (29.4%), professional (17.4%), semiskilled (17.4%), and sales (8.1%) positions. The sample included homemakers (6.0%), retirees (12.8%), and relatively few students (3.4%).

Of the usable questionnaires collected, approximately one fourth of the respondents had been assigned to the positive condition (25.6%) and one fourth to the negative condition (23.1%). The balance of the respondents, 51.3%, recounted salient service encounters with airlines. Chi-square tests confirmed that there was no systematic relationship between any of the demographic variables and the assigned conditions.

Measures

Service Encounter Satisfaction. Participants were asked to reflect upon the incident they had described. Then, satisfaction with the encounter was measured using nine 7-point scales. The items included a delighted/terrible scale (D/T) (Andrews & Withey, 1976), and six satisfaction items suggested by Oliver (1980). Two unipolar items were included (Westbrook & Oliver, 1991). The items measuring the construct are listed in Table 3.1.

Overall Service Satisfaction. Next, the respondent's overall satisfaction with the service provider was assessed. Respondents were asked to "step back" from the one encounter they had described and to think about *all experiences* with that specific service provider. Four items were used to measure the respondent's overall satisfaction with the service provider. All four items, listed in Table 3.1, were measured using 5-point scales. Following the scaled items, an open-ended question asked respondents to describe what led them to rate their overall service satisfaction/dissatisfaction as they had.

Service Quality. The respondents were then instructed to reflect on their *overall impression* of the organization. Respondents were prompted to consider their experience with the organization, as well as stories they had heard about others' interactions with the organization, the organization's advertising and public relations efforts, and anything else they knew about

TABLE 3.1 Construct Indicants

Encounter Satisfaction Measures

D/T	How did you feel about your service experience on this particular occasion?[a]
SATSERV	I was satisfied with that specific service experience.[b]
SATDEC	I was satisfied with my decision to obtain service from that specific organization on that particular occasion.[b]
DOAGAIN	If I had it to do over again, I would *not* have gone to that organization.[b*]
WISE	My decision to use that organiztion on that occasion was a wise one.[b]
FEELBAD	I feel badly about my decision to go to that organization for services that time.[b*]
DISSAT	I was *dis*satisfied with that specific service experience.[b*]
RIGHT	I think I did the right thing by going to that organization on that occasion.[b]
NOTHAPPY	I am *not* happy that I patronized that particular organization that time.[b*]

Overall Satisfaction Measures

ALLSAT	Based on *all of your own experience*, how satisfied overall are you with this organization's service?[c]
UNIDISS	Based on *all of my own experience* with this organization, I am:[d*]
COMPRSAT	Compared to other, similar organizations that you have done business with, how would you rate your satisfaction with this organization?[c]
GENSAT	In general, I am satisfied with this organization.[b]

Quality Measures

ALLQUAL	Based on *everything* you know about the organization, rate the overall *quality* of this organization:[e]
OUTSTNDQ	The quality of the service provided by this organization is outstanding.[b]
SUPERQ	When compared to other companies that provide the same type of service, this organization is:[f]

NOTES
[a] Fully anchored; end points: Delighted/Terrible.
[b] Anchored at end points: Strongly agree/Strongly disagree.
[c] Fully anchored; endpoints: Very satisfied/Very dissatisfied.
[d] Anchored at end points: Very dissatisfied/Not at all dissatisfied.
[e] Fully anchored; endpoints: Excellent/Poor.
[f] Anchored at end points: Superior/Inferior.
[*] Reverse scored.

the organization. Based on their overall impression, participants were asked to respond to three items, listed in Table 3.1, that assessed their perceptions of the quality of the organization. Each item used a 5-point scale. A open-ended question asked respondents to describe what led them to rate their quality perceptions as they had.

The sections addressing overall service satisfaction and the section addressing service quality were presented in alternating order in order to counteract any possible presentation bias, although previous research reported no evidence of bias due to the presentation order of constructs on the questionnaire (Westbrook, 1987). Thus, on half of the questionnaires, the service quality section preceded the overall service satisfaction section, and on the other half, the overall service satisfaction section preceded the quality section.

Analysis

Confirmatory Factor Analysis

The first proposition (P_1) states that service encounter satisfaction, overall service satisfaction, and service quality will exhibit significant independence. This proposition was tested by the development of a measurement model using confirmatory factor analysis.

Three separate confirmatory factor analyses were conducted. The three-factor solution, representing independence of the constructs, was compared to a two-factor solution and a single-factor solution. The two-factor solution combined overall service satisfaction and service quality onto one factor. This, in effect, would operationalize these two as a single construct. The other factor in the two-factor solution would be satisfaction with a specific encounter. The single-factor solution would specify satisfaction with the encounter, overall service satisfaction, and service quality as a single construct.

Two types of criteria were used to evaluate the models. First, global model fit was assessed using chi-square analysis, the adjusted goodness of fit index (AGFI), and the root mean square residual (RMR). An AGFI greater than 0.9 suggests that the tested model is meaningful (Bagozzi & Yi, 1988). The RMR indicates the average of the residual variances and covariances and can be used to compare the fits of different models to the same data (Bagozzi & Yi, 1988). Each of these criteria inform the evaluation of global model fit, that is, the overall adequacy of a model.

However, the global measures of fit do not provide information as to the nature of the internal structure of the model. It is possible that the global measurements will indicate a satisfactory model even though individual indicants are insignificant or have low reliability, for example, explained variance estimates < 0.5 (Bagozzi & Yi, 1988). Thus, the second criterion examined pertains to individual parameters, which reflect the internal structure of the model. Item reliabilities, and the squared multiple correlation of the individual item with the latent variable, will be compared among the three models assessed using factor analysis.

Content Analysis of Customer Thoughts

The second proposition posits that customers will express different types of thoughts when asked through open-ended questions to discuss service encounter satisfaction, service satisfaction, and service quality. Three different verbal responses were examined: the respondents' explanations for their interpretations of the incident described; the explanations for their overall service satisfaction ratings; and third, the explanations for their perceptions of service quality.

A coding system was developed in order to categorize the nature of thoughts expressed by the respondents in their verbal responses. Three categories of thoughts were conceptualized based on the definitions of the three constructs discussed above. Encounter-oriented comments were expected to center around the events of the specific service encounter (which had been described earlier in the questionnaire) or the respondent's reaction to those events. Overall service satisfaction comments would focus on all personal experiences beyond the service encounter that had been described. Service quality comments would include mentions of information about the company, its advertising policies, the perceived nature of its target market (e.g., appeal to upscale consumers), or perceptions of its positioning within the product class (e.g., a no-nonsense, no-frills airline) in addition to comments regarding personal experiences. Responses to the open-ended questions were then coded into one of the three categories (single-encounter thoughts, own personal experiences thoughts, and global impression thoughts) based on the primary emphasis of the response.

Results

Construct Independence

It was proposed that three distinct, yet correlated, constructs exist: service encounter satisfaction, overall service satisfaction, and service quality. Thus, a three-factor solution was sought.

Three-Factor Solution. All 16 items were loaded onto their respective factors: 9 items to a factor representing service encounter satisfaction, 4 items to a factor representing overall service satisfaction, and 3 items to a factor representing service quality. The model specified that the factors were correlated.

The resulting global fit was poor. The chi-square statistic was significant ($\chi^2_{(101)}$ = 379.86, $p < .0001$), indicating the model did a poor job of fitting the data. A significant chi-square test in and of itself is not too alarming because, when a large sample size is used, chi-square analysis is likely to reject true models as well as false ones. Thus, a significant chi-square may reflect sensitivity to sample size, rather than to an invalid model (Bagozzi & Yi, 1988). More compelling were the low AGFI (0.729) and high RMR (0.231). Low reliabilities of individual items were used to identify items that contributed to the poor global fit. Four encounter satisfaction items, DOAGAIN, FEELBAD, RIGHT, and NOTHAPPY, and one overall satisfaction item, UNIDISS, were eliminated for the second iteration of confirmatory factor analysis.

The second iteration provided a higher AGFI (0.840), although it remained below the normative acceptability level of 0.9. The RMR was 0.165, and the results of the chi-square analysis ($\chi^2_{(41)}$ = 133.76, $p < .0001$), remained significant. A third iteration was conducted, after once again eliminating the items with the lowest reliabilities, encounter satisfaction items DISSAT and WISE. The reliabilities for all of the items for both overall service satisfaction and quality exceeded 0.78 and were therefore retained in the model.

The results of the third iteration were much improved. The AGFI was 0.929 and the RMR was reduced to 0.077. The results of the chi-square analysis were approaching insignificance ($\chi^2_{(24)}$ = 40.60, $p = .018$). Examination of the item reliabilities revealed that they all exceeded 0.78, except the encounter satisfaction item SATDEC at 0.632. The other two encounter satisfaction reliabilities were 0.874 and 0.913 (D/T and SATSERV, respectively). Thus, the item SATDEC was eliminated from the model in the final iteration.

The final model exhibited a good fit with the data. The AGFI was 0.948 and the RMR was a low 0.024. The chi-square statistic was insignificant ($\chi^2_{(17)}$ = 22.07, $p > .15$), in spite of the large sample size. The internal structure was also very strong. All item reliabilities exceeded 0.75, and six of the eight exceeded 0.85. Thus, the three-construct model, operationalized by eight items, provided a strong fit with the data. The results of the final iteration are presented in Table 3.2.

TABLE 3.2 Results of the Final Iteration: Confirmatory Factor Analysis

	One Factor	Two Factors	Three Factors
Global Model Fit			
AFGI	.6533	.8501	.9479
RMR	.2712	.0361	.0235
χ^2 (df)	255.1606 (20)	68.8309 (19)	22.0729 (17)
p-value	.0001	.0001	.1819
Variance of the Endogenous Variables (R^2)			
Encounter Satisfaction:			
D/T	.5950	.8832	.8819
SATSERV	.6116	.9115	.9128
Overall Satisfaction:			
ALLSAT	.7807	.7846	.7968
COMPRSAT	.8028	.8092	.8542
GENSAT	.8350	.8412	.8812
Quality:			
ALLQUAL	.8441	.8452	.8711
OUTSTNDQ	.8455	.8437	.8780
SUPERQ	.7623	.7665	.7793
Interfactor Correlations			
Encounter/Overall-Quality	—	.80	—
Encounter/Overall	—	—	.77
Encounter/Quality	—	—	.79
Overall/Quality	—	—	.94

A low correlation among exogenous variables provides evidence of discrimination among constructs. In general, high interfactor correlations raise the question of whether or not the constructs are indeed distinct constructs. In this case, the interfactor correlations among all three of the constructs are very high. The correlation between encounter satisfaction and overall service satisfaction and between encounter satisfaction and service quality are almost identical (0.77 and 0.79, respectively). The correlation between overall service satisfaction and perceived quality is 0.94. This finding provides evidence for the notion that overall service satisfaction and service quality may be tapping elements of the same construct. Thus, a two-factor solution was sought.

Two-Factor Solution. The encounter satisfaction construct was operationalized by the nine items as before. The overall service satisfaction/service quality construct was operationalized by combining seven items, four from overall service satisfaction and three from service quality. The first confirmatory factor analysis used all 16 variables on the two factors as described. Global fit was poor: AGFI = 0.709, RMR = 0.231, and $\chi^2_{(103)}$ = 422.65, $p < .0001$. These results were not unexpected, and a second iteration was performed following the deletion of the items with the lowest reliabilities from the model (from encounter satisfaction: DOAGAIN, FEELBAD, RIGHT, and NOTHAPPY; and from overall satisfaction/service quality: UNIDISS.) The fit of the model with the data improved as a result, but remained unacceptably low. The AGFI was 0.791, the RMR was 0.165, and the chi-square analysis remained significant ($\chi^2_{(43)}$ = 179.84, $p < .0001$).

Three more encounter satisfaction items were deleted, based on their relatively low reliability scores: SATDEC, DISSAT, and WISE. The reliabilities of the six items making up overall service satisfaction/service quality each exceeded 0.75 and all six were retained in the model. The items included in the third iteration of the two-factor model were therefore the same items that remained in the final iteration of the three-factor model. The AGFI improved to 0.850; the RMR to 0.036. The chi-square statistic remained significant ($\chi^2_{(19)}$ = 68.83, $p < .0001$). At the same time, the reliability of each of the eight construct indicants remaining in the model exceeded 0.75. The high item reliabilities demonstrated a strong internal structure and indicated that the model would not be improved dramatically by the continued elimination of items. Thus, the final two-factor solution did not provide a model with as good a fit with the data as did the model provided by the three-factor solution.

The correlation between the two factors was .80 in the final iteration. This high correlation indicates little discrimination between the two factors. Therefore, a single-factor solution was sought next.

Single-Factor Solution. The single-factor solution implies that there is no discrimination among service encounter satisfaction, overall service satisfaction, and service quality. This model connotes that all of the items measured are reflective of a single construct, a general concept of service satisfaction and quality.

To assess this solution, all 16 of the items were loaded onto one, single factor. The solution indicated poor global fit. The AGFI was 0.446 and the RMR was 0.393. The chi-square analysis yielded significant results

$(\chi^2_{(104)} = 811.41, p < .0001)$. Once again, this was not unexpected and the individual item reliabilities were examined to determine which items should be eliminated from the model. The reliabilities of six individual items were below 0.5, the general rule of thumb used to assess acceptable item reliability (Bagozzi & Yi, 1988). Using these low reliabilities as a guide, six items were eliminated from the model: encounter items DISSAT, DOAGAIN, FEELBAD, RIGHT, and NOTHAPPY, and one overall satisfaction item, UNIDISS. The second iteration showed improved results, but the model fit with the data was still poor, as reflected by these global statistics: AGFI = 0.559, RMR = 0.318, and $\chi^2_{(35)}$ = 395.73, $p < .0001$. Again, using low item reliabilities as a guide to eliminate items, two more encounter items were eliminated from the model: SATDEC and WISE. The AGFI of the third iteration was 0.653, RMR was 0.271, with $\chi^2_{(20)}$ = 255.16, $p < .0001$. Thus, the model remained a poor fit with the data. An examination of the items revealed that those with the lowest reliabilities were the final two service encounter satisfaction items: D/T and SATSERV. These were eliminated for the final iteration. The resulting model fit with the data had once again improved, but remained a generally poor fit with the data. The AGFI was 0.785, well below the normative standard of 0.9. The RMR was 0.033 and the results of the chi-square analysis remained significant $(\chi^2_{(9)}$ = 62.07, $p < .0001)$. This final iteration yielded unacceptable empirical results, but more important, indicants of service encounter satisfaction were no longer included in the model, compromising the conceptualization of the model.

The squared multiple correlations of the items with the single factor (i.e., item reliabilities) all exceeded 0.7, indicating strong internal structure. Item reliabilities were high, but global model fit remained poor. This implied that continued elimination of items would not result in a better global fit. Thus, a representation of service satisfaction and quality as a single construct provided an unacceptable solution.

Summary. The three-factor solution was conceptualized, positing service encounter satisfaction, overall service satisfaction, and service quality as three distinct constructs. Results of confirmatory factor analysis found the three-factor solution to provide a good fit with the data, as reflected in the excellent global fit statistics. High item reliabilities indicated that the internal structure of the three-construct model was also strong. The solutions provided by the two-factor and single-factor models did not achieve a good fit with the data and were rejected as unacceptable, based on the confirmatory factor analysis. The high interfactor correlations in the three-factor solution provides evidence that the constructs, though distinct, are quite similar conceptually.

The Customer's Voice

Within the description of the service encounter, all of the respondents in the negative condition explained why they perceived the incident as negative. Only four respondents in the positive condition did not specifically express what led them to perceive the encounter as positive. Although the respondents in the airline condition were not explicitly prompted to provide an explanation for their evaluation of the specific service encounter, all but three respondents did so. The total number of respondents who supplied explanations for their evaluations of satisfaction with the encounter was 235 (97.1% of the total sample).

Respondents were asked in two separate questions to express what led them to respond as they had to the overall service satisfaction items and to the service quality items. There was a relatively high rate of response to these open-ended questions. The same number of respondents (193) supplied a response for each question (79.8% of the total sample), although not every participant responded to both questions.

Each verbal response (the explanation for satisfaction with the encounter, the explanation for the overall service satisfaction ratings, and the explanation for the service quality ratings) was categorized based on the primary emphasis of the comment. Each comment was placed into a single category: specific service encounter, cumulative personal experience, or global information/impression. A sample of the comments classified by the nature of the thought expressed is presented in Table 3.3. The breakdown of the classification of comments by construct is reported in Table 3.4.

Service Encounter Satisfaction. Ninety-five percent of those who provided explanations for their evaluation of satisfaction with the encounter focused their comments on the events of the encounter. This was not an unexpected finding. However, this statistic does provide a baseline comparison for the percentage of encounter-based comments that occurred in response to overall service satisfaction and service quality questions. Ten respondents (4.3%) emphasized experience beyond the bounds of the encounter in their evaluation of their satisfaction with the specific service

TABLE 3.3   Examples of Verbal Responses Classified by the Nature of the Thought Expressed

---

Comments Based on the Specific Service Encounter

"Very nice waitress and dealt with us very nicely."

"Made me feel I got a bargain."

"Employee was extremely helpful in searching files for helping us obtain a discount . . . although we were not members of any organization which was eligible for discount."

"I felt they took advantage of me because I was from out of town and in need of immediate repair service. Also to return the car to make them set it right would have been a major inconvenience."

"They tried to give me a bad deal and wasted my time."

Comments Based on Own Personal Experiences

"Based on my experience, I feel they are honest and competent. When they do repairs, it has always solved the problem."

"Always very accommodating to my needs, never feel that I am being overcharged or used."

"I have never had a good experience with this airline, and I thought I would give them a chance and they were awful again!"

"The employees are nice. Always there to be helpful in whatever my needs were. And very prompt."

"I have never had a positive experience with them."

"Several times they have been late, and once lost our luggage."

Comments Based on Global Information or Impressions

"Advertisement stating low fares."

"Most of the hotels show an interest in the traveling people and try to make your stay as close to home as they can."

"Poor service, old equipment, good business class seats."

"Their overall quality is better than my overall individual perception because several friends have had excellent satisfaction in dealing with [name of airline]."

"Customer service, knowledgeable salespeople, friendly (unintimidating) atmosphere, good selection of merchandise."

---

encounter. Only one respondent focused on information beyond the scope of her own personal experience, as shown in Table 3.4.

Overall Service Satisfaction. Almost half of those who provided an explanation for their ratings of the items addressing overall service satisfaction

TABLE 3.4 Classification of the Verbal Responses by Construct

| | In Response to Open-Ended Question on: | | | | | |
| | Service Encounter Satisfaction | | Overall Service Satisfaction | | Service Quality | |
Type of Thought Expressed	n	%	n	%	n	%
Single Encounter-Oriented	219	95.3	94	48.7	77	39.8
Own Personal Experiences	10	4.3	61	31.6	47	24.4
Global Information/Impression	1	.4	38	19.7	69	35.8
Total	230	100.0	193	100.0	193	100.0

centered their comments around the events of the specific service encounter they had described. Close to one third, 31.6%, focused on their own general personal experience to explain their overall satisfaction ratings, whereas just under 20% used global information or impressions to explain their overall service satisfaction, as reported in Table 3.4.

Service Quality. Forty percent of the participants who responded to the request for an elaboration of what led them to rate the quality items as they had focused on the events of the specific encounter. One fourth based their answer on their general previous experience. Almost 36% centered their response around global information or impressions, as shown in Table 3.4.

There was some evidence, however, that at least some of the respondents did not differentiate between overall service satisfaction and quality. Almost 9% of those who responded to the short-answer question addressing their overall service satisfaction ratings (17 of the 193) referred back to information provided either in the incident described or the comments given in response to the quality short-answer question. Nine percent of the responses to the service quality question referred the reader to either the overall satisfaction response or to information provided within the description of the incident. Seven percent of those responding to the overall service satisfaction and service quality short-answer questions wrote out exactly the same response (verbatim) for both the quality and overall satisfaction questions.

Summary. Fewer than 5% of the explanations for satisfaction with the service encounter focused on anything other than the events of the encounter itself. On the other hand, responses regarding the nature of overall service satisfaction referred to the specific encounter only half as often and were considerably more likely to emphasize the respondent's general personal experiences. Responses addressing the perceived quality of the service provider were more likely to focus on global information/impressions than in response to either of the other cues (almost 36%, compared to 20% for overall service satisfaction and less than 1% for encounter satisfaction).

These findings provide supporting evidence for P_2. When discussing encounter satisfaction, the respondents in this study overwhelmingly focused on events and employee behaviors within the specific transaction (P_{2a}). Respondents were most likely to refer to past personal experience when discussing overall service satisfaction with a service provider (P_{2b}). Global information/impressions were more likely to be the focus of the response when respondents were discussing the quality of the organization (P_{2c}).

However, the fact that both overall service satisfaction and overall quality contain a significant percentage of thoughts reflecting the other constructs (i.e., 24% of the service quality thoughts related to personal experiences and 20% of the overall service satisfaction thoughts related to global impressions) and both contain a significant percentage of thoughts related to a specific service encounter suggests that it may be difficult for consumers to differentiate between overall satisfaction and quality. In addition, verbatim responses to both short-answer questions provides further evidence that not all respondents differentiated the constructs. On the other hand, based on the types of thoughts expressed, service encounter satisfaction appears to be more easily discriminated from the consumer point of view.

Conclusion

Improving quality and increasing customer satisfaction are important goals in business practice today, and measurement and monitoring of quality and satisfaction are becoming increasingly common. Yet, frequently there is debate as to whether quality and satisfaction are *both* relevant measures of business success and whether the two are even distinguishable from the customer point of view.

The study presented here explored the concepts of service encounter satisfaction, overall satisfaction, and perceived service quality from the customer point of view to begin to understand whether and how consumers think about these concepts in their own words, as well as how they respond to quantitative scale measures of the three concepts. Results of the confirmatory factor analysis suggest that the three constructs are indeed distinct. Measurement models fit to the data revealed that the three-factor solution (including service encounter satisfaction, overall service satisfaction, and service quality as independent constructs) provided a good fit, better than either a two-factor or one-factor model. However, the constructs, although exhibiting independence, were highly correlated. This was especially true of overall service satisfaction and perceived quality. Service encounter satisfaction was not as highly correlated with overall satisfaction or service quality. The qualitative analysis of consumers' own thoughts about the three constructs revealed a similar pattern of results suggesting that service encounter satisfaction is much more easily distinguished from the other two constructs than they are from each other.

The results presented here are just a beginning for understanding the three service evaluation constructs. Based on the results of this study, it appears that the constructs do exhibit independence as defined. In particular, service encounter satisfaction appears to be quite distinct from overall satisfaction and perceived quality. Further, because the constructs as defined imply considerably different managerial actions, there is a strong practical justification for maintaining them as separate entities. Future research is needed to clarify the causal relationships among the variables, to understand whether certain kinds of experiences and encounters with a service firm might alter the relationships among the variables, and to discover which of the constructs are better predictors of later behaviors such as purchase loyalty and word of mouth.

References

Allport, G. W. (1935). Attitudes. In C. A. Murchinson (Ed.), *A handbook of social psychology* (pp. 798-844). Worcester, MA: Clark University Press.

Andrews, F. M., & Withey S. B. (1976). *Social indicators of well being.* New York: Plenum.

Babakus, E., & Boller, G. W. (1992). An empirical assessment of the SERVQUAL scale. *Journal of Business Research, 24,* 253-268.

Bagozzi, R. P., & Yi, Y. (1988). On the evaluation of structural equation models. *Journal of the Academy of Marketing Science, 16,* 74-94.

Bitner, M. J. (1990). Evaluating service encounters: The effects of physical surroundings and employee responses. *Journal of Marketing, 54,* 69-82.

Bitner, M. J., Booms, B. H., & Tetreault, M. S. (1990). The service encounter: Diagnosing favorable and unfavorable incidents. *Journal of Marketing, 54,* 71-84.

Bolton, R. N., & Drew, J. H. (1991). A multistage model of consumers' assessments of service quality and value. *Journal of Consumer Research, 17,* 375-384.

Carlzon, J. (1987). *Moments of truth.* Cambridge, MA: Ballinger.

Cronin, J. J., Jr., & Taylor, S. A. (1992). Measuring service quality: A reexamination and extension. *Journal of Marketing, 56,* 55-68.

Crosby, L. A. (1991). Expanding the role of CSM in total quality. *International Journal of Service Industry Management, 2,* 5-19.

Crosby, L. A., & Stephens, N. (1987). Effects of relationship marketing on satisfaction, retention, and prices in the life insurance industry. *Journal of Marketing Research, 24,* 404-411.

Czepiel, J. A., Solomon, M. R., Surprenant, C. F., & Gutman, E. G. (1985). Service encounters: An overview. In J. A. Czepiel, M. R. Solomon, & C. F. Surprenant (Eds.), *The service encounter: Managing employee/customer interaction in service businesses* (pp. 3-15). Lexington, MA: Lexington.

Day, R. L. (1984). Modeling choices among alternative responses to dissatisfaction. In T. C. Kinnear (Ed.), *Advances in Consumer Research* (Vol. 11, pp. 496-499). Provo, UT: Association for Consumer Research.

Garvin, D. A. (1991). How the Baldrige Award really works. *Harvard Business Review, 69,* 80-89.

Holbrook, M. B., & Corfman, K. P. (1985). Quality and value in the consumption experience: Phaedrus rides again. In J. Jacoby & J. Olson (Eds.), *Perceived quality* (pp. 31-57). Lexington, MA: Lexington.

Lindstrom, J. (1992). *SIQ and the Swedish national quality award.* Paper presented at the Quality in Service Symposium (QUIS 3), University of Karlstad, Karlstad, Sweden.

Oliva, T. A., Oliver, R. L., & MacMillan, I. C. (1992). A catastrophe model for developing service satisfaction strategies. *Journal of Marketing, 56,* 83-95.

Oliver, R. L. (1980). A cognitive model of the antecedents and consequences of satisfaction decisions. *Journal of Marketing Research, 17,* 460-469.

Oliver, R. L. (1981). Measurement and evaluation of satisfaction processes in retail settings. *Journal of Retailing, 57,* 25-48.

Oliver, R. L., & Swan, J. E. (1989). Equity and disconfirmation perceptions as influences on merchant and product satisfaction. *Journal of Consumer Research, 16,* 372-383.

Parasuraman, A., Zeithaml, V. A., & Berry, L. L. (1985). A conceptual model of service quality and its implications for future research. *Journal of Marketing, 49,* 41-50.

Parasuraman, A., Zeithaml, V. A., & Berry, L. L. (1988). SERVQUAL: A multiple-item scale for measuring consumer perceptions of service quality. *Journal of Retailing, 64,* 12-40.

Parasuraman, A., Zeithaml, V. A., & Berry, L. L. (1991). Refinement and reassessment of the SERVQUAL scale. *Journal of Retailing, 67,* 420-450.

Peacock, R. D. (1992). *The European quality award.* Paper presented at the Quality in Service Symposium (QUIS 3), University of Karlstad, Karlstad, Sweden.

Phillips, S., Dunkin, A., Treece, J. B., & Hammonds, K. H. (1990, March 12). King customer. *Business Week,* pp. 88-94.

Reimann, C. W. (1992). *Service quality, standards, and awards: The Malcolm Baldrige National Quality Award.* Paper presented at the Quality in Service Symposium (QUIS 3), University of Karlstad, Karlstad, Sweden.

Shostack, G. L. (1985). Planning the service encounter. In J. A. Czepiel, M. R. Solomon, & C. F. Surprenant (Eds.), *The service encounter: Managing employee/customer interaction in service businesses* (pp. 243-254). Lexington, MA: Lexington.

Surprenant, C. F., & Solomon, M. R. (1987). Predictability and personalization in the service encounter. *Journal of Marketing, 51*, 86-96.

The quality imperative. (1991, October 24). *Business Week* [Special issue].

Webster, F. E. (1988). The rediscovery of the marketing concept. *Business Horizons, 31*, 29-39.

Westbrook, R. A. (1987). Product/consumption-based affective responses and postpurchase processes. *Journal of Marketing Research, 24*, 258-270.

Westbrook, R. A., & Oliver, R. L. (1991). The dimensionality of consumption emotion patterns and consumer satisfaction. *Journal of Consumer Research, 18*, 84-91.

Zeithaml, V. A. (1988). Consumer perceptions of price, quality, and value: A means-end model and synthesis of evidence. *Journal of Marketing, 52*, 2-22.

Zeithaml, V. A., Parasuraman, A., & Berry, L. L. (1990). *Delivering quality service.* New York: Free Press.

CHAPTER FOUR

Price and Advertising as Market Signals for Service Quality

JAN-BENEDICT E. M. STEENKAMP

*Catholic University of Leuven, Belgium,
and Wageningen University, The Netherlands*

DONNA L. HOFFMAN

*Owen Graduate School of Management
Vanderbilt University*

Market signals, such as advertising and price, are information that firms transfer to their customers. A continuing question is the extent to which such signals are reliable. We examine this issue, focusing on the extent to which potential and current customers of a firm can rely on market signals in evaluating service quality. Our analysis draws heavily from the economic literature to develop a series of empirically testable hypotheses concerning services.

A continuing area of research in marketing and economics is the role markets can play in transferring information from firms to customers (Miller & Plott, 1985; Steenkamp, 1989). Important examples of such information, commonly called market signals, include advertising and price. Marketing academics have tended to concentrate on the firm's actual usage and influence of various market signals on customers' perceptions of quality (Jacoby & Olson, 1985; Kirmani & Wright, 1989; Rao & Monroe, 1989; Steenkamp, 1989). Economists, on the other hand, have concentrated on developing models that explain how and why the firm uses market signals to inform potential customers about the quality of its offering.

In this context, the question emerges as to the extent market signals are reliable. For example, a firm may be tempted to exploit customers' implicit theories about the relation between quality and market signals by charging noncompetitive prices or by spending large sums on advertising. In such cases, customers may be better off using sources of information not controlled by the firm, such as prior experience, expert opinion, and word of mouth.

In this chapter, we examine the extent to which potential and current customers can rely on market signals in evaluating service quality. In our analysis, we draw heavily from the economic literature on market signaling, despite the fact that economists have typically explored this issue in the context of product quality. As services tend to be neglected altogether, we introduce modifications as needed to develop a number of hypotheses relating to the issues. Our discussion is limited to the two market signals of greatest managerial relevance: price and advertising.

We organize the chapter as follows: First, we examine the construct of service quality and then consider the conditions under which advertising and price may be reliable market signals for service quality. To address this issue, the economic literature on market signaling is reviewed. We conclude with suggestions for future research.

Service Quality

We regard perceived service quality as an overall unidimensional construct concerning the fitness for consumption of the service. It is a higher level abstraction based on perceptions of the quality attributes composing the service. Following Nelson (1970) and Darby and Karni (1973), we may categorize service quality attributes as search, experience, and credence attributes (e.g., Parasuraman, Zeithaml, & Berry, 1985).

Search attributes can be ascertained prior to consumption of the service. Examples include the physical facility, appearance of personnel, and the company reputation. Some service quality attributes may be regarded as experience attributes because they can be ascertained on the basis of actual experience with the service (e.g., accuracy of billing, calling the customer back quickly, or performing the service at the designated time). Other service quality attributes cannot be ascertained even after repeated service encounters or without consulting an expert. Examples of such credence attributes include automobile repairs and the financial security of investments.

Search, experience, and credence attributes can be thought of as occupying positions on a continuum from "easy to evaluate" to "difficult to evaluate." It has been argued that compared to products, services tend to be difficult to evaluate (i.e., contain many experience and credence attributes) because services are intangible (Zeithaml, 1981).

In accord with work in the customer satisfaction area (Oliver, 1980, 1981), researchers in service quality (e.g., Boulding, Kalra, Staelin, & Zeithaml, 1993; Parasuraman et al., 1985) argue that perceptions of service quality (attributes) are based on both the customer's expectations about service quality and the actual service delivered. Expectations are based on many sources, including prior exposure to the service, word of mouth, and market signals such as advertising and price—the latter under the firm's control. In contrast, actual service delivered is composed of a number of objective factors (e.g., delayed departures of planes, accuracy of monthly account statements, waiting time at checkout line) for each service quality attribute (Boulding et al., 1993).

Objective measures of actual service quality are more difficult to obtain than objective measures of product quality, because the actual service delivered varies more from customer to customer than actual product quality. This is due in part to the fact that quality control procedures are currently more easily implemented in the product than the service context. Therefore, accurate estimates of the expected value of actual quality in the service context are likely to require repeated observations.

Advertising as a Market Signal for Service Quality

Two Opposing Views

Advertising can provide the customer with information about the quality of a service in at least two ways. First, an advertisement can convey information about the quality characteristics of the service, its price, and so on. Second, the basic fact that the service is advertised is relevant. Nelson (1970) argued that customers prefer advertisements that provide direct information about the characteristics of the service, provided they believe this information is valid. He posited that this belief will arise only for services that possess (at least predominantly) search attributes. Deceptive advertising for search items is therefore not advantageous to firms because the customer can easily verify the advertising claims prior to purchase. Moreover, deceptive advertising may damage a firm's reputation.

Thus, Nelson (1970) concluded that advertisements for search items provide predominantly direct information based on valid quality claims.

However, this is not the case for services possessing mainly experience attributes. Direct information about experience attributes cannot be verified prior to purchase. Firms can make exaggerated or even false claims to stimulate trial purchase behavior. Thus, advertising usually does not provide direct information that is of much assistance to the customer. Recognizing this, does advertising convey any information about the quality of a service at all? Nelson (1970) suggests the answer is a definitive yes: Quality information is provided by the level of advertising expenditures. To support this contention, Nelson argued that high-quality services elicit more repeat purchases, ceteris paribus, than low-quality services. Providers of high-quality services thus have more incentive to advertise than providers of low-quality services, which generates a positive relationship between the level of advertising and quality, regardless of the actual content of the advertisements.

Because few services predominantly consist of search attributes, we can conclude that the main information conveyed by advertising concerns the advertising expenditure level rather than any specific advertising content. Based on Nelson's (1970) model, imperfectly informed customers who wish to purchase a high-quality service should limit their sampling to heavily advertised services. The conclusion that there exists a positive relationship between the level of advertising and service quality is contested, however, by Comanor and Wilson (1979). Their work indicates that low-quality services generate fewer repeat purchases and therefore must compensate for this disadvantage by attracting greater trial. This implies that providers of low-quality services have more incentive to advertise than providers of high-quality services, resulting in a negative relationship between level of advertising and service quality. Following Comanor and Wilson's argument, the imperfectly informed customer looking for a high-quality service should purchase a service that is not heavily advertised.

Synthesis

The resolution of these two opposing views requires a formal model in which the different incentives for advertising can be mathematically specified. Such a model was developed by Schmalensee (1978). This model constitutes an important contribution to economic theory regarding the validity of advertising as a market signal; we discuss it in some detail in the service context.

Schmalensee (1978) considered a market that we can view as consisting of N service providers and Q customers, where all customers behave identically and each customer demands only one service transaction over each time period. Firms are assumed to maximize a discounted stream of profits. Customers do not optimize their behavior and can only obtain direct information about the quality of a service by engaging in a service transaction. Further, the model assumes that all firms charge the same price, P. The unit cost of production, $c(\beta)$ for a service with quality level β is assumed to be equal for all firms and can be formulated as:

(1) $c(\beta) = P[1 - (k/\beta^{\tau})]$

where $\beta \geq 1$, $0 < k < 1$ and $\tau \geq 0$; k is a constant and τ is a measure of the cost advantage of providing low-quality services.

The larger τ, the greater the cost advantage of providing low-quality services. Given P, this implies, ceteris paribus, that providing low-quality services is more profitable than providing high-quality services, due to higher margins. However, the probability that a customer will be satisfied following a low-quality service transaction is less than the probability of being satisfied after a high-quality service transaction.

Suppose a customer purchases service j in time period t. Then, it is assumed, with probability $[1 - 1/(\beta_j)]$, that the customer will be satisfied with service j and purchase it again in period $(t + 1)$. With probability $1/\beta_j$, the customer will be dissatisfied with the service and consider switching to another service provider in period $(t + 1)$.[1]

At this point, advertising enters the model. In Schmalensee's (1978) view, advertising is an attempt to lure dissatisfied customers from other firms. Following Nelson (1970), only advertising *expenditures,* not media content, are important. Let $A_i(t)$ denote the advertising expenditure of firm i in period t and $a_i(t)$ the conditional probability that a customer who becomes dissatisfied with a service transaction in time period t will switch to service transaction i in time period $(t + 1)$.

Schmalensee (1978) assumed that $a_i(t)$ is given by:

(2) $a_i(t) = A_i^e(t) / \sum_j A_j^e(t)$ $i,j = 1, \ldots, N$

where e measures advertising effectiveness, with $e \geq 0$. This parameter captures the confidence dissatisfied customers have (cf. Nelson's, 1970, notion) that advertising expenditure levels are positively related to the quality of the service. If $e = 0$, advertising is completely ignored by dissatisfied customers. If $0 < e < 1$, advertising has some, but a less than proportional, effect. If $e = 1$, dissatisfied customers are modeled as purchasing the service for which they are first exposed via advertising. If $e > 1$, the most heavily advertised service gains a disproportionately high share of currently dissatisfied customers (i.e., a_i is disproportionately large).[2]

Schmalensee (1978) combined $a_i(t)$ with the probability of dissatisfaction to model the probability, T_{ij}, that a customer who purchases service j in period t will switch to service i in period $(t + 1)$. For fixed values of a_i and β_i, the switching probabilities can be described by a first-order stationary Markov model:

$$(3) \qquad T_{ij} = [1 - (1/\beta_j)]\delta_{ij} + a_i(t)(1/\beta_j) \quad i,j = 1, \ldots, N$$

where δ_{ij} is the Kroneker delta (i.e., $\delta_{ij} = 1$ if $i = j$ and $\delta_{ij} = 0$ if $i \neq j$). If the $A_i(t)$ are fixed at A_i over time, theory establishes that in equilibrium the market share q_i for firm i is given by:

$$(4) \qquad q_i = \beta_i A_i^e / \sum_j \beta_j A_j^e \quad i,j = 1, \ldots, N$$

Implications of Schmalensee's Model

The model allows us to investigate whether advertising expenditures are positively correlated with service quality, as implied by Nelson's (1970, 1975) work, or negatively associated, as implied by Comanor and Wilson (1979). The answer depends on e and τ. Schmalensee (1978) showed theoretically that advertising expenditures will be inversely related to quality if $e\tau \geq 1$ and $\tau > 0$. These conditions imply that if advertising is very effective (i.e., e is large), and there is a large cost advantage to providing low-quality services (i.e., τ is large), it will be profitable to providers of low-quality services to advertise more than providers of high-quality services. Thus, the nature of the relationship between advertising expenditure and service quality is an empirical question.

Paradoxically, Schmalensee's (1978) model implies that Nelson's (1970) thesis would probably be proven wrong if customers viewed advertising expenditures as being positively related to quality. In such cases, e would be large and $e\tau$ would be more likely to exceed unity. At equilibrium, this results in a negative relationship between advertising and quality (assuming $\tau > 0$). A similar argument follows from customers behaving according to Comanor and Wilson (1979).

It is important to realize that Schmalensee's (1978) conclusion also depends on the necessary condition that higher quality entails higher unit costs of production (i.e., $\tau > 0$). In his model (as in Nelson's, 1970, model), advertising high-quality products is more profitable, ceteris paribus, than advertising low-quality products, due to the higher repeat purchase probabilities. This positive relation between quality and profitability is offset in Schmalensee's model by the negative relation between quality and profit per unit sold, as price is fixed in his model.

Note, however, that the basic assumption that high-quality services command lower absolute markups on top of unit costs may not be realistic (cf. Buzzell & Gale, 1987). This implies that for many services, the counterbalancing factor of lower markups for higher quality services in Schmalansee's (1978) model does not exist, and therefore, advertising expenditures and service quality may be expected to be positively correlated. The same conclusion was reached by Telser (1978), Shapiro (1983), and Kihlstrom and Riordan (1984). In sum, theoretical work in economics yields the empirically testable hypothesis that advertising expenditures and actual service quality are positively correlated.

Empirical Evidence

To our knowledge, no empirical research has examined the relationship between objective service quality and advertising expenditures, although several studies have investigated the association between advertising expenditures and product quality (Archibald, Haulman, & Moody, 1983; Marquardt & McGann, 1975; Rotfeld & Rotzoll, 1976). In such work, no distinction is made between search goods and experience goods. Obviously, that would be difficult, because most products contain both search and experience (and credence) attributes. In general, such studies appear to indicate that advertising and product quality are indeed positively correlated, as predicted by economic theory. However, the relation is far from perfect. Future investigations may extend this research to the service quality context.

Price as a Market Signal for Service Quality

Economic theory in general assumes a positive relationship exists between price and quality. The rationale is straightforward. In a competitive situation, a higher price reflects higher unit costs of production. If this were not the case, abnormally high profits would obtain, which would attract the entry of new firms. This, in turn, would cause abnormally high profits to disappear. Under the assumption of efficient production, unit cost of production is higher with increased levels of quality. Thus, higher quality should be accompanied by higher prices.

The positive relationship between price and quality is also perfectly logical if customers are completely informed about prices and quality attributes. Even in economic models that consider the case of imperfect information, it is typically assumed that price and quality are positively correlated. Nelson (1975) stated: "The customer quite properly assumes that there tends to be a positive relationship between price and quality" (p. 229). Hey and McKenna (1981) considered the possibility that quality is negatively correlated with price and stated: "This is highly unlikely in practice. A more realistic case is to assume that quality generally increases with price" (p. 62). Schwartz and Wilde (1985) assumed that in a competitive equilibrium, lower quality services sell for a lower price than higher quality services.

However, because at least some customers are imperfectly informed, it may be profitable for firms to capitalize on customers' tendencies to use price as a quality index by offering a service of low quality for a high price (Salop & Stiglitz, 1977; Scitovsky, 1945). Wolinsky (1983) formally analyzed this situation with a model in which some market information is obtained by customers without special effort, (e.g., as a by-product of the shopping process). Many service markets satisfy this requirement as services often possess search attributes. In Wolinsky's model, and in line with empirical evidence in marketing (Rao & Monroe, 1989), customers expect to find a certain quality at a certain price.

Now, it is possible that a firm charging a particular (high) price may cheat its customers by providing lower quality. However, some non-zero number of potential customers will discover this through information acquired via search attributes and will subsequently not purchase from the firm. Therefore, the firm must decide whether the loss of sales due to cheating is offset by the cost savings on the sales to the remaining customers.

Wolinsky (1983) showed theoretically that if the markup over the marginal cost of providing the quality signaled by price is sufficiently high, the loss of sales will outweigh the cost saved. Thus, at equilibrium, price is a valid signal of quality. Further, the size of the markup depends on the nature of the information received by customers: the poorer the information (e.g., the fewer search attributes), the higher the markup. This finding has the following interesting implication. Because services are typically considered to be relatively low in search attributes compared to products (Zeithaml, 1981), Wolinsky's model predicts that the markup should be higher for services than for products. One could test this hypothesis by comparing various measures of profitability for service-oriented and product-oriented firms.

Empirical Evidence Regarding the Price-Quality Correlation

Empirical evidence from various countries, including the United States, Japan, Canada, and the Netherlands indicates that price and actual product quality are indeed positively (though not necessarily highly) correlated (Bodell, Kerton, & Schuster, 1986; Gerstner, 1985; Steenkamp, 1988; Yamada & Ackerman, 1984). Illustrative are the findings of Tellis and Wernerfelt's (1987) meta-analysis of previous U.S. studies. They reported a highly significant ($p < .0001$), although modest, mean rank order correlation of .27; with a median of .31.[3]

The strength of the relation depends on the level of inflation, characteristics of the products involved, and price dispersion (Steenkamp, 1988; Tellis & Wernerfelt, 1987). The price-quality relation was stronger when inflation was low, for durables than for nondurables, and for markets exhibiting a large price dispersion.

Future research might investigate these issues for service quality, using objective measures or intersubjective measures. Of special interest would be a comparison of the veridicality of price as a market signal of quality for both products and services. There are two reasons why the strength of the price-quality relation may be weaker for services. First, services typically contain a higher proportion of credence attributes, which renders quality evaluation by customers even more difficult than for products. Second, objective sources such as *Consumer Reports* typically provide more information for products than services. Consequently, the proportion of well-informed customers that tend to "discipline" the market (Salop & Stiglitz, 1977) will be lower in service-oriented markets.

Thus, firms may have more opportunity to charge noncompetitive prices (Schwartz & Wilde, 1985).

Price and Advertising Considered Jointly

We have examined models that concentrate primarily on advertising or price and their relation to quality. However, these marketing variables should be considered jointly, as advertising can be used to maintain a certain price, and price impacts the level of advertising expenditures. Klein and Leffler (1981) developed an influential model that considered advertising and pricing decisions jointly. Quality, advertising, and price are set by the firm. If the quality of the service is less than that implied by its price, customers will cease to purchase from that firm. Klein and Leffler demonstrated theoretically that a firm will produce high quality if it is able to charge a price premium on top of the production cost of high-quality output. The price premium is necessary as compensation for the profit the firm foregoes by refraining from a hit-and-run strategy in which the firm would earn high profits for a short time by cheating customers through selling a low-quality service for a high price. Thus, the incentive to maintain quality comes through price premiums and repeat sales that are lost once cheating is discovered.

Market equilibrium requires that the profits generated by the price premium be spent so that no entry will occur. This is achieved by requiring firms to sink their profits on advertising, logos, and other firm-specific capital expenditures that are lost if the firm cheats on quality. In this way, advertising expenditures are positively correlated with quality. Therefore, according to Klein and Leffler (1981), advertising and price carry the same information about quality, and both can be used successfully as indicators of quality.

The model counterbalances the incentive to cheat with the profit potential from repeat purchase. An interesting and empirically testable implication is that the price premium for maintaining a high quality level is higher for those kinds of services that generate few repeat purchases because fewer potential repeat purchases reduce the counterbalancing influence of repeat sales vis-à-vis cheating.

Milgrom and Roberts (1986) developed a model applicable exclusively to newly introduced services consisting only of experience attributes. Quality is given, and price and advertising are set by the firm. The initial purchase decision is positively affected by the perceived quality of the service, but not by actual quality. Also, quality perceptions are modeled as a function of advertising and price, consistent with the marketing literature (e.g., Parasuraman et al., 1985). After the initial purchase, actual quality is revealed, and no perceptual distortions occur. In the Milgrom and Roberts (1986) model, repeat purchase increases with actual quality. Despite its different formulation, Milgrom and Roberts reach the same conclusion as Klein and Leffler (1981), namely that customers can infer quality from observing either price or advertising. The fact that two substantially different models yield the same conclusion increases confidence in the generalizability of the conclusions.

The work discussed here suggests that both advertising and price are equivalent in the strength of their relation to quality. Interestingly, Archibald et al. (1983) found support for this hypothesis in the product quality context. They found a rank order correlation of .203 for advertising and quality and .210 for price and quality in the running shoes category. Testing of this hypothesis for services awaits future research.

Conclusions

In this chapter, we have considered price and advertising as market signals of service quality. We have drawn on the economic literature on signaling in product markets to develop a series of empirically testable hypotheses concerning services. We hypothesized that advertising and price are both positively, although not perfectly, correlated with service quality. This implies that customers looking for high quality services may reliably employ this market information. Still largely unexplored is the question of whether customers might be better off using other sources of information. At a minimum, this appears to depend on idiosyncratic factors such as the extent of prior experience and the opportunity cost of time involved in conducting a thorough search of the market.

We further hypothesized that price and advertising carry essentially the same amount of quality information. Additionally, we expect the markup on costs to be higher for services than for products and the strength of the price-quality relationship to be weaker for services than for products. A corollary of this hypothesis, as well as our expectation that price and advertising carry essentially the same information value with respect to service quality, is that the advertising-quality relationship will be weaker for services than for products.

We believe that if services marketing is to continue to attract attention as a topic of academic inquiry, the field must move from exploratory studies toward empirical work based on rigorous theory. We hope the present chapter may provide some small impetus in this direction by drawing attention to the role service markets can play in transferring reliable information about service quality from the service provider to the customer.

Notes

1. This implies that the service possesses at least some credence attributes.
2. In the terminology of Smallwood and Conlisk (1979), customers in Schmalensee's (1978) model can only be weakly dissatisfied, because there is a non-zero probability that they can repurchase a brand of unsatisfactory quality. Schmalensee believed the case of strongly dissatisfied customers was completely intractable. Smallwood and Conlisk concluded similarly that the case of strongly dissatisfied customers would be very difficult to analyze.
3. Note that the rank order correlation coefficient typically used in this stream of research is consistent with the work of Wolinsky (1983) and Klein and Leffler (1981) that suggests a monotonically increasing but nonlinear relationship between price and quality.

References

Archibald, R. B., Haulman, C. A., & Moody, C. E., Jr. (1983). Quality, advertising and published quality ratings. *Journal of Consumer Research, 9,* 347-356.

Bodell, R. W., Kerton, R. R., & Schuster. R. W. (1986). Price as a signal of quality: Canada in the international context. *Journal of Consumer Policy, 9,* 431-444.

Boulding, W., Kalra, A., Staelin, R., & Zeithaml, V. A. (1993). A dynamic process model of service quality: From expectations to behavioral intentions. *Journal of Marketing Research, 30,* 7-27.

Buzzell, R. D., & Gale, B. T. (1987). *The PIMS principles.* New York: Free Press.

Comanor, W. S., & Wilson, T. A. (1979). The effect of advertising on competition: A survey. *Journal of Economic Literature, 17,* 453-476.

Darby, M. R., & Karni, E. (1973). Free competition and the optimal amount of fraud. *Journal of Law and Economics, 16,* 67-88.

Gerstner, E. (1985). Do higher prices signal higher quality? *Journal of Marketing Research, 22,* 209-215.

Hey, J. D., & McKenna, C. J. (1981). Consumer search with uncertain product quality. *Journal of Political Economy, 89,* 615-641.

Jacoby, J., & Olson, J. C. (Eds.). (1985), *Perceived quality.* Lexington, MA: Lexington.

Kihlstrom, R. E., & Riordan, M. H. (1984). Advertising as a signal. *Journal of Political Economy, 92,* 427-450.

Kirmani, A., & Wright, P. (1989). Money talks: Perceived advertising expense and expected product quality. *Journal of Consumer Research, 16,* 344-353.

Klein, B., & Leffler, K. B. (1981). The role of market forces in assuring contractual performance. *Journal of Political Economy, 89,* 615-641.

Marquardt, R. A., & McGann, A. F. (1975). Does advertising communicate product quality to consumers? Some evidence from *Consumer Reports. Journal of Advertising, 4,* 27-31.

Milgrom, P., & Roberts, J. (1986). Price and advertising signals of product quality. *Journal of Political Economy, 94,* 796-821.

Miller, R. M., & Plott, C. R. (1985). Product quality signaling in experimental markets. *Econometrica, 53,* 837-872.

Nelson, P. (1970). Information and consumer behavior. *Journal of Political Economy, 78,* 311-329.

Nelson, P. (1975). The economic consequences of advertising. *Journal of Business, 48,* 213-241.

Oliver, R. L. (1980). A cognitive model of the antecedents and consequences of satisfaction decisions. *Journal of Marketing Research, 17,* 460-469.

Oliver, R. L. (1981). Measurement and evaluation of satisfaction processes in retail settings. *Journal of Retailing, 57,* 25-48.

Parasuraman, A., Zeithaml, V. A., & Berry, L. L. (1985). A conceptual model of service quality and its implications for future research. *Journal of Marketing, 49,* 41-50.

Rao, A. R., & Monroe, K. B. (1989). The effect of price, brand name, and store name on buyers' perceptions of product quality: An integrative review. *Journal of Marketing Research, 26,* 351-357.

Rotfeld, H. J., & Rotzoll, K. B. (1976). Advertising and product quality: Are heavily advertised products better? *Journal of Consumer Affairs, 10,* 33-47.

Salop, S., & Stiglitz, J. (1977). Bargain and ripoffs: A model of monopolistically competitive price dispersion. *Review of Economic Studies, 44,* 493-510.

Schmalensee, R. (1978). A model of advertising and product quality. *Journal of Political Economy, 86,* 485-503.

Schwartz, A., & Wilde, L. L. (1985). Product quality and imperfect information. *Review of Economic Studies, 52,* 251-262.

Scitovsky, T. (1945). Some consequences of the habit of judging quality by price. *Review of Economic Studies, 12,* 100-105.

Shapiro, C. (1983). Premiums for high quality products as returns to reputations. *Quarterly Journal of Economics, 98,* 659-679.

Smallwood, D. E., & Conlisk, J. (1979). Product quality in markets where consumers are imperfectly informed. *Quarterly Journal of Economics, 93,* 1-23.

Steenkamp, J.B.E.M. (1988). The relationship between price and quality in the marketplace. *De Economist, 136,* 491-507.

Steenkamp, J.B.E.M. (1989). *Product quality.* Vernon, VA: Books International.

Tellis, G. J., & Wernerfelt, B. (1987). Competitive price and quality under asymmetric information. *Marketing Science, 6,* 240-253.

Telser, L. G. (1978). Towards a theory of the economics of advertising. In D. G. Tuerck (Ed.), *Issues in advertising: The economics in persuasion* (pp. 71-89). Washington, DC: American Enterprise Institute.

Wolinsky, A. (1983). Prices as signals of product quality. *Review of Economic Studies, 50,* 647-658.

Yamada, Y., & Ackerman, N. (1984). Price-quality correlations in the Japanese market. *Journal of Consumer Affairs, 18,* 251-265.

Zeithaml, V. A. (1981). How consumer evaluation processes differ between goods and services. In J. H. Donnelly & W. R. George (Eds.), *Marketing of services* (pp. 186-190). Chicago: American Marketing Association.

CHAPTER FIVE

How Consumers Predict Service Quality

What Do They Expect?

VALERIE S. FOLKES

School of Business,
University of Southern California

Consumers form expectancies that lead to predictions about service quality and so influence the evaluation of services. This chapter reviews some of the empirical research examining cognitive processes underlying the formation of expectancies. Memories of past service experiences can bias expectancies because the distinctiveness of the information, elaboration on the information, and affective responses associated with the information can make some material more easily recalled. Expectancies are also influenced by causal attributions for service outcomes. Antecedents of consumers' causal inferences for successful and unsuccessful service delivery and their consequences are examined with the emphasis on the temporal stability of the cause.

Consumer expectancies play a central role in understanding evaluations of service quality. The predominant models of service quality and customer satisfaction emphasize the role of expectancies (e.g., Oliver, 1977, 1980, 1989; Parasuraman, Zeithaml, & Berry, 1985; Zeithaml, Berry, & Parasuraman, 1988). When there is a negative gap between the service performed and customer expectancies, quality is judged to be poor (e.g., Bolton & Drew, 1991; Brown & Swartz, 1989). Similarly, when expectancies are disconfirmed by service performance falling short of customer anticipations, customer dissatisfaction is likely (e.g., Bearden & Teel, 1983; Oliver, 1980; Oliver & DeSarbo, 1988).

Given its centrality to understanding service quality, the expectancy construct deserves particular attention. How do consumers form expectancies for service performance? Understanding the cognitive processes influencing the formation of expectancies is important not only in understanding perceptions of service quality, but also in conceptualizing a variety of other domains. In this regard, an excellent overview of the various theoretical approaches to expectancies is provided in Oliver and Winer (1987). In this chapter I limit myself to elaborating on a few ways in which expectancies are formed and some empirical research that illustrates the underlying processes. This discussion is informed primarily by research in decision making and attribution theory.

For the purpose of this discussion, expectancies will be conceptualized as the consumer's beliefs about the range of likely outcomes of a service provision (see Oliver & Winer, 1987, for an in-depth discussion). This is similar to what Zeithaml, Berry, and Parasuraman (1993) termed predicted service or predictions about service. Service users often have some sense of the likelihood of various levels of service performance. For example, patients hold beliefs about the probability of accurate diagnoses from their physicians (e.g., Andreasen, 1985), investors about the likelihood of losses and profits by their brokers (e.g., Oliver & DeSarbo, 1988), restaurant patrons about getting the type of food they want (e.g., Swan & Trawick, 1981), and so on. Many service deliverers maintain that they provide a consistently high standard of service or a zerodefect standard. However, service is intrinsically difficult to standardize. As a result, consumers will almost inevitably encounter variance in the outcomes they receive from service delivery. Not all experiences will be evaluated as positively as others, leading to a perceived range of outcomes.

There is some difference of opinion as to the kinds of expectancies that influence perceptions of service quality and customer satisfaction. One perspective is that quality reflects expectations of what ought to be whereas satisfaction taps expectations of what is likely to be (e.g., Parasuraman et al., 1985). Yet, predicted service also influences expectations of what is considered desirable and what is only adequate, and so influences perceived quality (Zeithaml et al., 1993). Other investigators have suggested that expectations are drawn from various types of evidence, such as the performance of the best brand in the product class and the norms for the product class (Cadotte, Woodruff, & Jenkins, 1987). These are important distinctions. However, the complexities of these issues are beyond the scope of the present chapter.

The Role of Memory in Forming Expectancies

Expectancies are formed as a result of a variety of cognitive processes, some more complex than others. Past experience is one basis for forecasting future service performance. Consumers might predict the likelihood of poor service by reflecting on service received in the past, by themselves or others, and projecting that same rate of failure for future performance. For example, an airline passenger might count the number of times baggage was lost and assume that the same rate of failure will occur in the future.

Using past experience means that the consumer will search external or internal sources (Bettman, 1979). External sources could include written records and other consumers. For example, an investor could scan a checkbook or financial statements to identify payments to brokers. A friend might be asked about her experiences with a physician.

A reliance on internal search means that the consumer's memory will have considerable influence on the formation of expectancies. Although some investigators have emphasized the accuracy with which people encode information about the frequency of occurrence of events (Hasher & Zacks, 1984), others have noted the many ways in which memory is biased. Recency biases are one such mechanism: earlier events are generally more difficult to recall than subsequent events so a consumer might stop searching memory for additional events after recalling only recent ones. The newspaper subscriber remembering incidents of delivery failure will be more likely to sample recent service experiences than service received earlier. Other biases include distinctiveness and elaboration, discussed below.

Distinctiveness and Recall

The distinctiveness of the event facilitates recall (e.g., Gardner, 1983; Herr, 1989). Events that stand out and are easily distinguished from others will be sampled more readily by consumers when recalling service experiences compared to those that lack differentiation (Folkes, 1988). There are a variety of ways that service delivery can be made more distinctive and thus more memorable.

In one study examining the relationship between distinctiveness and forecasts of problems, people who regularly used an escalator in a six-story building were asked to provide expectancies for breakdowns (Folkes, 1988). As they approached the escalators, an interviewer asked them to estimate the percent of time the escalator was inoperable. The distinctiveness of the individual consumers' responses to past breakdowns varied.

The bank of escalators reached only to the fourth floor of the building. People going to the sixth floor had to both ride the escalator and climb stairs to reach their destination. Thus, climbing stairs was a familiar and typical experience for them regardless of whether the escalator was operative or not. In contrast, climbing stairs was a more distinctive experience for those going only to the fourth floor. Interrupted escalator service during repairs prevented their using their typical means of going to the fourth floor. Relative to those using the escalator to reach the sixth floor, those using the escalator to reach the fourth floor estimated that the escalator broke down more frequently, 54% versus 35% of the time.

The estimates of repair problems in the escalator study seem intuitively too high. This may reflect a bias toward recalling negative events more than positive events. Service failure is probably more distinctive than service success. Service problems occur less frequently than successes; therefore they should stand out more in memory relative to their actual occurrence. Further, events that have negative implications for a person's well-being attract more attention than do positive events (Pratto & John, 1991). Finally, service failure often requires an unusual response from the consumer to correct the problem (e.g., to seek out the appropriate person to complain to about service). Thus, expectancies should be biased in the direction of being pessimistic if consumers rely on recalling past experiences to forecast future problems.

Although to some extent distinctiveness is difficult for firms to control, distinctiveness of the service experience can be somewhat influenced by firms. In fact, most firms go to great lengths to distinguish their brand name, their style of service delivery, and the service itself from that of the competition. Golden arches, employee uniforms, packaging, and so forth help the consumer generate expectancies about McDonald's based on experiences with only individual franchisees' service. In contrast, distinguishing among experiences with different McDonald's outlets can be more difficult. The greater the number of similar experiences the more difficult is discerning among the experiences (cf. Hunt & Elliott, 1980). Thus, projections for future service are more likely to reflect actual past experiences when the context surrounding service delivery is distinctive.

Elaboration and Recall

Elaborating on an event also facilitates retrieval (e.g., Kiselius & Sternthal, 1986). As well as encoding a service delivery experience into memory, the consumer also stores associations with the experience. Most typically this involves elaborating on the meaning of the event. While waiting for an appointment for service, a consumer might ruminate on the implications for the delay on arriving for a subsequent appointment or think about similar experiences waiting for other services. When forming expectancies about future service delivery, such elaboration makes the experience more easily recalled and so more likely to be sampled. The nature of the elaboration can strengthen recall. Elaboration that is relevant to service performance facilitates recall more than irrelevant elaboration (Stein & Bransford, 1979). For example, the waiting consumer who spends time in the reception area relating the delay to the employee's attitude toward service delivery will more readily recall this experience when anticipating future service than the consumer who ruminates on the apparel of others in the reception area. Thus, relevant elaboration of good service experiences and irrelevant or no elaboration of poor service experiences will lead to more positive expectancies for future performance.

Elaboration can distort memories as well as facilitate recall. The process of associating service experience with other events in memory can lead the consumer to encode inaccurate information about the experience. For example, an airline passenger might recall a delay on a previous flight while waiting for a flight to board. This could lead to subsequent confusion over the current flight's actual departure time.

Distortion can also occur during recall, as when consumers fill in their gaps in remembering about a certain event by reconstructing the event (e.g., Helgeson & Beatty, 1987). For example, a patient might recall having an appointment and remember that there were other people in the waiting room, but forget whether there was a long delay before seeing the physician. The patient might use the number of people in the waiting room as a cue for assuming there had been a long wait. Thus, the memory of the incident is constructed rather than recalled exactly as it occurred.

Affective Reactions and Recall

The previous discussion about distinctiveness and elaboration suggests that another factor influencing recall ease is the valence associated with the event (Tversky & Kahneman, 1973). When strong affective reactions occur, individuals may give greater attention to the event, more thoroughly rehearse and ruminate over it, and find it easier to recall than when neutral reactions occur (Higgins, Kuiper, & Olson, 1981). Thus, a service problem that makes an individual angry should be easier to recall than a problem that does not arouse emotion. The relationship between affective reactions to service and recall has been examined for patrons of fast-food restaurants (Folkes, 1988). It appears that the negative feelings in response to a poor service experience are more easily remembered than the positive feelings due to a successful experience. This may be because a pleasant success lacks distinctiveness. For restaurant service, as for most other service outcomes, success is the typical outcome and pleasant feelings are the typical reaction to service delivery.

However, a good service experience that makes an individual feel particularly happy should be easier to recall than an experience unaccompanied by emotion. For example, restaurant patrons should more easily recall an experience when a strong positive affect occurred (e.g., when the customer is particularly delighted by the responsiveness of a firm's employee). The tendency for valence to influence memory suggests that forecasts based on recalled incidents will be affectively charged.

Summary

In sum, when consumers project the likelihood of future success or failure in service delivery based on past experience, their recall may be biased. Events that are distinctive and that elicit elaboration from the consumer are more easily recalled. Sometimes both these factors are present, as when strong affective reactions occur.

However, estimating future service outcomes by projecting from the occurrence of past events is only one means of arriving at expectancies. Recalling specific instances is often difficult, as when there are numerous nondistinctive events occurring over a lengthy time period. As an example, try to count the times in the past year that a pay telephone malfunctioned as a portion of all pay telephone usage. Even when the recall of incidents is such as to permit engaging in an enumerative procedure, the consumer may not be motivated to do so. In such situations, consumers often rely on heuristics or simple rules of thumb to arrive at expectancies. Heuristics are generally employed for less important information tasks and for simplifying complex tasks.

The Availability Heuristic

One means of assessing the likelihood of future events without recalling numerous events is to rely on the availability of an event in memory. The availability heuristic involves using the ease with which one can bring to mind exemplars of an event as a means of judging probability (Kahneman & Tversky, 1982; Tversky & Kahneman, 1973). Consumers using this decisional shortcut would not necessarily attempt to recall numerous service occasions, but instead would estimate the likelihood of problems with services by determining how easy it is to recall such incidents. When retrieval seems easy, problems are judged to be likely; when retrieval seems difficult, problems are judged to be unlikely. Ease of retrieval is influenced by the same factors described previously. Sometimes it is difficult to determine whether, in a given situation, estimates are based on a volume of incidents recalled or merely on the perceived ease of recall. For example, it may be that in the escalator study described earlier, people did not base their estimates of the likelihood of future problems on the number of incidents recalled, but instead on the ease of recalling an example of being without escalator service.

Frames of Reference

In a test of the availability heuristic, the effect of priming the type of event to be recalled was examined (Folkes, 1988). When people are asked about the probability of an event, they seek information about occurrences of the event more than nonoccurrences, unless the situation facilitates evenhanded consideration of both (e.g., Beyth-Marom & Fischhoff, 1983; Einhorn & Hogarth, 1981; Tversky & Kahneman, 1973). Consumers, when asked about the likelihood that food received in a restaurant will be different from what was ordered, determined that the ease of recalling occurrences (getting the wrong order—a failure) is greater than the ease of recalling nonoccurrences (getting exactly what was ordered) (Folkes, 1988). The ease of recalling an incident in which they received the wrong food was related to their estimates of the likelihood of not getting the correct order in the future rather than to estimates of getting what they wanted. Conversely, consumers asked about the likelihood that the food would be exactly what was ordered determined the ease of recalling those sorts of incidents rather than the ease of recalling getting the wrong order. The ease of recalling an instance when they received the food they ordered was related to their estimates of getting what they wanted in the future rather than to estimates of problems.

In short, when consumers are asked their expectancies for a service problem they determine the ease of recalling problem incidents, but neglect to consider equally the ease of recalling incidents of service successes, and vice versa. Problem estimates are related more strongly to the ease of recalling problem experiences than to the ease of recalling good experiences. Similarly, successful service is related more strongly to ease of recalling success experiences than to ease of recalling failure experiences. Thus, expectancies can vary depending on the frame of reference that is provided.

Summary

Consumers sometimes judge the probability of future service success and failure by assessing the ease of recalling exemplars of such occasions. Thus, the availability heuristic provides a shortcut to judging the probabilities of future outcomes. Other heuristics may also be used, such as the representativeness heuristic (see Oliver & Winer, 1987). On the other hand, judgments can be more complex than the processes identified so far. Expectancies are generated not just from a process of enumerating or attempting to enumerate experiences and projecting rates for the future, but also from the meaning extracted from a consumer's experiences. One particular type of inference making that has been shown to influence expectancies is causal inferences (i.e., attributions).

Attributions and Expectancies

Causal attributions are often integral to the way people and objects are evaluated. When consumers evaluate service delivery they infer reasons for their experiences with the firm. The hotel guest infers that the skill and training of the hotel staff led to a pleasant stay. The investor blames bad luck for a stock loss rather than holding the broker responsible.

Having an explanation provides a feeling of mastery over one's environment and so serves an adaptive function (Weiner, 1985). Nevertheless, causal inferences occur under some conditions more than others. Expectancies are a stimulus to forming attributions. Unexpected events lead to more causal inferences. This suggests that consumers who receive service that is much better or much worse than anticipated will engage in more attributional reasoning than those who get what they expect. Negative events are also more likely to trigger inferences about the reasons for performance (Folkes, 1982; Weiner, 1985). Thus, consumers who experience a problem with their service are more likely to search for an explanation. Further, outcomes must be sufficiently important to motivate the consumer to undertake a causal analysis. (Weiner, 1985)

Types of Causes

Considering that there are a variety of types of services and for each service there are many possible attributions for success and failure, understanding the effects of causal inferences on expectancies requires a means of classifying them. Based on logical and empirical analyses, Weiner (1990) has identified three major properties of perceived causes. These three causal dimensions are stability (stable or permanent versus unstable or temporary), locus of causality (internal to the person versus external to the person), and controllability (under one's control versus not under one's control).

Locus of causality and controllability have important consequences for firms and consumers, including feelings of anger, complaining behavior, and repurchase (e.g., Curren & Folkes, 1987; Folkes, 1990; Folkes, Koletsky, & Graham, 1987). However, stability is of particular interest for the purposes of this discussion. Causes of service success and failure have been categorized by their temporal stability as being permanent or unchanging versus temporary and fluctuating. For example, flight delays can be perceived as due to stable causes (e.g., constant understaffing or air traffic control problems) or to unstable causes (e.g., a temporary shortage of staff or a hailstorm) (Folkes et al., 1987).

Classification along the dimension of causal stability is particularly useful because stability influences expectancies for service performance. Attributing stable causes for service leads to more confidence that the same outcome will recur than do unstable causes (Folkes, 1984; Weiner, 1990). When an investor believes that a stock loss is due to the broker's poor training, similar losses are expected in the future. Similarly, a stock gain attributed to the broker's ability to pick good buys will suggest similar good outcomes in the future. When service outcomes are inferred to be due to unstable reasons (e.g., a stock loss due to bad luck), the consumer is more uncertain there will be future problems than when outcomes are attributed to stable reasons.

Attributions to Ability and Effort in Service Delivery

Two attributions are particularly important for understanding consumer evaluations of service delivery—the employee's ability or competence and the employee's effort or exertion. When evaluating people's performance in the achievement domain, these are two of the most common explanations given for successful and unsuccessful outcomes (see Weiner, 1986, for a review). In service delivery two components of success and failure are the ability of the personnel to perform the service and the attitude of the employees (Bitner, Booms, & Tetreault, 1990; Zeithaml et al., 1988).

Attributions About the Service Deliverer's Competence. Ability, in the sense of aptitude, is generally considered a stable attribution for performance (Weiner, 1986). For example, an accountant must have a certain aptitude for working with numbers and that aptitude is generally conceived as an enduring characteristic. However, ability can be considered unstable if learning is involved. For example, without losing confidence in the physician's basic aptitude, patients might expect a physician fresh out of medical school to make errors that more experienced physicians would not make.

For those services that involve customization to the individual consumer's needs, a pattern of performance over time that reflects learning might be expected. Initially, low-quality or otherwise unsatisfactory outcomes might be tolerated as long as improvement is demonstrated (cf. Oliva, Oliver, & MacMillan, 1992). Such a pattern might reflect a trial period as the service deliverer acquires a sense of the particular individual's needs. Later, poor service quality might not be tolerated, instead being taken as evidence of lack of effort or inability to learn. For example, an interior decorator's outrageous selections might be permitted more at the initial stage compared to later.

Consumers use a variety of cues to infer the competence of service personnel, including titles, certifications, demeanor, and so on. Cues from the service environment can imply competence in service delivery, which in turn implies stability of success and failure. A travel agent operating in a disorganized and messy establishment is thought to be more responsible for service failure than one in tidier surroundings (Bitner, 1990). As a result, continued poor service is thought more likely in the future.

Attributions About the Service Deliverer's Effort. The employee's effort in service delivery reflects the attitudinal component that is so important in service evaluation (Bitner, 1990). Effort demonstrated in service delivery gives some assurance of the employee's motivation. Thus, service that successfully meets the customer's wants is evaluated even more positively when the consumer perceives it to be a result of the service provider's hard work to satisfy the customer (Folkes & Spekman, 1992). Similarly, service problems are responded to less harshly when consumers feel that employees at least tried to deliver good service.

Effort can be either a stable attribution, as when a person can be characterized as a highly motivated person, or unstable, as when a person "goes the extra mile" to exert effort (Weiner, 1986). A variety of cues are used to infer effort. Physical and mental exertion can be suggested by beads of perspiration. Incentives such as high commissions or bonuses paid to service employees may convey to consumers that employees are highly motivated to provide good service.

As with ability, temporal patterns can be important in attributions of effort. Consumers may expect that service will be better if administered early in the day (when the employee is not tired) or after a coffee break (as the employee is alert), but worse just before closing time or before a holiday. For example, patients often prefer to schedule surgery early in the morning, expecting that surgeons will be less fatigued compared to later in the day.

Communications About Attributions

An important source of information about the reasons for service outcomes is communications from other consumers, from the media, and from service personnel themselves. Communications from other consumers are more likely to provide information suggesting stable causes for both success and failure. Consumers are more likely to complain about service performance to the firm and to other consumers when the reason for dissatisfaction is stable rather than unstable (Curren & Folkes, 1987). Similarly, compliments to service personnel and recommendations to other consumers are more likely when the reason for satisfaction is stable rather than unstable. Thus, expectancies are likely to be that service will remain the same.

The media are another source of information about causes of service performance. As with consumer communications, there is some evidence that media accounts are more likely to cite stable attributions for events (Andreassen, 1987). In at least one area, financial news, reporters tend to cite reasons for an increase in a stock price that are enduring rather than temporary. This leads investors to expect continued increases and so to purchase the stock.

Evidence of the influence of causal attributions for purchase comes from Andreassen's (1987) study in which people engaged in a simulated stock market game. Actual newspaper headlines were presented, some of which gave reasons for stock increases (e.g., gains due to a merger proposal) and some for decreases (e.g., declines due to a new competitor's entry into the market). Compared to headlines that did not provide explanations, reasons for falling prices lead people to sell the stock whereas reasons for increases led to stock purchases.

Service employees also communicate reasons for their firm's performance, particularly in the form of excuses, apologies, and justifications for poor performance. Excuses are a common means of maintaining disrupted social relationships (Weiner, 1992; Weiner, Amirkhan, Folkes, & Verette, 1987). Giving no excuse at all for failed service tends to have worse consequences for customer satisfaction than giving a poor excuse (Bitner, 1990). For example, a travel agent who gives no excuse for not finding an economical fare for the customer is evaluated more negatively than when the agent accepts blame.

Because a frequent goal of the excuse giver is to change the target's expectancies (Weiner, 1992), unstable attributions are typically communicated to the person who experiences negative outcomes. In their letters to shareholders, employees cite unstable reasons for poor performance (e.g., lower profits are attributed to unusual economic conditions) but stable reasons for good performance (e.g., high profits due to the firm's research and development efforts) (Bettman & Weitz, 1983). This contrasts with the tendency toward uniformly communicating stable attributions by other consumers and the media.

Summary

Consumers often go beyond the mere number of experiences they can recall to interpret and give meaning to those experiences. Inferences about the reasons for good and poor service are an important way to evaluate and predict outcomes. By classifying consumers' causal attributions by temporal stability, expectancies for the future can be predicted. Causal inferences are, in turn, influenced by a variety of factors, including other consumers, the media, and service personnel themselves.

Overview

There are a variety of means by which consumers arrive at expectancies for service, some cognitively complex, some rather simple. For each of these, perceived expectancies are influenced by consumers' own experiences and beliefs and by their ability and motivation to use various types of information. Thus, consumer expectancies for service quality can be quite different from what those who deliver service to the client believe they should be.

References

Andreasen, A. R. (1985). Consumer responses to dissatisfaction in loose monopolies. *Journal of Consumer Research, 12,* 135-141.

Andreassen, P. B. (1987). On the social psychology of the stock market: Aggregate attributions' effects and the regressiveness of prediction. *Journal of Personality and Social Psychology, 53,* 490-496.

Bearden, W. O., & Teel, J. E. (1983). Selected determinants of consumer satisfaction and complaint reports. *Journal of Marketing Research, 20,* 21-28.

Bettman, J. R. (1979). *An information processing theory of consumer choice.* Reading, MA: Addison-Wesley.

Bettman, J. R., & Weitz, B. A. (1983). Attributions in the board room: Causal reasoning in corporate annual reports. *Administrative Science Quarterly, 28,* 165-183.

Beyth-Marom, R., & Fischhoff, B. (1983). Diagnosticity and pseudo-diagnosticity. *Journal of Personality and Social Psychology, 45,* 1185-1195.

Bitner, M. J. (1990). Evaluating service encounters: The effects of physical surroundings and employee responses. *Journal of Marketing, 54,* 69-82.

Bitner, M. J., Booms, B. M., & Tetreault, M. S. (1990). The service encounter: Diagnosing favorable and unfavorable incidents. *Journal of Marketing, 54,* 71-84.

Bolton, R. N., & Drew, J. H. (1991). A longitudinal analysis of the impact of service changes on customer attitudes. *Journal of Marketing, 55,* 1-9.

Brown, S. W., & Swartz, T. A. (1989). A gap analysis of professional service quality. *Journal of Marketing, 53,* 92-98.

Cadotte, E. R., Woodruff, R. B., & Jenkins, R. L. (1987). Expectations and norms in models of consumer satisfaction. *Journal of Marketing Research, 24,* 305-314.

Curren, M. T., & Folkes, V. S. (1987). Attributional influences on consumers' desires to communicate about products. *Psychology and Marketing, 4,* 35-45.

Einhorn, H. J., & Hogarth, R. M. (1981). Behavioral decision theory: Processes of judgment and choice. *Annual Review of Psychology, 32,* 53-88.

Folkes, V. S. (1982). Communicating the reasons for social rejection. *Journal of Experimental Social Psychology, 18,* 235-252.

Folkes, V. S. (1984). Consumer reactions to product failure: An attributional approach. *Journal of Consumer Research, 10,* 398-409.

Folkes, V. S. (1988). The availability heuristic and perceived risk. *Journal of Consumer Research, 15,* 13-23.

Folkes, V. S. (1990). Conflict in the marketplace: Explaining why products fail. In S. Graham & V. S. Folkes (Eds.), *Attribution theory: Applications to achievement, mental health, and interpersonal conflict* (pp. 143-160). Hillsdale, NJ: Lawrence Erlbaum.

Folkes, V. S., Koletsky, S., & Graham, J. L. (1987). A field study of causal inferences and consumer reaction: The view from the airport. *Journal of Consumer Research, 15,* 534-539.

Folkes, V. S., & Spekman, R. (1992). *Measuring customer satisfaction.* Working paper, University of Southern California.

Gardner, M. P. (1983). Advertising effects on attributes recalled and criteria used for brand evaluations. *Journal of Consumer Research, 10,* 310-318.

Hasher, L., & Zacks, R. T. (1984). Automatic processing of fundamental information: The case of frequency of occurrence. *American Psychologist, 39,* 1372-1388.

Helgeson, J. G., & Beatty, S. E. (1987). Price expectation and price recall error: An empirical study. *Journal of Consumer Research, 14,* 67-75.

Herr, P. M. (1989). Priming price: Prior knowledge and context effects. *Journal of Consumer Research. 16,* 67-75.

Higgins, E. T., Kuiper, N. A., & Olson, J. M. (1981). Social cognition: A need to get personal. In E. T. Higgins, C. P. Herman, & M. P. Zanna (Eds.), *Social cognition* (pp. 395-420). Hillsdale, NJ: Lawrence Erlbaum.

Hunt, R. R., & Elliott, J. M. (1980). The role of nonsemantic information in memory: Orthographic distinctiveness effects on retention. *Journal of Experimental Psychology: General, 109,* 49-74.

Kahneman, D., & Tversky, A. (1982). *Judgment under uncertainty: Heuristics and biases.* New York: Cambridge University Press.

Kiselius, J., & Sternthal, B. (1986). Examining the vividness controversy: An availability-valence interpretation. *Journal of Consumer Research, 12,* 418-431.

Oliva, T. A., Oliver, R. L., & MacMillan, I. C. (1992). A catastrophe model for developing service satisfaction strategies. *Journal of Marketing, 56,* 83-95.

Oliver, R. L. (1977). Effect of expectation and disconfirmation on postexposure product evaluations: An alternative interpretation. *Journal of Applied Psychology, 62,* 480-486.

Oliver, R. L. (1980). A cognitive model of the antecedents and consequences of satisfaction decisions. *Journal of Marketing Research, 17,* 460-469.

Oliver, R. L. (1989). Processing of the satisfaction response in consumption: A suggested framework and research propositions. *Journal of Consumer Satisfaction, Dissatisfaction and Complaining Behavior, 2,* 1-16.

Oliver, R. L., & DeSarbo, W. S. (1988). Response determinants in satisfaction judgments. *Journal of Consumer Research, 14,* 495-507.

Oliver, R. L., & Winer, R. S. (1987). A framework for the formation and structure of consumer expectations: Review and propositions. *Journal of Economic Psychology, 8,* 469-499.

Parasuraman, A., Zeithaml, V. A., & Berry, L. L. (1985). A conceptual model of service quality and its implications for future research. *Journal of Marketing, 49,* 41-50.

Pratto, F., & John, O. P. (1991). Automatic vigilance: The attention-grabbing power of negative social information. *Journal of Personality and Social Psychology, 61,* 380-391.

Stein, B. S., & Bransford, J. D. (1979). Constraints on effective elaboration: Effects of precision and subject generation. *Journal of Verbal Learning and Verbal Behavior, 18,* 769-777.

Swan, J. E., & Trawick, I. F. (1981). Disconfirmation of expectations and satisfaction with a retail service. *Journal of Retailing, 57,* 49-67.

Tversky, A., & Kahneman, D. (1973). Availability: A heuristic for judging frequency and probability. *Cognitive Psychology, 5,* 207-232.

Weiner, B. (1985). "Spontaneous" causal thinking. *Psychological Bulletin, 97,* 74-84.

Weiner, B. (1986). *An attributional theory of motivation and emotion.* New York: Springer-Verlag.

Weiner, B. (1990). Searching for the roots of applied attribution theory. In S. Graham & V. S. Folkes (Eds.), *Attribution theory: Application to achievement, mental health, and interpersonal conflict* (pp. 1-16). Hillsdale, NJ: Lawrence Erlbaum.

Weiner, B. (1992). Excuses in everyday interaction. In M. McLaughlin, M. J. Cody, & S. J. Read (Eds.), *Explaining oneself to others: Reason-giving in a social context* (pp. 131-146). Hillsdale, NJ: Lawrence Erlbaum.

Weiner, B., Amirkhan, J., Folkes, V. S., & Verette, J. (1987). An attributional analysis of excuse giving: Studies of a naive theory of emotion. *Journal of Personality and Social Psychology, 53,* 316-324.

Zeithaml, V. A., Berry, L. L., & Parasuraman, A. (1988). Communication and control processes in the delivery of service quality. *Journal of Marketing, 52,* 35-48.

Zeithaml, V. A., Berry, L. L., & Parasuraman, A. (1993). The nature and determinants of customer expectations of service. *Journal of the Academy of Marketing Science, 21,* 1-12.

CHAPTER SIX

Managing Services When
the Service Is a Performance

JOHN DEIGHTON

*Graduate School of Business,
University of Chicago*

In the instant of delivery, all services are staged performances. Producers and marketers of services, accordingly, have the many resources of dramatistics at their command to amplify the sense consumers make of service encounters. This chapter examines how audiences judge a staged performance to be a success or a failure. The result is a revised conception of service quality. In particular, satisfaction depends on involvement. The chapter explores how to use involvement to heighten the consumption experience and concludes with prescriptions for managing services as performances.

Performances present marketers with some unfamiliar problems. Whenever transactions involve *doings of actors* rather than *possession of objects,* as they clearly do in domains like sport, entertainment, politics, and professional services like management consulting and law, the classical prescriptions of marketing do not seem to get to the essence of the managerial challenge. Even the services marketing literature does not have much to say about how to stage a good "show." The rules for successful marketing of performance tend to be vested in practitioner lore, not academic texts. Except for a seminal paper by Boissac (1987), some symbolic interactionist theory applications (Solomon, 1983), and work in the tradition of Erving Goffman (Grove & Fisk, 1983), the topic of performance marketing has been barely explored.

What Is and What Is Not a Performance?

It is a truism to say that all services are performed. To say that all services are performances, however, is to say something slightly different and more interesting. To go further and claim that all services are staged performances is very different and quite provocative. In this chapter, I am concerned first with exploring the claim that services are intrinsically staged activities. Second, I aim to identify managerial prescriptions that apply whenever a service is a performance and is staged.

The definitions of performance to be used in this paper are adapted from and justified in Deighton (1992). By a *contractual performance,* I mean nothing more than an action done to fulfill an obligation, a debt, or a contract to another party. Performances stand in contrast to mere occurrences, which are events that "just happen" without any intention to satisfy another party. By a *staged performance,* I mean one that is put on with deliberate concern for the impression it will make on the other party and without any sly attempt to hide the staging. An actor stages a performance when he or she acts in a way that is overtly shaped by presentational concerns.

Given this definition, it is hard to imagine a marketed service that is not a staged performance. Is any service provider in a competitive market indifferent to what the service buyer thinks of the delivery? Clearly some hide their apprehension better than others, and some services are less overtly staged than others. Entertainment, for example, is usually quite blatant about its stagedness. By contrast, professional service providers such as surgeons usually try to hold themselves aloof from the concerns of putting on a good show. Yet even the most task-oriented surgeon knows what it means to behave like a surgeon and has enough innate stagecraft to avoid looking too much like a butcher or a motor mechanic.

The value of thinking about service provision as a matter of performance is not found, however, by asking what kind of performance the provider thinks he or she is putting on. The crucial point is what kind of performance *consumers* think they are seeing. As the following discussion will show, shifts in the way the consuming audience sees the performance, whether as staged or contracted or even as a random, unplanned occurrence, are resources for managing the impact of the service.

Contractual Performance

Compare the sentence, "The lawyer cross-examined" to "The lawyer performed a cross-examination." The latter is the marked case in a semantic sense: It is less concise and by implication carries more information about the action. What is the new information? First, performance implies an *audience*. It draws attention to the idea that someone is watching. Second, the action in the marked case becomes something of an *act*, almost a rite or ritual, assumed to be a familiar pattern of action to the person hearing the report. (Hear how odd it sounds when this transformation is used on an action that does not have canonical status, as in "The waiter poured the water" and "The waiter performed the pouring of the water.") Third, the marked sentence implies that the action may be *held to some standard* of normality or excellence. The speaker of the marked sentence might be hinting that the lawyer was not just doing the task, but was putting on a show of professional skill. It is plausible that one could say of oneself that "I performed the cross-examination," referring to oneself as both actor and audience. This happens when one acts with the intention of looking evaluatively at that action, as distinct from acting unself-consciously.

The conclusion is that an action becomes a performance when there is an audience that thinks it can hold the actor to a standard. I use the expression *contractual performance* to describe this kind of judgment about an event. Consumers can usually interpret the things that service producers do for them as performances in this sense. They arise from transactions, so obligations are inescapable.

But it is the consumer, not the service performer, who decides what is or is not a performance, and the performer cannot escape the consumer's right to judge. As Lovelock (1991) notes with respect to Federal Express, customers buy whatever they think they are buying. If a consumer thinks that some stray occurrence is actually part of a contractual performance, then it is. If the consumer fails to realize that some action belongs in the performance, then the marketer will get no credit for it. The Sir Francis Drake Hotel in San Francisco, for example, launders all its coins each night so that the hotel can give its guests clean money. If a guest fails to recognize that a bright coin is part of the hotel's performance, then it is in fact not. It is just something that happened, a chance event that earns the hotel no goodwill.

Hence the importance that service marketers have traditionally attached to managing expectations. When consumer and producer share the same expectations, then they agree on what counts and what does not count toward a satisfactory performance. In the standard formulations of customer satisfaction, first the consumer and the producer strike a contract, whether explicitly or implicitly, to embody mutual expectations. Then the service provider performs. Finally a consumer rates the performance against the contract, forming a satisfaction judgment (e.g., Oliver, 1980). In this view, management of service quality consists simply of bringing performance and expectations into alignment. In the next section of this chapter, I argue that there is much more to successful service performance than matching expectations. In particular there are the devices and stratagems of staging.

Staged Performance

If we say that an orthopedic surgeon performs a successful operation, we usually are making a quite simple judgment: The outcome sought by both the actor and ourselves was realized or exceeded. The judgment is simple because we are assured that the actor's goals were set without regard to our goals. It would be a very different matter if we thought that knowledge of our goals influenced the intentions of the surgeon. Then we might fear that the surgeon was trying to please us or impress us, rather than solve our problem, and it would be hard to feel much confidence in a judgment that the operation appeared to be successful.

To the extent that the consumer perceives a motive on the actor's part to produce a calculated effect in his or her actions, the performance is no longer merely contractual, but a *staged performance*. Such actions are dramatistics (Sarbin, 1986). The audience reads the conduct of the actor with forewarning that it is deliberate and intended to contrive an effect.

Recognizing that a performance is staged for effect can destroy it. The value of the performance may be dismissed as mere pandering, or worse, as deception or fraud. On the other hand, stagedness can be accepted indulgently, even avidly, as one accepts entertainment, or exploitatively, as one accepts flattery or servility from service providers. The discovery that something is staged is not in itself a clue to how it will be evaluated. That depends on the audience's perception of the actor's *motive*. Thus there are two elements to judgments of staged performance quality. First, the audience recognizes that the action is not just a chance occurrence, but is performance, and so can be held to a standard. Second, the audience recognizes that it is contrived and makes an attribution of motive, which is either benign or hostile to the judgment of quality. Effective management of staged performance calls for scrupulous control of both parts of this consumer judgment.

Motives for Staging a Performance

When an actor is seen to be "putting on a show," the discovery is not necessarily threatening to the audience. Consistent with the signaling view of advertising (Darby & Karni, 1973; Nelson, 1974), a signaling view of staging would assert that its purpose is to offer the consumer evidence that the performer of the service believes in the quality of the service and is investing in staging as a bond or pledge of quality. The significance of staging is richer than this, however. Different kinds of staging suggest different motives for staging. Deighton (1992) finds four kinds of staging. First there is the distinction between ceremonial and festive staging. Ceremonies tend to be planned and rehearsed, to require proper behavior from the audience, and to have a plotlike structure. Festivals tend to be more uninhibited and fun, and to be more enjoyable if they involve other people. This dimension is the *observation-to-participation* dimension. A second dimension distinguishes contests and spectacles on one hand from ceremonies and festivals on the other. The former are grounded in the here and now; the latter take the audience out of itself, transporting it to a hypothetical, idealized time. This is a *realism-to-fantasy* dimension. Although both extremes may use uncertainty, realism deals in risk and fantasy in suspense. Each quadrant of the space so formed can be labeled, defining four kinds of motive for staging the show.

Skill performance is the staged display of competence in a naturalistic setting for the benefit of a passive observer. This is the kind of performance aspired to by professional service providers such as lawyers and accountants.

Show performance delivers entertainment to a passive observer who must be persuaded to accept a nonrealistic context for the action. Stage and motion picture entertainment are examples.

Thrill performance refers to active participation by the consumer in naturalistic activity, in which the staging, although present, is not intrusive. White water rafting expeditions and safaris are extreme examples.

Festive performance involves active consumer participation in a built context created by deliberate staging and costuming. Examples include the performance of rituals such as Christmas and Halloween, and structured play such as cruise vacations and Mardi Gras.

Figure 6.1 describes the logic of the classification and gives more examples. It emphasizes that when we ascribe a motive to an actor for

INFLUENCES ON
THE CONSUMER'S ROLE

			Emphasize Observer Role	Emphasize Participant Role
			Passive, segregated audience, *Focus on actors,* *Constrained set of audience responses.*	*Involved, integrated audience,* *No single focus,* *Flexible audience roles.*
INFLU-ENCES ON THE EVENT'S PURPOSE	Emphasize Event's Realism	*Naturalistic setting, Tension and uncertainty, Values under test.*	**SKILL PERFORMANCE** Chess, golf, tennis, boxing, jury trial, management consulting.	**THRILL PERFORMANCE** Rafting, safari, fraternity rush, convention, class reunion.
	Emphasize Event's Fantasy	*Artificial setting, Ritualistic, predictable, Affirmation of values.*	**SHOW PERFORMANCE** Opera, ballet, pro wrestling, theater, cinema.	**FESTIVE PERFORMANCE** Mardi gras, pageant, Christmas, Halloween, theme park.

Figure 6.1. Kinds of Staged Performance

SOURCE: Reproduced from Deighton (1992, December). The Consumption of Performance. *Journal of Consumer Research, 19,* 367. © 1992 by The Journal of Consumer Research, Inc. Used with permission of The University of Chicago Press.

staging a performance, we also learn how to judge the performance. If I imply to you that my motive is to perform skillfully, you will hold me to standards of honesty that you would not have used if I had suggested that my motive was to perform entertainingly. For example, the music performers Milli Vanilli presented themselves as skillful singers. When it emerged that the voices in their recordings were not their own, their performance flopped. Perhaps a show frame might have saved them by encouraging the audience to enjoy the spectacle, not the skill.

What Do Consumers Want From Performances?

How Do Consumers Judge Performances as Failures?

Two ways that performances can fail are if they appear incompetent or if they are discovered to be deceptive. Consumers want first that the action should achieve its goal (competence) and second that the staging should not misrepresent in some way (deception). The precise meaning of each of these terms, however, depends on the motive or intention imputed to the act of staging.

Incompetence for a skill performance is simply a failure to perform to the expected level of skill or the discovery that the feat is not as difficult as expected. For a show or thrill performance, incompetence has to do with boring an audience or the failure to be impressive or spectacular (show) or exciting or stirring (thrill). A festival lacks competence when its audience is detached and does not participate.

Deception for a skill or thrill performance occurs when the audience finds that the outcome is bogus or in some way rigged. This is no problem for a show performance, as in the theater, where effects are understood to be contrived. Here deception involves plagiarism or the representation of work as original when it is not. Festive performance can be deceptive if it uses audience plants, shills, or other contrivances to engineer audience participation. For example a commercial service in New York hires out unemployed actors to party givers to play interesting characters at social gatherings. A service in Japan invites grandparents to hire surrogate grandchildren for weekend visits to impress upon the neighbors that the grandparents are not neglected.

What Makes a Performance Successful?

When we think of the satisfactions that performance can deliver, the scope is vast. It would be convenient managerially if a single criterion of success existed for all performance, so that a single quality scale might be constructed. A man who shines shoes gives value if he gets the shoes to shine. If he has personality and some dexterity with the cloth, the performance gives even more value. It can be more than just utilitarian; it can be engaging. But can we place the finest shoe shine on the same scale as a performance by the Chicago Bulls or Itzak Perlman? Is there a single attribute that consumers seek from performances of all kinds?

Audiences often subjectively describe great performances in terms that suggest that they have been uplifted, taken out of themselves, exhilarated, or otherwise transformed. They talk of minor performances in less transcendent terms, but still imply that their attention has been captured, diverted, or engaged. I want to argue that the quality that unites these experiences, the measure of success in every performance from the mundane to the transcendent, is *involvement* (Deighton, 1993). To succeed, a performance must involve the audience in the sense of capturing its attention and controlling it for a time. The audience must yield up its autonomy to the agenda of another, the performer. More important, the audience must like what it gets well enough to remain engaged until the performer is finished. The ambiguous delight of surrendering control is suggested in words that everyday language uses to describe satisfying performance: arresting, riveting, entrancing, or captivating.

A performance can be thought successful when the audience is persuaded to live for a while within the drama constructed by the architects of the production. We might say, for example, that a successful salesperson induced customers to act in his or her play. Good performance is more than the imposition of beliefs, as in the conventional view of persuasion. It is a presentation that draws the consumer, even if only for a moment, into an integrated web of beliefs, values, aspirations, scripted scenes, and roles. The performance entertains the audience, and in exchange the audience entertains the performer's view of the world.

Why is involvement in the experience of watching, say, the World Series more or less intense than the experience of attending a Little League game? Or more pragmatically, how would one influence an audience's involvement with a particular performance? What are the determinants of involvement intensity? Sarbin (1986) offers a way to think about this question. Performance imposes a *role* on its audience, for example, to dress soberly and behave with decorum in an opera, to be exuberant at a rock concert, or to join in the fun of a Mardi Gras. He claims that involvement becomes more intense as the gap between role and self narrows. When the self is detached from the role and one is merely going through the motions of the role, one is uninvolved. As role and self merge, so involvement increases. The body expends more effort to meet the role's demands, and more organic systems are in play. One moves "out of oneself" and into the role. One loses self-consciousness and inhibitedness. At an extreme of involvement, the role becomes the self, as in bewitchment or trance states. The audience gives itself over entirely to the performance.

Figure 6.2 develops these ideas in the context of service encounters. Five degrees of involvement with the performance of a service are identified for the consumer.

Detached Role Taking. The consumer interacts with the performer in a perfunctory way. Consider the experience of having one's hair cut by a person who makes no conversation and gets on with the job. The con-

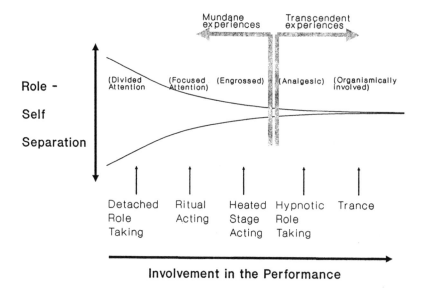

Figure 6.2. Degrees of Involvement in a Performance

sumer conforms to the dictates of the consumer's role by being compliant, but his or her thoughts are elsewhere. Such a performance may be very satisfying, judged as a contractual performance, because it depends simply on whether expectations are met or not. But the staged performance is unappreciated because, in a cognitive sense, the consumer did not attend to it. The performance succeeds if the consumer knows how to judge a good haircut as a purely utilitarian outcome and judges it as satisfactory. If the outcome is ambiguous, however, the consumer is left in doubt. There are none of the pleasures of a good staged performance to suffuse the memory of the experience and help to resolve the ambiguity.

Ritual Acting. At the next level of involvement, the consumer is drawn more tightly into the performance, accepting and executing a more involving role. The parties to the transaction do not merely exchange performances as they do in the previous stage: Their performances interact with one another. Consumers at fast-food restaurants learn the vocabulary and ritual of each particular ordering system. They learn to decode "Here or t'go?" This involvement may contribute very little to the evaluation of the performance beyond helping it to run more smoothly, and in that sense ritual acting is an enabling condition for good performance, but is in no way sufficient. In some situations it may contribute to a sense of belonging or familiarity that gives a merchant an advantage with regular customers. The consumer who says he feels at home in a particular hotel, or who judges Bloomingdale's as "my kind of store" expresses a sense of competence in the interactions demanded of that performance. The consumer who feels "out of place" feels that way because he or she does not know how to play with or finesse the part demanded by the rituals.

It is paradoxical that a mannered or heavily stylized performance of a ritual action may be judged to be more real than a sincere or authentic performance. A French chef who speaks good English might, for example, do better to emphasize a French accent when talking to English-speaking patrons.

Heated Stage Acting. The next degree of involvement occurs when the consumer takes on a role quite deliberately, for rhetorical effect and to accomplish some instrumental purpose. When a shopper wants to register a complaint, he or she will adopt a standard code for making a fuss. Italian opera audiences and U.S. professional wrestling fans employ quite different physical codes to express similar visceral responses. Bars, taverns, and nightclubs offer their patrons stages for a range of social performances. More than in the previous stages, consumers coproduce the performance. They play roles with an enthusiasm that begins to become its own reward. Satisfaction depends less on the utilitarian outcome of the service and more on the expressive rewards of the performance.

Hypnotic Role Taking. To a basketball fan at a tense moment in a game, a child meeting Mickey at Disneyland for the first time, or a tourist confronting a leopard on the African veld at dawn, the self is transported. The performance dominates consciousness to the exclusion of self-consciousness, pain, hunger, and the concerns of the body. These are transcendent experiences, in which the self is taken over entirely by the demands of the situation. Judgments of satisfaction depend entirely on memory of expressive gratification recollected later.

Trance States. Serving more as a marker on the scale of involvement than as a likely consequence of a normal service encounter, trance states are states in which the most intense and durable migration of self into role occurs. Examples of persons in such states are religious ecstatics, soldiers in battle, and some pop concert customers. These transported actors are similar to hypnotic role takers, but the duration of the experience is much longer.

Most of the responses consumers feel in response to the performances they encounter in everyday life are ordinary or mundane. We ride taxis, have our hair cut, or attend social gatherings so bland that there is nothing to take note of. In the language of Dilthey (1976), these are *mere* experiences. At some pitch of involvement between heated acting and hypnotic role taking, a transition occurs. We move to what Dilthey calls *an* experience (see also Abrahams, 1986; Turner, 1986). These are the experiences that stand out from the sameness of life and are remembered later for their significance as life transitions or told as anecdotes to convey the flavor of a phase of one's personal history. They carry important private meaning. They involve not just cognition, but emotional states like willing, desiring, and feeling. Service performances seldom achieve this intensity of response, but service advertising often seeks to attach a brand name to such experiences. Some McDonald's advertising, for example, has identified the restaurant with coming-of-age experiences. AT&T's "Reach out and touch someone" campaign involved the telephone service with intensely involving interpersonal experiences.

Managing Performance

What does it mean to manage a staged performance? Grove and Fisk (1992) have already cataloged some useful prescriptions that flow from adopting a dramaturgical model of service performance. A different set of prescriptions can be built from the terms developed in this chapter.

The managerial task can be described by attending to two features of the positioning of the performance. First, we must notice how its meaning is framed as one of the skill, thrill, show, or festive categories. Management must attempt to *amplify the event's meaning* by permeating the boundaries between realism and fantasy, observation and participation, so that the event takes on a more varied, rich, and complex significance. Second, we must try to intensify audience involvement. A performance begins with a default capacity to involve its audience, one that probably lies to the left of the center of the scale. Management's task is to try to *intensify involvement with the event*. The audience is drawn into a tighter sense of identification with the action.

Strategies to Amplify Meaning

1. Permeate the Boundaries Between Performance Types. Performances are episodic. Although a particular performance may be preponderantly a skill show, individual episodes may take the consumer beyond that frame and into another. I contend that these excursions outside the frame are powerful ways to enrich meaning. The effect need not be to change the essential character of the performance, but to supply the perceptual event that precipitates a more complex comprehension.

For example, a festival locates its consumer in the show—on the stage as it were. In Disneyworld, Colonial Williamsburg, or a Harvard Business School classroom during a case session, consumers are persuaded to adopt active roles and absorb a hypothetical environment. Fantasy and participation are the strong features of the format. Opportunities may exist, therefore, for excursions into realism and passive observation.

If a theme park employs a sky-mounted video camera to show patrons a view of the entire park, it temporarily takes them out of the festive (participant) frame and allows them to comprehend what they are doing as a spectacle (observer frame). A business school case discussion becomes a more varied and satisfying performance if the participants are moved back and forth between realism and fantasy, between skill displays and festive performance.

2. Develop the Audience's Sense of Uncertainty. Boissac (1987) proposes that a sense of outcome uncertainty is one dimension of the meaning of a performance. One buys a musical recording (product) expecting it to be exemplary, but one experiences a live show (performance) hoping it will not be flawed. In realistic performance, this uncertainty is termed risk or danger or jeopardy, and in fantasy it has the character of suspense or tension.

Advertising and press publicity are often used to develop uncertainty. Boissac describes how circus advertising arouses apprehension at the challenge faced by lion tamers and trapeze artists, and press coverage intensifies the sense of riskiness. They build a narrative that lacks closure, so that only attending the show can resolve the uncertainty. Advertising, he claims, is therefore a functional part of a satisfying dramatistic performance in a way that is not so for products. He claims, paradoxically, that although the result of product purchase is usually advertised to be perfect, no such promise should be made for risky performance. This kind of performance is promoted not by sampling, but by *teasing:* Will the narrative reach a successful closure this time?

3. Exchange Responses. When participants are persuaded to express to other audience members either affective or judgmental or even simple elaborative responses to a performance, they start a process that can amplify what the event comes to mean to them. If an audience member sees a performance, but has no occasion to exchange responses, first, his or her own response will be attenuated, and second, the others will not have been provoked into accepting or rejecting that response.

Often teachers and seminar leaders encourage audiences to share emotional reactions. Waiters interrupt diners to ask, "Is everything OK?" Television entertainment uses canned audience laughter, gasps, and cheers. Each of these devices is an occasion for the consumer to form and air opinions about the service experience. Provided the performance is going well, the effect is reinforcing.

Strategies to Intensify Involvement

1. Increase Performer-Audience Interaction. Performance, because it relates to a transaction, has at least some minimal level of interaction. The script of a service performance always implies a role for the audience. The role may be as solitary and passive as that of a passenger in a taxicab, or as richly interactive as the role of a skier who makes use of the many services of a ski lodge. As the consumer becomes more interactive, it is difficult not to become more involved.

There is, for example, a qualitative difference between the experience of attending a live sporting event and viewing it on television. One source of that difference is the opportunity for direct interaction among the actors in the live event, namely fans with each other (for example the coordinated audience activity known as the wave) and fans with athletes (applause). Fans often report that they can have a good time in the stands even if the game is not particularly rewarding.

2. Design for More Coproduction. A consumer's role in the interactions may be reactive, as in mere responses to the producer's initiatives, or it may be creative, initiating elements of the service and shaping its form. In general, the more the role is designed to make the consumer accept responsibility for coproduction of the performance, the more involved he or she will be.

A patient undergoing surgery encounters a service with apparently little opportunity for co-creation of the outcome. Yet Shouldice Hospital (Heskett, 1983), a Canadian facility specializing in the treatment of hernias, has designed a performance in which the patient has an active role. Patients perform limited self-diagnosis, they do their own presurgery preparation, they walk into and out of the operating room, and after surgery they meet with the next day's incoming patients to brief them on the procedure and prepare the patients for their role.

Coproduction lets the consumer feel that he or she is affecting the outcome of the service. The consumer feels empowered, or at least, avoids the sense of incompetence that comes from enforced passivity. If the performance is successful, the consumer can take some pride of authorship.

3. Create a More Expressive Role for the Consumer. I have conceived of involvement as what happens when the self migrates into a role. The more the role expresses aspects of an aspirational self, the more tempting it will seem to try it on, and the more likely this migration is to occur.

Altercasting is the term sociologists use (Weinstein & Deutschberger, 1964) for the process by which one actor sets the scope of another's role. A shrewd auto salesperson, a restaurant maitre d', or an investment advisor infers the aspirations of a client or customer and altercasts the customer into that role. Advertising too can transform the service experience into one that expresses aspirations of the customer. For Federal Express users and recipients, advertising has made the red, white, and blue envelope into a prop in the role of time-pressed business executive.

Conclusion

This chapter has been concerned with the resources and strategies that a marketer can use to craft a performance that satisfies consumers, beginning with distinguishing between performances that are perceived to be merely contractual and those that are overtly staged.

For contractual performance, the expectancy confirmation/disconfirmation paradigm guides service managers well. When the idea of satisfaction is applied to staged performance, however, this chapter has pointed to some ways in which conventional views of quality and customer satisfaction are incomplete. Satisfaction is not simply a matter of ensuring that the event conforms to expectations (see Oliver 1989).

For instance, when the term *satisfaction* is applied to performances, there is usually some ambiguity. It is unclear who should get the credit, the actor who performs or the object with which he or she performs or even the service institution within which the performance occurs. When the customer becomes an actor in the performance, as for example in the experience of eating in a restaurant, the question of who gets the credit for a good experience becomes even more complicated. In the restaurant example, an astute marketer might shift credit for a successful evening from congenial guests to the chef, the ambiance, or some other aspect of the restaurant.

Further, satisfaction with performance is an interactive concept. The actions of the audience feed on those of the actor and vice versa. In festive performances, the audience becomes part of the production, and success depends on how enthusiastically the audience plays its role. The audience at a rock concert or presidential nominating convention is part of the show and carries joint credit or blame for the outcome. Skillful marketing can draw the audience into the show and save a poor performance in a way that is not possible in product consumption. On the other hand, failure to recruit the audience can damage an otherwise good performance. Satisfaction on one occasion is therefore no guarantee of satisfaction on a subsequent occasion.

Viewing services as staged performances is not metaphorical. It is of the essence of service management that the customer and all the actors who are involved in delivering the service share and sustain "a single definition of the situation in the face of a multitude of potential disruptions," to borrow Goffman's (1959) definition of a successful social encounter. Viewing service provision as theater would be metaphorical, and it has not been my intention here to advocate that we do so. Theater is only one kind of staging, one that explicitly lacks the real consequences that flow from most service transactions. Theater is a game played in the currency of illusion. We insult the consumer if we imagine that staging the illusion of a satisfying transaction can substitute for the staging of the real thing.

References

Abrahams, R. D. (1986). Ordinary and extraordinary experiences. In V. W. Turner (Ed.), *The anthropology of experience* (pp. 45-72). Champaign: University of Illinois Press.

Boissac, P. (1987). The marketing of performance. In Jean Umiker-Sebeok (Ed.), *Marketing and semiotics* (pp. 391-406). Amsterdam: Mouton de Gruyter.

Darby, M. R., & Karni, E. (1973). Free competition and the optimal amount of fraud. *Journal of Law and Economics, 16*, 67-88.

Deighton, J. (1992). The consumption of performance. *Journal of Consumer Research, 19*, 362-372.

Deighton, J. (1993). *Fraud, seduction and entertainment.* Working paper, University of Chicago Graduate School of Business.

Dilthey, W. (1976). *Selected Writings* (H. P. Rickman, Ed.). Cambridge, UK: Cambridge University Press.

Goffman, E. (1959). *The presentation of self in everyday life.* New York, NY: Doubleday.

Grove, S. J., & Fisk, R. P. (1983). The dramaturgy of services exchange: An analytical framework for services marketing. In L. L. Berry, G. L. Shostack, & G. D. Upah (Eds.), *Emerging perspectives on services marketing* (pp. 45-49). Chicago: American Marketing Association.

Grove, S. J., & Fisk, R. P. (1992). The service experience as theater. In J. F. Sherry Jr., & B. Sternthal (Eds.), *Advances in consumer research* (Vol. 19, pp. 455-461). Provo, UT: Association for Consumer Research.

Heskett, J. L. (1983). Shouldice Hospital Limited (Harvard Business School Case No. 9-683-068). Boston: Harvard Business School.

Lovelock, C. H. (1991). *Services marketing.* Englewood Cliffs, NJ: Prentice-Hall.

Nelson, P. (1974). Advertising and information. *Journal of Political Economy, 81*, 729-754.

Oliver, R. L. (1980). A cognitive model of the antecedents and consequences of satisfaction decisions. *Journal of Marketing Research, 17*, 460-469.

Oliver, R. L. (1989). Processing of the satisfaction response in consumption: A suggested framework and research propositions. *Journal of Consumer Satisfaction, Dissatisfaction and Complaining Behavior, 2*, 1-16.

Sarbin, T. (1986). Emotion and act: roles and rhetoric. In R. Harre (Ed.), *The social construction of emotion* (pp. 83-97). Oxford: Basil Blackwell.

Solomon, M. R. (1983). The role of products as social stimuli: A symbolic interactionism perspective. *Journal of Consumer Research, 10*, 319-329.

Turner, V. W. (1986). Dewey, Dilthey and drama: An essay in the anthropology of experience. In V. W. Turner (Ed.), *The anthropology of experience* (pp. 33-44). Champaign: University of Illinois Press.

Weinstein, E. A., & Deutschberger, P. (1964). Tasks, bargains and identities in social interaction. *Social Forces, 42*, 451-456.

CHAPTER SEVEN

Beyond Smiling

Social Support and Service Quality

MARA B. ADELMAN

Northwestern University

AARON AHUVIA

*School of Business Administration,
University of Michigan*

CATHY GOODWIN

University of Manitoba

The argument of this chapter is that social support is an important aspect of service quality. The chapter begins with a discussion of three trends that will increase future demand for social support: changing social values, the growing number of single consumers, and the graying of America. A definition of social support is then proposed based on previous research and this definition is used to understand social support in service encounters. Next addressed is the importance of intercustomer interactions in shaping consumer experience, followed by a look at the implications of the analysis for service quality and the pros and cons of trying to increase social support as a services marketing strategy.

When asked what "quality in services" means to them, consumers' Number 1 answer was employee contact skills such as courtesy,

AUTHORS' NOTE: The authors contributed equally to this work and are listed alphabetically. They would like to thank Rich Oliver; Syd Bernard; David Aron; Sheri Frankel; and Joseph Nowak, Assistant Vice President of Merrill Lynch, for their help and support with this chapter.

attitude, and helpfulness (Gallup Organization, 1988). The existence of this close relationship between service quality and positive interpersonal contact is supported in Parasuraman, Zeithaml, and Berry (1988), who found that empathy was one of the five key service attributes that customers associated with quality. Findings by these and other researchers[1] reinforce the commonsense position that the quality of interpersonal contact is vital in service encounters. In the pioneering stages of services marketing research, identifying the key variables consumers use to judge service quality was a major advance. As services marketing research moves forward, it becomes necessary to take a more in-depth look at these variables.

This chapter provides an extended discussion of what it means for consumers to have positive interpersonal contact with a service provider. We center this discussion on the construct of social support, which has been heavily researched in social psychology, sociology, public health and epidemiology, and communications. Broadly speaking, customers receive social support when service providers' verbal or nonverbal communication does at least one of three things: (a) reduces clients' uncertainty, thus increasing their sense of control; (b) improves their self-esteem; or (c) creates a sense of social connection to others (this definition will be further developed below).

The integration of social support literature into services marketing literature has several potential benefits. First, it allows the extensive literature on social support to be brought to bear on services marketing problems. Second, it provides a customer-centered perspective on service quality by looking at the customer needs being met through social activity with service providers. Third, this customer-centered perspective allows researchers to address basic managerial concerns such as customer satisfaction, as well as more diverse client benefits such as increased self-esteem or a sense of community integration. Finally, social support is most applicable to those service encounters that have been shown to lead to high levels of satisfaction (Bitner, Booms, & Tetreault, 1990). Conceptualizing good service in terms of smiles and polite manners is probably sufficient to describe the majority of acceptable service encounters. However, Bitner et al. (1990) found that high levels of customer satisfaction were most common when service providers went beyond their basic role definition. Because social support is a construct developed to explain the social interactions that have a significant (if sometimes subtle) impact on the individual, it is well suited to explain these kinds of more substantive social encounters.

We begin with a discussion of macro environmental trends that we believe will increase the demand for social support in the coming years. We then look at the nature of social support itself, focusing on the functions of social support in service encounters and how social support can be understood from a variety of analytic perspectives. Next we discuss the role of intercustomer interactions in creating social support, emphasizing that many services involve more than a one-on-one interaction between the client and the service provider. Finally we look at the implications of our analysis for service quality and service marketing.

The Macro Environment and Demand for Social Support

We believe that the need for research in this area is particularly pressing given the combination of three social trends that promise to increase the demand for social support from services and an important economic trend that could increase the number of businesses capable of supplying social support to their clients. The macro environmental trends include: (a) an increased preference among people born after World War II for warm, personal interactions over formal, impersonal ones; (b) an increase in the number of singles; and (c) an increase in the number of elderly consumers. These social trends are enhanced by an important economic trend: the rapid growth in the number of small businesses that are particularly well suited to provide social support to their clients.

A recent shift in cultural values away from materialism has been widely noted (Crimmins, Easterlin, & Saito, 1991; Dimma, 1991; Huey, 1993; Schwartz, 1991; Van Gorder, 1990). Inglehart (1990) reviews over 20 years of research and provides a compelling explanation for this and related phenomena. He argues that the values of North Americans and Europeans born after World War II were shaped by coming of age in a period of political stability and economic prosperity. This formative experience has contributed to a secure and lasting assumption that their economic needs will be met, and hence, allows them to focus more energy on higher order needs such as attaining meaningful relationships and belonging to a community. Therefore, when compared with people who experienced the Depression or World War II, younger North Americans and Europeans are more concerned with warm, informal interpersonal relationships and community ties and less concerned with financial success[2] than are their elders. This means that younger consumers will demand interactions with service personnel that meet their higher order emotional and psychological needs as well as satisfy their economic concerns.

Inglehart (1990) also provides evidence to suggest that these differences in values between younger and older cohorts reflect lasting personal orientations that remain relatively unchanged for life. As the buying power of post-World War II generations grows with time, the impact of their preferences will become more strongly felt by the economy. Future services will need to adapt to customers' increased sensitivity to the nature of their interpersonal interaction with service providers.

The personalized nature of service encounters can be an essential part of our sense of community and social integration. Although our more profound interactions often lie with close relationships, marketplace ties are among the ties that bind individuals to community life (Adelman, M. R. Parks, & Albrecht, 1987; Fischer, 1982; Stone, 1954; Wellman, 1979). Given younger generations' often conflicting desires for personal freedom and strong community (Inglehart, 1990), the voluntaristic nature of service interactions can offer people a sense of community that does not threaten individual autonomy. Hence, services may play an increasingly important role in helping people form a sense of community that leaves their individual autonomy intact.

The need for service encounters to contribute to a sense of community may be felt with great intensity among the rapidly growing singles population.[3] In the process of preparing a series of articles on singles and singles' services (Adelman & Ahuvia, 1991b; Ahuvia & Adelman 1992, in press; Ahuvia, Adelman, & Schroeder, 1991), the authors found that singles frequently felt alienated from the larger adult community. Not only does marriage provide a sense of rootedness and belonging, but many ways of tying into the larger community such as religious affiliation are too family centered for some adult singles. Although further research is needed to determine the extent of these feelings, service interactions may be especially key in fostering a sense of community for singles. Further, community integration is just one aspect of social support that singles may be disproportionately likely to seek from service providers. Although close friends and dating partners fulfill most of the social functions that would otherwise be performed by a spouse, service providers can be a marginal but significant source of casual conversation, social comparison, or confidential self-disclosure.

Although the post-World War II generations' values will remain relatively constant as they age, for both today's and tomorrow's elderly, aging brings changes that increase the likelihood of seeking social support through services. Currently, about 12% of the U.S. population is 65 or older. Between 2010 and 2030 when the baby boom generation moves into retirement, the percentage of the population over 65 is expected to almost double (Leech, 1992). The graying of America is likely to create a demand for many more personal care services such as independent or group living facilities and home delivery of everything from groceries to medical attention. These expanded markets will not only increase the scope of the service industry, but will provide more personalized contexts for service encounters that in turn make the provision of social support easier. Dychtwald (1990) provides a glimpse into the nature of personalized services targeting mature consumers:

> For [older] consumers, the interpersonal experience matters a great deal. In fact, in many retirement-area locations, banks offer refreshments and a comfortable air-conditioned lounge. They encourage people to visit and to take as much time as they'd like at the bank. This concept would never occur to a retail-banking manager who had cut his or her teeth on busy yuppies.(p. 288)

If "the interpersonal experience matters a great deal" to today's elderly, it should be even more important in the future when the baby boom and baby bust generations bring their heightened sensitivity to interpersonal interactions into retirement.

These three trends indicate that the demand for social support from service providers could grow sharply in the years ahead. Yet not all businesses are equally well situated to meet this demand. At a minimum, a business must allow for extended interpersonal contact between the service provider and the client, that is, be an "interpersonal service" (Bitner, 1992). Beyond this basic requirement, it is also advantageous to have norms of interaction that allow for personal communication and a reasonable assumption of anonymity or confidentiality. For example, lawyers, tax accountants, financial advisors, hairdressers, real estate agents, cab drivers, teachers, bartenders, doctors, funeral home directors, and even matchmakers all perform services with norms that encourage self-disclosure. Finally, some service providers, such as divorce lawyers, funeral home directors, or matchmakers, are in especially good positions to provide social support because the nature of their businesses almost ensures that clients coming to them will be under stress and therefore in special need of support.

Generally speaking, small owner-operated and entrepreneurial businesses are in a better position to meet these criteria for providing social support than are larger more impersonal organizations. It is, therefore, important to note that entrepreneurial businesses have been providing much of our economic growth. If this historic growth in small businesses continues, then the area of social support and services provision should take on increasing importance as demand and supply simultaneously increase in the coming decades.

What Is Social Support?

Historically, interest in social support began with epidemiological studies on how social ties impact physical and mental well-being (Gottlieb, 1981). For example, in a 9-year follow-up study of widows, Berkman and Syme (1979) found evidence for the role of supportive relationships in increasing longevity. Within the last decade, multidisciplinary research has expanded, and several books have been devoted to this topic (Albrecht, Adelman, & Associates, 1987; Duck & Silver, 1990; Gottlieb, 1981; Pilisuk & S. H. Parks, 1986). Although the bulk of these studies have focused on distressed populations (e.g., persons experiencing unemployment, life-threatening illness, bereavement, drug abuse, eating disorders, rape, divorce), studies of social support for everyday functioning has also been examined.

The Three Schools of Social Support

Recently, Hobfoll and Stokes (1988) characterized social support as "a generic term for that 'right stuff' that is gained by being socially connected" (p. 498). Efforts to move beyond vague or tautological definitions to develop a more rigorous construct have resulted in a plethora of functionally based definitions that reflects the multidimensional aspects of social support. Prior reviews of this literature (Albrecht & Adelman, 1984; Hobfoll & Stokes, 1988) suggest that various definitions for social support can be classified according to three themes: uncertainty reduction and control, self-acceptance, and social integration (see Table 7.1).

First, much of the literature on social support is grounded in models of coping with stress. Because a central tenet in the stress and coping literature is the need to seek control over oneself and the stressful situation (Albrecht & Adelman, 1987a; Fisher, 1984; Lazarus & Launier, 1978), concepts related to cognitive uncertainty and need for control have been central to these definitions of social support. Second, social support

TABLE 7.1   Selected Overview of Social Support

	Uncertainty Reduction and Control	*Self-Acceptance*	*Social Integration*
Definitions	"Communication . . . that reduces uncertainty . . . and functions to enhance a perception of personal control." (Albrecht & Adelman, 1987a, p. 19)	"Provide(s) individuals with opportunities for feedback about themselves and for validations of their expectations about others." (Caplan, 1976, p. 19)	"Information leading the subject to believe that he is cared for and loved . . . esteemed and valued . . . that he belongs to a network of communication and mutual obligation." (Cobb, 1976, p. 300)
Functions	Facilitates personal goals Aids in personal coping	Enhances self-esteem	Confirms sense of belonging
Example: Real Estate Agent	Couple experiences uncertainty and anxiety about taking care of young children during a move. Real estate agent helps find day care.	Real estate agent assures embarrassed couple that petty bickering is often the outcome of a stressful move.	Real estate agent introduces newcomer to friends.

SOURCE: Adapted from Thoits (1985) and Albrecht and Adelman (1987a).

can be conceptualized as a response to the need for self-acceptance, validation, and self-esteem. These self-acceptance definitions stress the value of significant loving relationships for promoting self-esteem (Wills, 1987) and facilitating social comparison. Third, whereas self-acceptance conceptions approach social ties from a dyadic perspective, social integration definitions emphasize social networks and relationships set in the context of the larger community. These definitions point to the importance of patterns of social interaction within communities and the ways larger social groups affect support benefits. Clearly, these three types of definitions frequently overlap. However, the themes of uncertainty reduction, self-acceptance, and social integration do provide conceptual boundaries for understanding the process and functions of social support.

Social Support Is in the Mind of the Receiver

When one person undertakes an action intended to help another alleviate stress, enhance self-esteem, or identify with a community, the recipient always interprets the action from his or her own perspective. Therefore it is necessary to distinguish between objective and subjective support. Objective support occurs when tangible goods such as money or intangible goods such as information are exchanged. However, many theorists argue that the subjective experience of the exchange, not the objective value of the goods received, determines whether an action is perceived as social support. For example, the service provider who offers to extend credit may be viewed as supportive or nonsupportive depending on the recipient's causal attributions about the lender. These attributions can range from, "This person is acting as a friend," to "S/he just wants more of my business." This example shows that "The effect of social support is mediated by the perception of meaning that the recipients of support assign to what they receive" (Hobfoll & Stokes, 1988, p. 503). This subjective, meaning-based perspective suggests that social support is "a process inextricably woven into communicative and symbolic behavior" (Albrecht & Adelman, 1987c, p. 14) and is not synonymous with objective exchanges of goods, information, or services. Indeed, Wethington and Kessler (1986) suggest that perceptions of social support may be as helpful as actual support in relieving stress.

Social Support in the Service Encounter

Research on social relationships has emphasized intimate ties such as family and close friendships, thus reflecting an "ideology of intimacy" (M. R. Parks, 1982; Sennett, 1977) that is prevalent in U.S. culture. Taking superficial relationships seriously by looking at the important role of commercial contacts, acquaintances, and other passing encounters has received far less attention in the study of social relationships (Lofland, 1989) and supportive relationships (Adelman et al., 1987).

Yet, several writers have identified sources of support that emerge in impersonal urban areas to augment the range of social support found in closer social ties (Kelly, 1964; Lofland, 1989; Milgram, 1977). This growing literature on public places that fosters interaction among friends and strangers also addresses their unique role in escaping from everyday identities and enhancing a sense of community life (Brissett & Oldenburg, 1982; Lofland, 1973; Oldenburg, 1989). Although these authors do not focus on the commercial nature of most of these relationships and places, their work is highly relevant to readers concerned with service quality and services marketing.

Adelman et al. (1987) draw upon the work of Granovetter (1973, 1982) to distinguish between strong ties and weak ties in understanding the unique role of service providers. Using the Adelman et al. expanded definition of weak tie support, we examine the functions of weak tie support in service encounters, particularly the role of service providers in quasi-therapeutic interactions.

Strong Versus Weak Ties

Granovetter (1982) differentiates weak and strong ties on the basis of network density. Density refers to the degree that various members of a particular network (e.g., work, social) are interconnected with each other. For example, an individual's close friends are likely to be in touch with each other, forming a densely knit cluster of strong ties. However, new acquaintances or service providers who are not integrated with the individual's network of close friends constitute weak ties.

In his work on "the strength of weak ties," Granovetter (1973, 1982) argued that weak ties (e.g., persons not connected to the primary network) can extend resources of the individual's primary network (i.e., close friends and family). Weak ties can also facilitate the diffusion of new information, decrease conformist pressure inherent in more insulated networks, and facilitate community and societal cohesion. It is important to point out that Granovetter defines weak ties by their loosely coupled position vis-à-vis the primary network, not by the level of intimacy. Thus, even a very close relationship with one's lawyer may constitute a "weak tie" if that service provider is not connected to the primary, social network.

Adelman et al. (1987) expand the notion of weak ties and redefine it as "an umbrella concept that covers a wide range of potential supporters who lie beyond the primary network of family and friends" (p. 126). This expanded definition of weak ties is developed in Table 7.2 and will be used throughout this chapter. Overall, weak tie features serve to minimize obligation and limit relational development while simultaneously expanding access to resources that could not be obtained from more intimate relationships.

TABLE 7.2   Weak Versus Strong Ties

	Weak Ties: Service Providers	Strong Ties: Family and Friends
Dyadic	Limited mutual interdependence Concrete forms of social exchange for maintaining equity More restricted types of information exchange	High levels of mutual interdependence Ongoing relational exchange norms Less restricted types of information exchange
Network	Distance from the primary social network gives access to new information and insures anonymity	Central to social network
Social Context	Confined times and settings shape the range of social interaction	Interaction in a wider variety of settings and times

The Functions of Weak Tie Support[4]

Weak ties, such as service providers, both extend the forms of social support found in closer relationships and play a unique role in providing forms of support not available through strong ties. One of the key functions of weak ties is their ability to extend access to information that would otherwise be unavailable. This information is sometimes of an instrumental nature (e.g., what job openings are available), but it can also be friendly chitchat that allows for psychologically valuable social comparison with dissimilar others. Our strong tie networks are so often filled with people like ourselves that it is only through weak ties that we gain a larger perspective on the world. The homogeneity of many strong tie networks not only limits social comparison and access to other types of information, but it can often discourage "trying on" new social roles. Weak tie relationships offer the opportunity to develop new "possible selves" (Markus & Nurius, 1986).

Weak ties also play an important role in fostering a sense of community. As the service economy grows, consumers interact with a larger number of service providers and do so on a more frequent basis. When these interactions go beyond a pleasant smile to become a genuine though circumscribed relationship, the consumer may feel more wedded to the community as a whole.

Weak ties can also provide support during periods when stronger ties are disrupted (e.g., due to a death, divorce, unemployment, relocation).

For example, Cowen (1982) found that divorce lawyers often played the role of confidant for troubled spouses. Weak ties can also provide channels of sociability for those who do not desire stronger social relationships or who lack the skills for initiating and sustaining intimate ties. Persons suffering from extreme shyness, mental illness or chronic homelessness or even those with preferences for a highly private life-style may rely on weak ties for social contact. Similarly, people whose professions entail constant mobility (e.g., sales, consulting) may seek sociability from interactions with strangers.

Finally, because weak ties are removed from the primary social network, they can provide a measure of anonymity and confidentiality, thus facilitating the confessorial and advice-giving role or simply allowing clients to vent their feelings (Albrecht & Adelman, 1987a). A bartender quoted by Adelman et al. (1987) illustrates the way role expectations and social boundaries facilitate low-risk discussion of high-risk topics:

> During my training I learned several important lessons. When a customer offers to buy you a drink, it's more than a token tip—he's buying your time and the opportunity to talk. I was told to always pour the drink in front of him, set it there, and try to get back and exchange a few words occasionally. Also, never assume the type of relationship a customer has with another person. He may have spent nights talking about his wonderful wife and five kids, but don't assume the woman he suddenly brings in is her. Finally, what is said one night is often best forgotten by the next.

Social Support and the Technical/Functional Quality Distinction

In the services marketing literature, Grönroos (1982) distinguishes "technical" quality of services, such as a good meal or acceptable style of hairdressing, from what he identifies as "functional quality," the way technical quality is transferred to the consumer. Previous research suggests that friendliness and courtesy (Parasuraman, Zeithaml, & Berry, 1985) and service personalization (Surprenant & Solomon, 1987) contribute to functional quality and consumer satisfaction; therefore, because these variables are also related to social support, it is tempting to view social support as simply one aspect of functional quality. However, the previous discussion of the functions of weak ties indicates that social support might better be conceptualized as a separate supporting service (Grönroos, 1987), which is a set of benefits in its own right, rather than a style of transferring the core service benefits (see Table 7.3).

TABLE 7.3   Social Support and the Technical/Functional Quality Distinction (hairdresser example)

	Core Service	Supporting Service: Social Support Provision
Technical quality: What the customer receives as the outcome	Cuts hair well	Extends access to information Facilitates social comparison with dissimilar others Allows for low-risk discussion of high-risk topics Fosters a sense of community
Functional quality: The way the task function is transferred to the consumer	Delivers haircut in a friendly and pleasant manner	Support is perceived to be given in a nonjudgmental and confidential manner

Service Professionals as Quasi-Therapeutic Providers

The use of service providers for quasi-therapeutic interactions is particularly central to the construct of social support and hence is deserving of special attention. Although most service providers are not in the business of dispensing therapy or referrals, they can offer stigma-free, low-cost comfort and aid (Cowen, 1982; Wills, 1987). Although this quasi-therapeutic role has been documented by psychological researchers, we suggest it is also important to service marketers.

Ahuvia, Adelman, and Goodwin (1992) identify three attributes of the service encounter that allow for this form of social support. First, there must be extended interpersonal contact. Cowen et al. (1979, p. 636) suggest that hairdressers attract confidences because customers interact with them on a regular basis and the service itself allows "sizable conversational time units." Second, interaction norms must support personal communications; for example, norms of supermarket interactions differ substantially from those of farmers' markets (Heisley, McGrath, & Sherry, 1991; R. Sommer, Herrick, & T. R. Sommer, 1981) and flea markets (Sherry, 1990). Third, the customer must feel anonymous (as when a passenger tells his life story to a flight attendant) or believe the conversation will remain confidential.

In contemporary Western society, open discussion of one's problems often elicits comparisons with psychotherapeutic processes. For example, customers of a matchmaking service drew analogies between psychotherapy and interviews with the matchmaker (e.g., "I related to her as though she could be my therapist") (Adelman & Ahuvia, 1991a). Mental health professionals are often horrified at the amount of advice that is dispensed by untrained service providers; however, in the case of lawyers, Doane and Cowen (1981) note that they are involved whether they like it or not.

Social support functions offered by service providers differ from professional therapists in a number of ways. First, simply presenting oneself for therapy may signal the presence of a significant mental health problem. Once a person is labeled with a disorder (e.g., alcoholic or depressive), social interactions with others become affected by the pejorative impact of the label, leading persons to feel discredited or stigmatized (Goffman, 1963). Other costs of help seeking include embarrassment and damage to self-esteem, particularly if the problem derives from inadequacy on a dimension that is central to one's identity (Shapiro, 1984; Wills, 1987). Talking to a service provider allows a customer to avoid self-labeling as a help seeker and obtain "stigma-free assistance" (Adelman et al., 1987). Thus, a widow may prefer to discuss her grief with the funeral director rather than seek help from a psychotherapist in order to avoid the potential stigma of "having a problem."

Use of these "stigma-free" substitutes for psychotherapy is fairly common. Cowen et al. (1979; Cowen, McKim, & Weissberg, 1981) summarize data from a variety of sources suggesting that: (a) although 70% of middle-class Americans tend to take psychological problems to physicians and clergy, only 15% of low-income people do so; and (b) hairdressers, lawyers, and bartenders believed that active involvement with clients' "moderate to serious psychological problems" was a part of their job that they performed effectively.

Second, support from service providers differs from psychotherapy in that sharing a tale of woe with the bartender calls for a different type of discourse. Albrecht and Adelman (1987a) identify ventilation as a central function of social support. Venting is "a way to relieve internalized pressures but also to create through talk imagery that crystallizes somewhat unknown cognitions into known and shared entities" (p. 33). This process also takes place in both psychotherapy and service encounters. However, in psychotherapy, it is only one part of a complex therapeutic intervention, whereas in service encounters it often constitutes the entirety of the interaction.

Third, some researchers believe that nonprofessionals can help as effectively as those in designated helping professions (Wills, 1987). In some cases, nonprofessionals may be uniquely qualified to offer specific types of support. For example, an informal network, based in a bar, was more successful in helping homeless men than the official rescue agencies (Oldenburg, 1989). Although it is difficult to measure success in any form of therapeutic interaction, Wills (1987) suggested that the client's perception of the therapist is a critical factor. Therefore, it is not surprising that the well-liked service provider may be seen as extremely effective. Further, the fact that a provider is not compensated for listening can create a perception of sincerity and hence influence the meaning that the support receiver places on the interaction. Therefore, a lawyer may be more credible than a therapist as a source of reassurance or perspective shifting (e.g., "My other divorce clients do this too").

Intercustomer Social Support

Understanding the social support function of services directs attention to clients' interaction with fellow customers. People who are seen regularly and strangers who offer anonymity for confidences ("familiar strangers" as described by Milgram, 1977) are also important sources of social support in many kinds of service encounters.

Both popular and academic researchers have observed that certain environments facilitate customer interaction. Lofland (1973) suggests that three factors influence the willingness of city dwellers to initiate or reply to a conversation with strangers: the desirability of the person or encounter; legitimacy of circumstances for interaction; and appropriateness of setting. These three conditions seem to occur when the shared element of the encounter represents an aspect of self that is positively valued. Thus, secondhand clothing stores (Wiseman, 1979), certain laundromats (Graham, 1990; Kenen, 1982), and waiting lines for movies (Reisman, 1985) will facilitate interactions; on the other hand, patrons of pornographic movies (Donnelly, 1981) prefer to remain anonymous despite apparent communality of interests. Bars and coffee shops that facilitate informal social gathering have been labeled "third places" (Oldenburg, 1989) because they are neither home nor work settings. These third places allow people to maintain a situation-specific, place-specific social identity that offers an outlet from everyday concerns.

In addition to Lofland's conditions, intercustomer support may be facilitated by unstructured blocks of time, anonymity, service provider mediation, and physical surroundings. Unstructured blocks of time that are not perceived as distasteful stimulate conversation. People seem to tolerate waits for pleasure-related activities better than for necessity-related activities (Hui & Bateson, 1991). In some cities, a long line for a movie becomes part of the entertainment (Reisman, 1985). Similarly, customers seem to resent waiting in supermarket lines, but enjoy the relaxed setting of farmers' markets as they line up for food (R. Sommer et al., 1981).

Anonymity or a reasonable belief in confidentiality is essential for the level of self-disclosure necessary for venting among strangers. Lofland (1989) used the term "unpersonal/bounded relationships" to refer to relationships that are "simultaneously characterized by both social distance and closeness" (p. 469). One example of these relations is the "stranger on the plane" phenomenon (Adelman et al., 1987, p. 141), where any closed, captive setting draws out disclosures among strangers. Besides providing anonymity, these settings stimulate conversation through low levels of reciprocity, minimal expected future interaction, and often a fair measure of boredom.

The service provider's role as an intermediary between customers can also be critical. The bartender's role can vary from serving drinks impersonally, to receptive listening, to serving as matchmaker for favorite customers. In laundromats, conversations between a customer and an employee can lead to intercustomer conversations (Kenen, 1982). Conversely, the conspicuous absence of a service provider may force customers to seek help from one another (Wiseman, 1979).

Finally, physical surroundings or "servicescapes" (Bitner, 1992) may influence customer interactions. Wiseman (1979) suggests that in a used clothing store, the arrangement of merchandise, shortage of mirrors, and limited dressing rooms lead to "fairly close social mingling of strangers" (p. 39). Similarly, in farmers' markets, wide aisles facilitate mingling and small parcels allow closer physical proximity than shopping carts (R. Sommer et al., 1981).

Some situations that combine several factors seem particularly powerful in promoting intercustomer associations. In a detailed participant-observer study, Gross (1986) describes the way patients at the Mayo Clinic develop a unique supportive association. First, though illness ordinarily represents an aspect of self that would be devalued, it is an appropriate—even desirable—topic and source of bonding at the Mayo Clinic. Second, Mayo patients have taken time out from their usual routines and have limited recreational options in Rochester, Minnesota. Therefore, the author finds, patients see waiting time as an opportunity for extended interaction rather than an annoyance. Third, the temporary nature of relationships promotes anonymity. Finally, the close proximity of patients in the waiting room and the opportunity to overhear conversations with the receptionist encourage conversation.

The bars and coffeehouses described by Oldenburg (1989) and Nathe (1976) initially seem very different from the clinical setting of the Mayo Clinic, but similar forces operate to promote interaction. These third places allow people to maintain situation-specific, place-specific social identities that offer outlets from everyday concerns. There is a sense of timelessness—not waiting, but hanging out. Patrons are not anonymous, but tend to have limited, bounded relationships. Interaction is promoted by the casual arrangements of tables and chairs as well as the crowded conditions.

Although this discussion has emphasized the positive role of inter-customer support, it is essential to recognize that customers differ in their willingness to engage in supportive interactions. Kenen (1982) addresses this difference indirectly, noting that middle-class patrons of a laundro-mat will be less likely to socialize than persons in lower class neighbor-hoods who share a common ethnicity. Interestingly, Wiseman (1979) and Gross (1986) do not address the possibility that people might be embar-rassed, angry, or uncomfortable as they participate in the rituals of a used clothing store or a clinic. Airline passengers (Zurcher, 1979) and library patrons (B. B. Brown, 1987) adopt behavior patterns to distance them-selves from fellow customers, hanging an intangible but unmistakable "Do not disturb" sign around their space. Similar strategies, as well as the motivations to enact these behaviors, should be studied in other service contexts as well.

Implications for Service Quality and Services Marketing

When services marketing researchers investigate the social support function of services, they can be expected to address different issues from those studied in psychological and communications frameworks. A mar-keting orientation directs attention to elements of service quality and satisfaction, as well as issues of social responsibility. In this section we look at reasons why a firm may (or may not) wish to increase its provision of social support. We then discuss possible ways in which a firm might increase the quality and quantity of social support it provides to its clients.

Should a Firm Encourage Social Support?

Social support is generally presented as a phenomenon that emerges spontaneously in a service encounter. However, there are at least three general reasons why a firm may consciously choose to increase or decrease the level of social support it provides. Social support may increase profits by improving customer loyalty and perceived quality of service. Providing social support may also be an ethically responsible act that augments the service provider's sense of mission. However, social support also has potential negative consequences both for providers and clients.

Social Support and the Bottom Line

Does providing social support increase profit-related measures such as perceived quality, satisfaction, or customer loyalty? Although most current research on service delivery has not explored social support directly, some findings have implications for understanding the relationship between social support and service quality. "Empirical research in both service quality and service satisfaction affirms the importance of quality of customer/employee interactions in the assessment of overall quality and/or satisfaction with services" (Bitner et al., 1990, p. 72). Parasuraman et al. (1988)[5] found five factors underlying service quality: tangibles, reliability, responsiveness, assurance, and empathy. Empathy, defined as "caring, individualized attention the firm provides its customers" (p. 23), appears to be quite similar to social support. Although empathy was the least important predictor of perceived quality, the authors cautioned that some of its importance may have been masked by multicollinearity. Further, empathy had statistically significant simple correlations with overall quality, ranging from 0.20 to 0.40. Most important, Parasuraman et al. (1988) studied industries where customer-provider interactions tend to be brief and discontinuous: appliance repair and maintenance, retail banking, long-distance telephone, securities brokerage, and credit cards. The importance of empathy as a predictor can be expected to increase when researchers study service interactions that meet the criteria for social support provision, as discussed earlier.

Researchers have emphasized that perceptions of service quality are influenced by interpersonal interactions with the provider (S. W. Brown & Swartz, 1989; Crosby & Stephens, 1987; Day & Bodur, 1978; Quelch & Ash, 1981; Westbrook, 1981). Specifically, perceived quality can be enhanced through personalization (Surprenant & Solomon, 1987) and respect (Bitran & Hoech, 1990), both of which are related to social support. Bitner et al. (1990) found that many behaviors associated with social support also led to memorable and extremely positive service encounters.

In addition to situations where service professionals performed their expected roles exceptionally well, for example, "The flight attendant helped me calm and care for my airsick child" (p. 77); "43.8% of satisfactory encounters are a result of customer delight with unprompted and/or unsolicited employee actions" (p. 80). The authors conclude that "The importance of spontaneous interactive quality in service delivery cannot be overemphasized" (p. 81).

The finding that service providers' actions transcending customers' expectations led to extremely positive service encounters is fully consistent with the notion of social support as transcending core service activities. Arnould and Price (1991) found that customers evaluated raft trips more highly when they viewed their guide as a friend rather than simply as an employee of the firm.

Although social support is likely to have the strongest positive impact on perceived quality when it is seen as going beyond the call of duty, many consumers have come to expect some forms of social support from particular types of service providers. Future research is needed to identify dimensions of service categories associated with these expectations, but it is reasonable to assume that disappointment may result if these expectations are not met. For instance, medical consumers frequently expect caring providers who are good listeners; at the same time, the provider's training, temperament, or cost constraints may lead to assembly line, impersonal service delivery. A health club that attracts busy people who want to get in and out quickly may lose potential customers who associate workouts with a more supportive environment.

To date, the only research to specifically measure social support in a service encounter has found it to be the key variable in predicting service satisfaction (reported in Adelman, 1987; Adelman & Ahuvia, 1991a; Ahuvia et al., 1992). This investigation chose a matchmaking agency as the research site, because it provides a highly personalized service and the clients would be likely to desire social support in dealing with the stresses of dating. The core benefits of the service were operationalized as the number of dates received and the quality of those dates as rated by the respondents. Social support was measured by a 12-item scale developed specifically for this study, which included such items as "I felt assured I'm a worthwhile person" and "I shared and reflected on personal information." The results of this study indicated that long-term psychological changes such as feeling more in control of one's life were influenced by social support provision ($\beta = 0.22$, $p < .05$), but were much more strongly influenced by the core service function, for example, the quality of the dates ($\beta = 0.44$, $p < .001$). At the same time, satisfaction with the service was more strongly related to social support received ($\beta = 0.41$, $p < .001$) than it was to either the quality ($\beta = 0.25$, $p < .005$) or quantity ($\beta = 0.16$, $p < .10$) of dates. Thus, although social support in this service setting only moderately impacted on long-term psychological states, results suggest that given the right conditions, it can have an extremely powerful influence on service satisfaction.

In addition to improving customer perceptions of service quality, social support provision may directly increase consumer loyalty. Stryker (1987) notes that increased commitment to a relationship will increase costs associated with leaving the relationship. Social support may create commitment by increasing the intensity of a relationship with the service provider—what Stryker calls "affective commitment." The insurance industry has even been criticized by the FTC (Lynch & Mackay, 1985) and others (Cooper, 1987) for relying on affective commitment generated through relationship marketing to charge excessive prices (for a rebuttal see Crosby & Stephens, 1987).

Increased loyalty can also come about when customers bond with one another. For example, Harley-Davidson Motorcycles has enhanced customer loyalty by supporting clubs for motorcycle enthusiasts. These clubs facilitate intercustomer friendships and thus increase the number of social relationships associated with the "biker" identity, creating what Stryker calls "interactional commitment." Just as important, these clubs help create a peer network in which the use of their product is esteemed (Schouten & McAlexander, 1992). Thus, customers who experience core service failures may be reluctant to exercise the exit option or even to risk the friendly relationships with the service provider or other customers by voicing criticism. At times, however, intercustomer support can be problematic for the provider who has little or no control over these interactions.

Finally, customers sometimes participate in the service production process, even serving as partial employees (Mills & Morris, 1986), but remain "free actors" compared to the employees on the firm's payroll

(Bowen & Schneider, 1988). When customers support each other, they take over some of the functions of the service provider. Those in second-hand clothing stores will fill the clerk's customary function of advising and encouraging a clothing purchase (Wiseman, 1979). Customers in bars and cafes provide their own entertainment (Oldenburg, 1989). Members of a health club or fitness class can encourage new members ("You'll be less sore by tomorrow") and sometimes demonstrate the equipment to novice users. Sometimes customers will be even more effective than paid employees; they are more readily available, and the absence of a profit motive will lend credibility to their advice.

Social Mission

In addition to increasing profits, service providers may also see providing social support as the right thing to do for ethical reasons. At its essence, adding social support to a commercial relationship changes the norms that govern the interaction. In conventional commercial relationships, people expect an emphasis on self-interest (by both the service provider and the consumer) constrained by the law, the desire for future transactions, and it is hoped, personal values that preclude severe exploitation. In communal relationships (Clark & Mills, 1979) such as friendship and family, different norms apply. These norms include the "need norm" (O'Connell, 1984) in which giving a benefit in response to a need is seen as appropriate, rather than only giving a benefit in direct exchange for another benefit. These two sets of norms can be seen as existing at opposite ends of a continuum. By adding social support into what had previously been a purely commercial context, the provider moves the norms that govern the interaction more in the direction of communal exchange.

This shift in norms has many positive outcomes. Among other potential benefits, it may build a sense of community, add warmth to social interactions, and allow service providers to believe they genuinely help the people with whom they come into contact. At the same time, a caveat is in order. Communal exchange norms require a level of trust not found in many business transactions. In shifting the ground rules of the relationship by providing social support, service providers take on the moral obligation not to exploit that trust in ways that would harm the client. If the service provider cannot make that kind of a commitment, she or he is better off from an ethical standpoint keeping the relationship on a purely businesslike footing.

Even if the consumer gets a good product at a fair price, social support can still be problematic for recipients who appear to be paying money in order to obtain an affective relationship. This feeling can lead to both a sense of exploitation and to unhealthy consumption patterns. In their study of compulsive buying, O'Guinn and Faber (1989) noted that shopping interactions were often valued for their social content: "Some compulsive buyers indicated they received little positive attention from other people outside the shopping environment. . . . Salespeople were referred to by some of the informants as if they were very close friends" (p. 154).

In a humorous example, a "Cathy" cartoon shows the heroine succumbing to the retail salesperson's compliments, "You're different! You're unique!" Her parting words reflect a successful reciprocity strategy (Cialdini, 1985): "Desperate to feel special to someone, the shopper spends another $43 endearing herself to a salesclerk she hopes she never sees again" (Guisewite, 1991).

Much earlier, Stone (1954) identified the "personalizing shopper" who shops primarily as an interpersonal activity, preferring local merchants who "get to know you." Shoppers with this orientation "lacked access to formal and informal channels of social participation." They were often newcomers who lacked local friends, suggesting the establishment of what Stone calls a "quasi-primary" relationship with local merchants.

In brief, some service providers may see social support as a social responsibility that comes out of treating their customers as people, not just sources of financial gain. But by going beyond a purely economic understanding of the transaction, the service provider must be careful not to abuse the trust that social support can engender or exploit the emotional needs of customers in other ways. Weak tie support is a bounded relationship that need not become a generalized friendship. Within the boundaries of weak tie support, however, a level of sincerity is still ethically required. Weak tie support is a limited friendship, not a "McFriendship."

The Down Side of Social Support

Social support may contribute positively to customer evaluations of service encounters. However, there are risks associated with both promising and attempting to deliver social support (Albrecht & Adelman, 1987b). Practitioners and theorists must be alerted to the possible negative outcomes of social support for both the service firm and the client. Several of these possible problems are listed below.

Increased Work Load and Expense. Hiam and Schewe (1992) criticize the trend of companies trying to improve service quality by adding more and more supporting services to supplement their core service offering (see Table 7.3). They argue that increasing supporting services adds to long-term costs while only providing short-term improvements in customer satisfaction. In contrast, they claim that quality improvements in the core service increase satisfaction and may reduce costs over the long run. We have argued that social support is best seen as a supporting service, and we recognize that increasing social support will require time, money, and energy. However, we contend that social support is not a gimmick and its benefits will not be short lived. Even so, one needs to carefully weigh the costs of adding to the service provider's job requirements.

Provider Stress. Emotion management can be stressful even when the provider is simply required to be cheerful and polite to rude customers (Hochschild, 1983). Therefore, those required to go "beyond a smile and nod" may experience even greater difficulty. The river raft guide described by Arnould and Price (1991) has to deal with fearful customers attempting a new skill in a dangerous situation. Lawyers often see people at times of major life stress, such as death, divorce, and bankruptcy. Unlike professional caregivers, these providers may lack training in managing their own responses and may be ill equipped to handle distressed clients. At times, the demands of being supportive can be so burdensome that providers are forced to disengage from clients. Bissonette (1977) notes that bartenders have developed tactics to lower their involvement with certain customers, such as refusing to respond to conversational overtures.

Conflicts Between Support and Core Service Delivery. A contact person may also experience conflict between his/her own caregiving attitude and management's emphasis on profit. For example, the time requirements of providing social support may conflict with the pressure to be efficient. Alternatively, the interests of the clients may diverge from those of management. For example, Lovelock et al. (1992) identified a waitress who experienced resentment when management ordered her to tempt a dieting patron with a dessert tray.

Measurement Difficulties. The impact of social support on profit will be difficult to detect. Banks and supermarket clerks are often evaluated on the basis of quantitative efficiency measures (Schneider, 1980). Firms in a variety of industries often monitor telephone calls, evaluating both length and content of each call. This management approach conflicts with the provider's social support functions. At the same time, Adelman et al. (1987) note that support from weak ties can be hard to detect, let alone measure, because of the fleeting nature and low involvement of the contact. Thus, firms may have difficulty assessing the impact of social support on customer satisfaction and loyalty.

Misplaced Loyalties. Providing social support may increase customer loyalty, but the object of that loyalty may be a particular employee and not the firm as a whole. From the management point of view this type of loyalty can be a double-edged sword (Oliva, Oliver, & MacMillan, 1992). For example Bissonette (1977) observed that customers will sometimes follow a popular bartender who moves to another bar.

Unwanted Intrusions. Providing social support is a delicate endeavor, the effectiveness of which is highly dependent on the situation and desires of the individual customer. Just as customers differ in their preference for formality during service encounters (Goodwin & Smith, 1990), their responses to social support may range from gratitude to feelings of intrusion. As noted above, Bitner et al. (1990) found that situations in which service personnel go beyond their professional role can lead to highly positive evaluations. However, another study (Surprenant & Solomon, 1987) found making small talk with clients can be seen as intrusive and lead to negative evaluations of the service. Future research is needed to determine what conditions are likely to lead to either of these effects.

How to Increase Social Support Provision

The manager who wants to incorporate social support into service delivery faces unique obstacles due to the paradoxical nature of social support. As we discussed earlier, customers will assign their own meanings to actions of the service provider. Attributions of sincerity and voluntariness will increase the likelihood that these actions are perceived as supportive. Therefore, mandating social support is a little like mandating spontaneity. At the same time, managers can enhance employees' capacity to respond supportively to clients, as well as develop environments that encourage intercustomer support. In this section we discuss several possible ways social support provision might be increased, along with the many obstacles that complicate this process.

Integrate Social Support in Corporate Philosophy

The first step in increasing social support provision is to make a conscious decision that this is something worth doing. Businesses that have formal corporate mission statements should integrate social support provision into that document. However, many service providers are too small to have formal mission statements. For them, a conscious decision that providing social support is part of their business, not something that interferes with their business, is a necessary first step.

Recruitment and Training of Personnel

One of the best ways that a service provider may increase the quality and quantity of social support to clients is hiring personnel with the needed aptitudes and attitudes (Schneider, Wheeler, & Cox, 1992). No matter whether it is facilitating intercustomer support or providing support directly to the clients, some people seem to have social skills that others lack. Making these social talents a hiring qualification may be the best way to develop a work force that is consistent with the desire to provide social support.

Training employees is also an option that might complement a social support-oriented hiring policy (Goodwin, 1988). For instance, research has found that bartenders rely on their personality rather than psychological techniques when addressing sensitive topics (Bissonette, 1977). As mentioned above, this has led to attempts to train service personnel in psychological techniques or offer them free consultations with mental health professionals (Cowen et al., 1981). However, these efforts have met with mixed success (Cowen, 1982); for example, hairdressers were more open to this help than bartenders. Further, this training may alter the nature of the provider/client interaction with negative consequences. Wiesenfeld and Weis (1979) report that hairdressers exposed to a mental health training program increased their use of feeling-reflection techniques as compared to advice giving; however, they note that a sudden change of interaction style may be unsettling to the client. We emphasize the importance of market research to identify the type of interaction desired by clients: People may turn to hairdressers precisely because they like the advice-giving approach and find it helpful. Overall, they may expect a nontherapeutic interaction style when dealing with nontherapists.

Creating Proper Environment

Cues in the physical surroundings will encourage customers to interact, hang out, or limit themselves to straightforward business transactions. The arrangement of chairs, type of music, and even lighting can facilitate or inhibit interaction (Bitner, 1992). Serving food can encourage sociability even in places not traditionally associated with friendly interaction, such as laundromats (Kenen, 1982). Health clubs often offer juice bars or place chairs strategically in the locker room to encourage members to socialize.

However, simply enhancing opportunities for interaction may not lead to social support. Some people do not want to be bothered by interaction with others as they eat a meal, do laundry, or undertake other activities of daily life. One New York city bar owner set up a 12-person table to allow parties of one to dine communally with strangers; however, his mature, affluent customers refused to participate (Schoolsky, 1990). Similarly, some clients may prefer to talk to one another on a superficial or task-specific level ("May I borrow your detergent?") without offering information or creating a sense of community. Therefore, social support provision will, of necessity, be a niche marketing strategy that appeals only to certain customers.

Market Research on Social Support Needs

Solicitation and responsiveness to customer opinions is highly correlated ($r = 0.54$) with those items on the SERVQUAL measure most closely related to social support (Schneider, Wheeler, & Cox, 1992). This may be because frequent communication with service providers about client needs can create a culture in which customer needs are valued. In addition, market research can play a key role in determining if the current clientele desire social support, and if so, what type. For instance, travel-related businesses may find that because their clients are in situations of high uncertainty and are distanced from established ties, they may be particularly receptive to a wide range of support. Thus, airlines, hotels, and vacation resorts provide staff to help with all kinds of problems. Market research can also be used to target potential populations that are particularly receptive to offers of support (e.g., single mothers, elderly, dual-career couples, etc.). Segmenting the market by the type of relationship clients want with the service provider is key to using social support as part of a successful business strategy (Oldano, 1987).

Advertising Social Support Provision

Whether deliberate or not, we frequently find evidence of social support in advertising service quality. Claims that "we care," "we listen," "we're here for you," and so on abound in commercial messages. For example, as part of the "We Love to Fly" campaign, Delta Airlines depicted a flight attendant who stayed with an elderly lady as she waited for her ride at her destination.

Explicitly featuring a service as a source of support may be appealing to some customers, but if done improperly it may stigmatize future participation. People choose to confide in hairdressers, bartenders, and lawyers because these occupations lack the stigma of psychotherapy. A service that advertises an opportunity to discuss personal problems may lose this stigma-free positioning. Similarly, a coffee shop or bar that is positioned as "a great place to meet people" may inadvertently be perceived as a singles' meeting place, and people who utilize singles' places can be perceived as socially inadequate (Adelman & Ahuvia, 1991b). Therefore, any advertising of social support benefits must be done in a subtle and careful manner.

It also needs to be stressed that advertising social support is not a substitute for providing it. It is much easier to create an ad campaign that says "we care" then it is to create a genuinely caring work force or a corporate orientation that facilitates support. As with any advertising claim, the firm must work hard to back it up both to avoid creating deception and to avoid dissatisfaction resulting from overselling.

Conclusion

If all our service encounters that make up daily life were reduced to only commercial exchanges, we would be left with a bleak image of social relations. In their search for objectivity, scholarly writings rarely convey the transient yet deeply felt quality of service encounters that touch the lives and well-being of those involved. We conclude therefore, with a literary excerpt that serves as a reminder of the "strength of weak ties."

In reminiscing about the encounters with his barber that took place over a period of many years, Fulghum (1986) provides a rich, personal description of this relationship created by a "peculiar distance."

> We started out as categories to each other: "barber" and "customer." Then we become "redneck ignorant barber" and "pinko egghead minister." Once a month we reviewed the world and our lives and explored our positions. We sparred over civil rights and Vietnam and a lot of elections. We became mirrors, confidants, confessors, therapists, and companions in an odd sort of way. We went through being thirty years old and then forty. We discussed and argued and joked, but always with a certain thoughtful deference. After all, I was his customer. And he was standing there with a razor in his hand. . . . I never saw him outside the barber shop, never met his wife or children, never sat in his home or ate a meal with him. Yet he became a terribly important fixture in my life. Perhaps a lot more important than if we had been next-door neighbors. The quality of our relationship was partly created by a peculiar distance. . . . Without realizing it, we fill important places in each other's lives. (pp. 76-77)

Telling others about the supportive role of service encounters often elicits stories of incidences or relationships like Fulghum's (1986) with his barber. We believe these encounters are more than anecdotes or exceptional tales. These fleeting moments are vital to daily life and keep it in repair.

Notes

1. For applications of theories of interpersonal interactions to services, see Bitran and Hoech (1990); Crosby, Evans, and Cowles (1990); Felcher (1992); Solomon, Surprenant, Czepiel, and Gutman (1985); and Surprenant and Solomon (1987). For applications of theories of interpersonal interactions to sales, see Oliver and Swan (1989), Soldow and Thomas (1984), Webster (1968), and Williams and Spiro (1985). For the effect of empathy on salesperson performance, see Dawson, Soper, and Pettijohn (1992).

2. A notable exception to this general trend is the people who came of age during the major recession of the 1970s. Due to these economically hard times, this cohort did not develop an ingrained sense of economic security and hence now places a relatively high value on financial success.

3. Recent history has seen such a huge rise in the number of singles that Stern, Gould, and Barak (1987) labeled them a "megasegment" (p. 6). Between 1975 and 1985, the population of singles increased from 47 million to 68 million (Bennet, 1989). Between 1960 and 1987,

the proportion of unmarried women ages 25-44 almost doubled to become "the highest rate ever experienced in U.S. history" (Fuchs, 1988, pp. 17-18). Similarly, in just the 7 years between 1980 and 1987, the number of unmarried men aged 25-44 increased by 65% to 12 million (Cutler, 1989).

4. This section draws heavily on Adelman et al. (1987).

5. This work was based on Parasuraman et al. (1985), who originally found 10 key determinants of service quality. Of these, courtesy (politeness, respect, consideration, and friendliness) and understanding/knowing the customer (making the effort to understand the customer's needs and providing individualized attention) seem related to social support.

References

Adelman, M. B. (1987, May-June). *Love's urban agent: Social support and the matchmaker.* Paper presented at the Iowa Conference on Personal Relationships, University of Iowa, Iowa City, IA.

Adelman, M. B., & Ahuvia, A. C. (1991a). *Matchmakers as urban agents: A multimethod study.* Paper presented at the Annual Conference of the International Communications Association, Chicago.

Adelman, M. B., & Ahuvia, A. C. (1991b). Mediated channels for mate seeking: A solution to involuntary singlehood? *Critical Studies in Mass Communication, 8,* 273-289.

Adelman, M. B., Parks, M. R., & Albrecht, T. L. (1987). Beyond close relationships: Social support and weak ties. In T. L. Albrecht, M. B. Adelman, & Associates (Eds.), *Communicating social support* (pp. 126-147). Newbury Park, CA: Sage.

Ahuvia, A. C., & Adelman, M. B. (1992). Formal intermediaries in the marriage market: A typology and review. *Journal of Marriage and the Family, 54,* 452-463.

Ahuvia, A. C., & Adelman, M. B. (in press). Market metaphors for meeting mates. In R. Belk (Ed.), *Research in consumer behavior: A research annual* (Vol. 5). Greenwich, CT: JAI.

Ahuvia, A. C., Adelman, M. B., & Goodwin, C. (1992, March). Social support as a source of service satisfaction. In R. T. Rust & R. L. Oliver (Chairs), *Service quality, service satisfaction, and services marketing.* Conference sponsored by the TIMS College on Marketing and the Center for Services Marketing at Vanderbilt University and the Owen Graduate School of Management, Nashville, TN.

Ahuvia, A. C., Adelman, M. B., & Schroeder, J. E. (1991). Two views of consumption in mating and dating. In R. H. Holman & M. R. Solomon (Eds.), *Advances in consumer research* (Vol. 18, pp. 532-537). Provo, UT: Association for Consumer Research.

Albrecht, T. L., & Adelman, M. B. (1984). Social support and life stress: New directions for communication research. *Human Communication Research, 11,* 3-32.

Albrecht, T. L., & Adelman, M. B. (1987a). Communicating social support: A theoretical perspective. In T. L. Albrecht & M. B. Adelman (Eds.), *Communicating social support* (pp. 18-39). Newbury Park, CA: Sage.

Albrecht, T. L., & Adelman, M. B. (1987b). Dilemmas, applications, and new directions for research. In T. L. Albrecht & M. B. Adelman (Eds.), *Communicating social support* (pp. 240-274). Newbury Park, CA: Sage.

Albrecht, T. L., & Adelman, M. B. (1987c). Rethinking the relationship between communication and social support. In T. L. Albrecht & M. B. Adelman (Eds.), *Communicating social support* (pp. 13-16). Newbury Park, CA: Sage.

Albrecht, T. L., Adelman, M. B., & Associates (Eds.). (1987). *Communicating social support.* Newbury Park, CA: Sage.

Arnould, E. J., & Price, L. L. (1991, October). *River magic: Hedonic consumption and the extended service encounter.* Paper presented at the Annual Meeting of the Association for Consumer Research, Chicago.

Bennet, J. (1989, February 13). The data game. *New Republic,* pp. 20-22.

Berkman, L. F., & Syme, S. L. (1979). Social networks, host resistance, and mortality: A nine-year follow-up study of Alameda County residents. *American Journal of Epidemiology, 109,* 186-204.

Bissonette, R. (1977). The bartender as a mental health service gatekeeper: A role analysis. *Community Mental Health Journal, 13,* 92-99.

Bitner, M. J. (1992). Servicescapes. *Journal of Marketing, 56,* 57-71.

Bitner, M. J., Booms, B. M., & Tetreault, M. S. (1990). The service encounter: Diagnosing favorable and unfavorable incidents. *Journal of Marketing, 54,* 71-84.

Bitran, G. R., & Hoech, J. (1990). The humanization of service: Respect at the moment of truth. *Sloan Management Review, 31,* 89-96.

Bowen, D. E., & Schneider, B. (1988). Services marketing and management: Implications for organizational behavior. *Research in Organizational Behavior, 10,* 43-80.

Brissett, D., & Oldenburg, R. (1982). Friendship: An exploration and appreciation of ambiguity. *Psychiatry, 45,* 325-335.

Brown, B. B. (1987). Territoriality. In D. Stokols & I. Altman (Eds.), *Handbook of environmental psychology* (pp. 505-533). New York: John Wiley.

Brown, S. W., & Swartz, T. A. (1989). Gap analysis of professional service quality. *Journal of Marketing, 53,* 92-98.

Caplan, G. (1976). The family as a support system. In G. Caplan & M. Killilea (Eds.), *Support systems and mutual help* (pp. 19-36). New York: Grune & Stratton.

Cialdini, R. B. (1985). *Influence: Science and practice.* Glenview, IL: Scott-Foresman.

Clark, M. S., & Mills, J. (1979). Interpersonal attraction in exchange and communal relationships. *Journal of Personality and Social Psychology, 37,* 12-24.

Cobb, S. (1976). Social support as a moderator of life stress. *Psychosomatic Medicine, 38,* 300-314.

Cooper, M. N. (1987). *Confusion and excess cost: Consumer problems in purchasing life insurance.* Unpublished report, Consumer Federation of America, Washington, DC.

Cowen, E. L. (1982). Help is where you find it: Four informal helping groups. *American Psychologist, 37,* 385-395.

Cowen, E. L., Gesten, E. L., Boike, M., Norton, P., Wilson, A. B., & DeStefano, M. A. (1979). Hairdressers as caregivers: A descriptive profile of interpersonal help-giving involvements. *American Journal of Community Psychology, 7,* 633-648.

Cowen, E. L., McKim, B. J., & Weissberg, R. P. (1981). Bartenders as informal, interpersonal help-agents. *American Journal of Community Psychology, 9,* 715-729.

Crimmins, E. M., Easterlin, R. A., & Saito, Y. (1991). What young adults want. *American Demographics, 13,* 24-33.

Crosby, L. A., Evans, K. R., & Cowles, D. (1990). Relationship quality in services selling: An interpersonal influence perspective. *Journal of Marketing, 54,* 68-81.

Crosby, L. A., & Stephens, N. J. (1987). Effects of relationship marketing on satisfaction, retention and prices in the life insurance industry. *Journal of Marketing Research, 24,* 404-411.

Cutler, B. (1989). Bachelor party. *American Demographics, 11,* 22-26, 55.

Dawson, L. E., Jr., Soper, B., & Pettijohn, C. E. (1992). The effects of empathy on salesperson effectiveness. *Psychology & Marketing, 9,* 297-310.

Day, R. L., & Bodur, M. (1978). Consumer response to dissatisfaction with services and intangibles. In H. K. Hunt (Ed.), *Advances in consumer research* (Vol. 5, pp. 263-272). Ann Arbor, MI: Association for Consumer Research.

Dimma, W. A. (1991). Decline of ethics. *Business Quarterly* (Canada), *55,* 8-10.

Doane, J. A., & Cowen, E. L. (1981). Interpersonal help-giving of family practice lawyers. *American Journal of Community Psychology, 9,* 547-558.

Donnelly, P. (1981, October). Running the gauntlet: The moral order of pornographic movie theatres. *Urban Life, 10,* 239-264.

Duck, S., & Silver R. C. (1990). *Personal relationships and social support.* London: Sage.

Dychtwald, K. (1990). *Age wave.* New York: Bantam.

Felcher, M. E. (1992). *"Professors," "get-me-done's," and "moochers": The struggle for control between car salespeople and their customers.* Unpublished manuscript, Northwestern University, Medill School of Journalism, Evanston, IL.

Fischer, C. S. (1982). *To dwell among friends: Personal networks in town and city.* Chicago: University of Chicago Press.

Fisher, S. (1984). *Stress and the perception of control.* London: Lawrence Erlbaum.

Fuchs, V. R. (1988). *Women's quest for economic equality.* Cambridge, MA: Harvard University Press.

Fulghum, R. (1986). *All I really need to know I learned in kindergarten.* New York: Ivy.

Gallup Organization, Inc. (1988). *Consumers' perceptions concerning the quality of American products and services* (Survey conducted for the American Society for Quality Control; ASQC Publication No. T711).

Goffman, E. (1963). *Stigma: Notes on the management of spoiled identity.* Englewood Cliffs, NJ: Prentice-Hall.

Goodwin, C. (1988). I can do it myself: Training the service consumer to enhance productivity. *Journal of Services Marketing, 2,* 71-78.

Goodwin, C., & Smith, K. L. (1990). Friendliness and courtesy: Conflicting goals for the service provider. *Journal of Services Marketing, 4,* 5-20.

Gottlieb, B. H. (1981). Introduction. In B. H. Gottlieb (Ed.), *Social networks and social support* (pp. 11-42). Newbury Park, CA: Sage.

Graham, E. (1990, March 7). Recipe for romance: A box of Duz, a cup of bleach and thou. *Wall Street Journal,* p. A1.

Granovetter, M. S. (1973). The strength of weak ties. *American Journal of Sociology, 78,* 1360-1380.

Granovetter, M. S. (1982). The strength of weak ties: A network theory revisited. In P. V. Marsden & N. Lin (Eds.), *Social structure and network analysis* (pp. 105-130). Newbury Park, CA: Sage.

Grönroos, C. (1982). An applied service marketing theory. *European Journal of Marketing, 16,* 30-41.

Grönroos, C. (1987). Developing the service offering—A source of competitive advantage. In C. Surprenant (Ed.), *Add value to your service: The key to success* (pp. 81-85). Chicago: American Marketing Association.

Gross, E. (1986, July). Waiting at Mayo. *Urban Life, 15,* 139-164.

Guisewite, C. (1991, December 5). Cathy [cartoon strip]. *Winnipeg Free Press,* p. A17.

Heisley, D. D., McGrath, M. A., & Sherry, J. F., Jr. (1991). To everything there is a season: A photoessay of a farmers' market. In R. W. Belk (Ed.), *Highways and buyways* (pp. 141-166). Provo, UT: Association for Consumer Research.

Hiam, A., & Schewe, C. D. (1992, December 7). It's time for Santa, the marketing genius. *Marketing News, 26,* p. 4.

Hobfoll, S. E., & Stokes, J. P. (1988). The process and mechanics of social support. In S. W. Duck (Ed.), *Handbook of personal relationships* (pp. 497-517). New York: John Wiley.

Hochschild, A. R. (1983). *The managed heart.* Berkeley: University of California Press.

Huey, J. (1993). Finding new heroes for a new era. *Fortune, 127,* 62-69.

Hui, M. K., & Bateson, J.E.G. (1991). Perceived control and the effects of crowding and consumer choice on the service experience. *Journal of Consumer Research, 18,* 174-184.

Inglehart, R. (1990). *Culture shift in advanced industrial society.* Princeton, NJ: Princeton University Press.

Kelly, J. G. (1964). The mental health agent in the urban community. In L. H. Barteneirer *Urban America and the planning of mental health services* (pp. 474-494). New York: Group for the Advancement of Psychiatry.

Kenen, R. (1982). Soapsuds, space and sociability: A participant observation of a laundromat. *Urban Life, 11,* 163-184.

Lazarus, R., & Launier, R. (1978). Stress related transactions between people and environment. In L. A. Pervin & M. Lewis (Eds.), *Perspectives in interactional psychology* (pp. 287-327). New York: Plenum.

Leech, E. (1992, July 5). Satisfying the customer of the '90s. *Chicago Tribune,* section 6, p. 1.

Lofland, L. H. (1973). *A world of strangers: Order and action in urban public space.* New York: Basic Books.

Lofland, L. H. (1989). Social life in the public realm: A review. *Journal of Contemporary Ethnography, 17,* 453-482.

Lovelock, C. H., et al. (1992). Ten service workers and their jobs. In C. H. Lovelock (Ed.), *Managing services: Marketing, operations and human resources* (2nd ed., pp. 373-383). Englewood Cliffs: Prentice-Hall.

Lynch, M. P., & Mackay, R. J. (1985). *Life insurance products and consumer information* (FTC Staff Report, pp. 280-300). Washington, DC: U.S. Government Printing Office.

Markus, H., & Nurius, P. (1986). Possible selves. *American Psychologist, 41,* 954-969.

Milgram, S. (1977). *The individual in a social world.* Reading, MA: Addison-Wesley.

Mills, P. K., & Morris, J. H. (1986). Clients as "partial employees" of service organizations: Role development in client participation. *Academy of Management Review, 11,* 726-735.

Nathe, P. A. (1976, April). Prickly Pear coffee house: The hangout. *Urban Life, 5,* 75-104.

O'Connell, L. (1984). An exploration of exchange in three social relationships: Kinship, friendship and the marketplace. *Journal of Social and Personal Relationships, 1,* 333-345.

O'Guinn, T. C., & Faber, R. J. (1989). Compulsive buying: A phenomenological exploration. *Journal of Consumer Research, 16,* 147-157.

Oldano, T. L. (1987). Relationship segmentation: Enhancing the service provider/client connection. In C. Surprenant (Ed.), *Add value to your service: The key to success* (pp. 143-146). Chicago: American Marketing Association.

Oldenburg, R. (1989). *The great good place.* New York: Paragon House.

Oliva, T. A., Oliver, R. L., & MacMillan, I. C. (1992). A catastrophe model for developing service satisfaction strategies. *Journal of Marketing, 56,* 83-95.

Oliver, R. L., & Swan, J. E. (1989). Consumer perceptions of interpersonal equity and satisfaction in transactions: A field survey approach. *Journal of Marketing, 53,* 21-35.

Parasuraman, A., Zeithaml, V. A., & Berry, L. L. (1985). Conceptual model of service quality and its implications for future research. *Journal of Marketing, 49,* 41-50.

Parasuraman, A., Zeithaml, V. A., & Berry, L. L. (1988). SERVQUAL: A multiple-item scale for measuring consumer perceptions of service quality. *Journal of Retailing, 64,* 12-40.

Parks, M. R. (1982). Ideology in interpersonal communication: Off the couch and into the world. In M. Burgoon (Ed.), *Communication yearbook 5* (pp. 79-107). New Brunswick, NJ: Transaction Books.

Pilisuk, M., & Parks, S. H. (1986). *The healing web: Social networks and human survival.* Hanover, NH: University Press of New England.

Quelch, J. A., & Ash, S. B. (1981). Consumer satisfaction with professional services. In J. H. Donnelly & W. R. George (Eds.), *Marketing of services* (pp. 82-85). Chicago: American Marketing Association.

Reisman, M. (1985). Lining up: The microlegal system of queues. *University of Cincinnati Law Review, 54,* 417-449.

Schneider, B. (1980). The service organization: Climate is crucial. *Organizational Dynamics, 9,* 52-65.

Schneider, B., Wheeler, J. K., & Cox, J. F. (1992). A passion for service: Using content analysis to explicate service climate themes. *Journal of Applied Psychology, 77,* 705-716.

Schoolsky, R. (1990, April). Bar associations. *Restaurant Hospitality, 74,* 174-176.

Schouten, J. W., & McAlexander, J. H. (1992). *Hog heaven: The structure, ethos and market impact of a consumer subculture.* Paper presented at the International Conference of the Association for Consumer Research, Amsterdam.

Schwartz, M. (1991). Materialism declining in U.S.: Survey. *National Underwriter, 95,* 14.

Sennett, R. (1977). *The fall of public man.* New York: Vintage.

Shapiro, G. E. (1984). Help seeking: Why people don't. *Research in the Sociology of Organizations* (Vol. 3, pp. 213-236). Greenwich, CT: JAI.

Sherry, J. F. (1990). A sociocultural analysis of a midwestern American flea market. *Journal of Consumer Research, 17,* 13-30.

Soldow, G. F., & Thomas, G. P. (1984). Relational communication: Form versus content in the sales interaction. *Journal of Marketing, 48,* 84-93.

Solomon, M. R., Surprenant, C., Czepiel, J. A., & Gutman, E. G. (1985). A role theory perspective on dyadic interactions: The service encounter. *Journal of Marketing, 49,* 99-111.

Sommer, R., Herrick, J., & Sommer, T. R. (1981). The behavioral ecology of supermarkets and farmers' markets. *Journal of Environmental Psychology, 1,* 13-19.

Stern, B. B., Gould, S. J., & Barak, B. (1987). Baby boom singles: The social seekers. *Journal of Consumer Marketing, 4,* 5-22.

Stone, G. P. (1954). City shoppers and urban identification: Observations on the social psychology of city life. *American Journal of Sociology, 60,* 36-45.

Stryker, S. (1987). Identity theory: Developments and extensions. In K. Yardley & T. Honess (Eds.), *Self and identity: Psychosocial perspectives* (pp. 89-103). New York: John Wiley.

Surprenant, C. F., & Solomon, M. R. (1987). Predictability and personalization in the service encounter. *Journal of Marketing, 51,* 86-96.

Thoits, P. A. (1985). Social support and psychological well being: Theoretical possibilities. In I. G. Sarason & B. R. Sarason (Eds.), *Social support: Theory, research and applications* (pp. 51-72). Dordrecht: Martinus Nijhoff.

Van Gorder, B. E. (1990). Satisfying the customer of the '90s. *Credit, 16,* 10-15.

Webster, F. E., Jr. (1968). Interpersonal communication and salesman effectiveness. *Journal of Marketing, 32,* 7-13.

Wellman, B. (1979). The community question: The intimate networks of East Yonkers. *American Sociological Review, 84,* 1201-1231.

Westbrook, R. A. (1981). Sources of consumer satisfaction with retail outlets. *Journal of Retailing, 57,* 68-85.

Wethington, E., & Kessler, R. C. (1986). Perceived support, received support and adjustment to stressful life events. *Journal of Health and Social Behavior, 27,* 78-89.

Wiesenfeld, A. R., & Weis, H. M. (1979). Hairdressers and helping: Influencing the behavior of informal caregivers. *Professional Psychology, 10,* 786-792.

Williams, K. C., & Spiro, R. L. (1985). Communication style in the salesperson-customer dyad. *Journal of Marketing Research, 22,* 434-442.

Wills, T. A. (1987). Help-seeking as a coping mechanism. In C. R. Snyder & C. E. Ford (Eds.), *Coping with negative life events: Clinical and psychological perspectives* (pp. 19-50). New York: Plenum.

Wiseman, J. P. (1979, April). Close encounters of the quasi-primary kind: Sociability in urban second hand clothing stores. *Urban Life, 8,* 23-51.

Zurcher, L. A. (1979, January). The airline passenger: Protection of self in an encapsulated group. *Qualitative Sociology,* pp. 77-99.

CHAPTER EIGHT

Linking Customer Satisfaction to
Service Operations and Outcomes

RUTH N. BOLTON

JAMES H. DREW

GTE Laboratories Incorporated

Organizations have traditionally managed services by manipulating engineering and operational attributes and observing market outcomes. In recent years, customer satisfaction ratings have become an important component in this process. Hence, managers are keenly interested in the effect of service changes on customer satisfaction, customer behavior, and revenues. This chapter develops a framework that describes the theoretical relationships among service operations, customer assessments, and market outcomes. It also discusses the methodological and managerial issues that tend to arise during an investigation of these relationships. Three case studies offer models of aggregate customer complaint behavior, perceived service quality, and customer satisfaction with a specific service encounter. These illustrate how the effects of service changes can be examined by estimating statistical models based on company records and survey data. The advantages and disadvantages of different approaches are outlined.

Organizations have traditionally managed service delivery processes by manipulating "objective" features that are typically measured by engineering or operational records, such as the answer time of customer service representatives, repair clearing intervals, minutes of system downtime, and noise metallic readings on telephone cables. These measures share one characteristic in common: They are calculated by machinery and staff situated within the organization. As such, they can be described

173

as "internal" measures of the service delivery process. This nomenclature distinguishes them from "external" measures that originate from customers, such as satisfaction or complaint data, purchase transactions, sales volume, and revenues.

Initial customer satisfaction efforts by many service organizations tend to focus on tracking customer survey ratings over time or benchmarking them against competitors' ratings. Customer satisfaction ratings become, in effect, a goal in their own right. However, when organizations attempt to incorporate the "voice of the customer" into the service delivery process, they quickly discover a need for diagnostic information that predicts how service changes will affect customer satisfaction, revenues, and profits. Customer satisfaction ratings become one element in a loop that links service operations and outcomes, as shown in Figure 8.1. Consequently, organizations have become interested in the relationship between service operations, primarily characterized by internal measures, and market outcomes, which are primarily characterized by external measures.

Managers have become interested in the relationships between internal and external measures because they would like to: (a) *predict* how service changes will affect customer satisfaction and (ultimately) revenues or profits, (b) *diagnose* low customer ratings, or (c) use customer ratings to *evaluate* the effectiveness of personnel and organizational units. For example, suppose a service organization surveys customers and finds that perceived waiting time has an important influence on customer satisfaction ratings (e.g., Clemmer & Schneider, 1989). The manager of a customer service center is likely to ask the following kinds of questions: Will a decrease in average answer time (i.e., the average number of times the telephone rings before a representative answers) decrease average *perceived* waiting time? If not, what will be the impact of altering other features of the service delivery process, such as the speed of the computerized order entry system? How will these changes affect customer satisfaction ratings, costs, and revenues?

In this chapter, we discuss how customer assessments of services can be linked to service operations and outcomes. In the first section, we develop a theoretical framework by addressing the following questions:

1. What are the key constructs that characterize customer assessments of services?

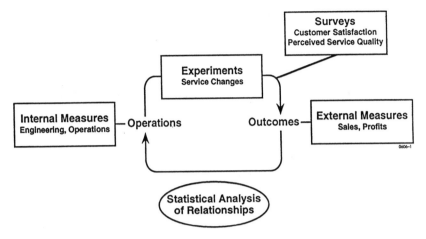

Figure 8.1. Customer Satisfaction Loop

2. What are the antecedents of customer assessments of services?
3. How should key constructs, such as customer satisfaction and service quality, be measured?
4. What are the relationships among customer perceptions, customer dis/ satisfaction, perceived service quality and value, customer purchase intentions, and loyalty?
5. What are the linkages between service operations and customer assessments of services?
6. What are the linkages between customer assessments of services, purchase behavior, and revenues?

In the second section, we discuss how this theoretical framework can be applied to practical problems. Three case studies are described: a model of aggregate customer complaint behavior, a model of perceived service quality, and a model of customer satisfaction with a specific service encounter. These examples illustrate how the links among customer assessments of services, service operations, and outcomes can be investigated by estimating the statistical relationships among internal and external measures. The strengths and weaknesses of different approaches are discussed.

Theoretical Framework

Conceptualization of Customer Assessments of Services

Most research in services marketing has relied on two key constructs to characterize customer assessments of services: customer satisfaction and perceived service quality. Research on customer satisfaction/dissatisfaction (CS/D) has focused on customer assessment of a *specific transaction* involving a product or service (Holbrook & Corfman, 1985; Oliver, 1981; Olshavsky, 1985). In contrast, research on service quality has examined customer assessment of the *overall excellence* or superiority of a service (Zeithaml, 1988). However, CS/D and customer attitudes about services are intrinsically related. In a dynamic framework, customer satisfaction with a specific service encounter depends on preexisting or contemporaneous attitudes about service quality (Anderson & Sullivan, 1993; Cronin & Taylor, 1992; Oliver, 1977) and customer post-usage attitudes depend on satisfaction (Bitner, 1990; Bolton & Drew, 1992; Oliver, 1980). These relationships have been explained by a variety of theories (Oliver, 1981; Inman & Dyer, 1992).

Perceived service value and purchase intentions are useful constructs to link customer assessments of services to their purchase behavior—and ultimately company revenues. Several studies find that consumer satisfaction is positively related to repurchase intentions (e.g., Anderson & Sullivan, 1993; Bearden & Teel, 1983; Oliver, 1980; Oliver & Swan, 1989a). Both Bitner's (1990) travel story experiment and Cronin and Taylor's (1992) survey research showed that service encounter satisfaction *and* perceived service quality are positively related to behavioral intentions. Bolton and Drew's (1992) study of small business customers indicated that perceived service value is positively related to behavioral intentions. LaBarbera and Mazursky's (1983) longitudinal study supports the role of satisfaction in influencing purchase intentions *and* behavior.

Application Issues. Companies typically link customer assessments to service operations and outcomes through programs that track average customer ratings on key survey questions over time. In this context, the conceptualization of the above constructs—particularly the subtle distinction between CS/D and perceived service quality—can be useful (if somewhat confusing) to managers. For example, because CS/D focuses on a specific transaction, customer satisfaction measures tend to be sensitive to service changes. Hence, if the goal of the program is to detect the effects of service improvements or failures in a timely fashion, managers should track customer satisfaction and its ingredients. (Managers have found control charts useful in tracking how company actions have impacted survey ratings.) In contrast, attitudes about service quality tend to change slowly over time (Bolton & Drew, 1991a). Hence, if the goal is to compare the performance of different organizational units—where employee compensation or incentives may be tied to changes in results—managers should probably track perceived service quality or a less volatile index.

Antecedents of Customer Assessments of Services

CS/D is considered to be a function of disconfirmation arising from discrepancies between prior expectations and actual performance (Cardozo, 1965; Oliver, 1977, 1980; Olshavsky & Miller, 1972; Olson & Dover, 1976). Favorable disconfirmation (when performance exceeds expectations) can positively affect satisfaction. Expectations and perceptions of performance levels can affect CS/D directly, as well as indirectly via subjective disconfirmation (Oliver, 1980, 1989; Tse & Wilton, 1988). Other antecedents of CS/D with products or services are customer attributions about unexpected events (e.g., Bitner, 1990; Folkes, 1984), their perceptions about the fairness (i.e., equity) of the exchange process (e.g., Huppertz, Arenson, & Evans, 1978; Oliver & DeSarbo, 1988; Oliver & Swan, 1989a,b), mood or affect (e.g., Westbrook, 1987), and usage frequency and situation (Ram & Jung, 1991).

Oliver (1989) argues that there are at least five different consumption modes that give rise to satisfaction. Different affect descriptions are appropriate for different modes, and different antecedents operate for different modes. The latter notion is consistent with studies that indicate that expectations, performance evaluations, and subjective disconfirmation do not necessarily have independent, additive effects for every product and service (e.g., Churchill & Surprenant, 1982). For example, customer expectations about continuing services, such as public utilities, may be passive.

Parasuraman, Zeithaml, and Berry (1985, 1988) conceptualized perceived service quality as a "gap," similar to disconfirmation, between expectations and perceptions of performance. In their framework, word-of-mouth communications, personal needs, past experience, and external communications influence expectations or perceptions of performance; expectations and perceptions of performance indirectly affect perceived service quality via the gap. More recently, Cronin and Taylor's (1992) empirical work supports an attitude-based conceptualization of service quality in which perceived service quality depends on customer perceptions of performance rather than the gap between perceptions and expectations about performance. They note that some models of service quality are primarily performance based and closely akin to conventional multiattribute models (Wilkie & Pessemier, 1973).

Antecedent Issues. Researchers do not entirely understand how various antecedents, such as expectations, affect customer assessments. Two common conceptualizations of expectations are normative expectations, the customer's standard for the evoked set of competitive alternatives (Woodruff, Cadotte, & Jenkins, 1983), and predictive expectations, the customer's probabilistic assessment of the focal service's attributes. Although there is some agreement about the measurement of predictive expectations (e.g., Oliver, 1981), the measurement of normative expectations poses certain problems.

As customers are likely to bring different frames of reference to different consumption situations, different (and multiple) conceptualizations of expectations may be appropriate for different service contexts (e.g., Barbeau, 1985; Boulding, Kalra, Staelin, & Zeithaml, 1993; Tse & Wilton, 1988). Further, Woodruff et al. (1983) suggest that the customer's subjective disconfirmation may only operate when perceived performance lies outside a "zone of indifference." Attributions about "unexpected" service successes/failures might operate similarly (Oliver, 1989). The observation that expectations are difficult to operationalize and that antecedents may be passive in certain consumption modes may explain why certain models of CS/D and service quality have been primarily performance based.

Measurement of Key Constructs

Marketing conceptualizations of CS/D and service quality critically affect their measurement. Survey items cannot distinguish between these two constructs simply by asking customers questions that include either the word "satisfaction" or "quality" (see Oliver, 1993). In fact, certain conflicting empirical results can be reconciled by examining the different measures used in different studies.

Measures of CS/D should elicit the customer's evaluation of a specific transaction—not a global evaluation of a service organization or process. In other words, the survey question should refer to the customer's specific, personal experience with a service. As satisfaction is a summary psychological state that soon decays (Oliver, 1980), the *timing* of the measurement should be soon after the transaction. As it is considered to be an evaluation of an emotional experience (Hunt, 1977), more affective measures may be appropriate. Researchers have used a variety of "satisfied/dissatisfied" scales. Westbrook (1980) argues for a delighted/terrible scale. When multiple measures of CS/D are desirable, Likert or semantic differential scale items have higher reliabilities and convergent and discriminant validities than other satisfaction scales (Oliver, 1980; Westbrook & Oliver, 1981). Different scale items may be appropriate for different service contexts (Oliver, 1989).

Because perceived service quality is conceptualized as the customer's attitude about the excellence of a service, many researchers have relied on a single overall quality question with a poor/excellent scale. The identification of multiple measures of perceived service quality have turned out to be more problematic. Parasuraman et al. (1988) suggested a multi-item scale called SERVQUAL, but the five underlying dimensions of service quality identified in their research have not been found reliably in other service contexts (e.g., Cronin & Taylor, 1992). Because different service dimensions are relevant in different industries, it is incumbent upon the manager or researcher to develop multiple scale items to adequately capture a particular study context.

Application Issues. Numerous practical issues beset field studies designed to link customer assessments to service operations and outcomes. First, the design of a CS/D or service quality questionnaire must accommodate certain corporate realities. Managers control the engineering and operations attributes of the service delivery process, such as staffing and response speed, whereas customer perceptions of service attributes are benefit oriented, such as "courteous representatives" and "easy to do business with." Managers typically would like to be able to link attributes, such as the signal-to-noise ratio on a telephone line, to customer perceptions of (say) sound quality. Because most companies are (as yet) unable to link engineering/operations attributes to customer perceptions of services through statistical models, managers tend to prefer survey items that reflect specific attributes. Hence, the wording of specific questions tends to reflect a compromise between language that is meaningful to customers and language that seems actionable to managers.

Second, the entire survey design must minimize total survey error (Assael & Keon, 1982). This goal entails obtaining cooperation from a representative sample of customers, maintaining respondent interest to elicit high quality responses, and so forth. Within the constraints imposed by the method of survey administration (mail, phone, personal interview) and the design (particularly length and structure) of the questionnaire, it may not be possible to obtain multiple measures of all key customer assessment constructs, perceptual ratings of relevant service process attributes, and respondent classification information. As a result, it may be necessary to measure certain constructs with global measures or indices—and these can be difficult to operationalize.

Relationships Among Customer Assessments of Services

Marketing's theoretical models of customer assessments of services have become increasingly sophisticated. Figure 8.2 depicts the structural relationships described in the preceding paragraphs. This structural model is characterized by a system of relationships, with simultaneous linkages, including reciprocal causation. In particular, there seems to be a simultaneous relationship between CS/D with a service encounter and pre- and posttransaction attitudes about service quality. These causal links are difficult to trace except in rare, longitudinal studies. Hence, the relationship between CS/D and perceived service quality has yet to be completely resolved (Anderson & Sullivan, 1993; Bitner, 1990; Cronin & Taylor, 1992; Oliver, 1993).

In general, there is an underlying tension between structural models of CS/D, which tend to capture the richness of customers' cognitive processes, and structural models of service quality, which tend to reflect (via customer perceptions) a rich set of service attributes. Because these two constructs are related, *reduced form* models of CS/D and perceived service quality may appear to be very similar—a frustrating situation for an empirical researcher. However, certain variables (e.g., perceptions of particular attributes) may affect CS/D, but not perceived quality, or vice versa. Further, the coefficients (i.e., importance weights) of the predictor variables will certainly be different. Hence, although reduced form models of CS/D and perceived quality may be similar, they will *not* be identical.

The links between customer assessments of services, service operations, and outcomes can be investigated by estimating the statistical relationships among internal and external measures. Although Figure 8.2 does not depict any measurement relationships, it does give some indication of the scope of the estimation problem. Because the model includes simultaneous structural relationships, simple estimation methods such as ordinary least squares may not be appropriate. If each construct has a

Figure 8.2. Links Among Customer Assessments, Service Operations, and Outcomes

single measure, simultaneous equation methods, such as two-stage least squares (Johnston, 1972), can be utilized (e.g., Bolton & Drew, 1991a,b). If some constructs have multiple measures, path analysis (e.g., Bitner, 1990) or structural equation modeling (e.g., Cronin & Taylor, 1992; Oliver & Swan, 1989a) are suitable.

Drew and Bolton (1991) have documented the existence of survey effects (e.g., question order) that can potentially confound the estimation of structural relationships. Because it is not always feasible to modify the survey structure to remove these effects, their results imply that the researcher must account for relatively complicated measurement relationships in order to obtain unbiased estimates of the structural parameters linking CS/D, perceived service quality, and their antecedents or consequences. For example, when certain measures share common scales, it may be necessary to introduce a method factor(s) in Figure 8.2. A final complication arises if the researcher believes that most measurement scales have ordinal rather than interval properties. In this circumstance, robust estimation methods that do not require strong distributional assumptions, such as partial least squares (e.g., Fornell & Bookstein, 1982), may be preferred over maximum likelihood estimation of structural equation models (e.g., as embodied in LISREL). Alternatively, the researcher might consider transforming the data to better match distributional assumptions.

Links Between Service Attributes and Customer Assessments

If managers desire to enhance customer satisfaction and service quality, they need to understand how service features affect customer assessments. The overall relationship between product/service features and affect is typically investigated using conjoint analysis (Green & Wind, 1975), quality function deployment (Hauser & Clausing, 1988), or other decompositional techniques. However, these techniques are more suitable for investigating new product/service design issues than for describing how complex features of an existing service delivery process affect customer assessments of service.

The linkage between service features and customer assessments of services can be considered a two-stage process (Brunswick, 1952; Holbrook, 1981). "The first link in the chain represents the psychophysical relationships between product features and subjective attribute perceptions, whereas the second link represents the . . . impact of attribute perceptions on affect" (Holbrook, 1981, p. 14). Numerous studies have used compositional techniques, particularly multiattribute attitude models, to investigate the second link, namely how perceptions influence affect (e.g., Crosby & Stephens, 1987). In contrast, there are only a few studies that focus on the link between features and perceptions. They include research that relates service attributes to customers' perceptions of outpatient health services (Neslin, 1983), educational services (Chapman & Jackson, 1987), and so forth (e.g., Louviere, 1988), as well as research that relates product features to subjective perceptions (e.g., Hauser & Simmie, 1981; Narasimhan & Sen, 1990).

Different theories have been proposed to explain the influence of service features in terms of customer-employee (Oliver & Swan, 1989b;

Solomon, Surprenant, Czepiel & Gutman, 1985) and customer-environment interactions (Bitner, 1992). Laboratory experiments have focused on constructs that mediate between service features and CS/D with service encounters, such as personalization strategies (Surprenant & Solomon, 1987) and perceived control (Hui & Bateson, 1991). Bolton and Drew (1991a) conducted a longitudinal analysis of a field experiment that directly related a change in service features (upgrading of plant and equipment) to customer perceptions and attitudes about service quality. In a survey-based approach, Bitner, Booms, and Tetreault (1990) use the critical incident method to study how customers distinguish satisfactory/unsatisfactory service encounters.

Application Issues. Managers are frequently interested in how internal measures are related to customer perceptions. To estimate appropriate descriptive models, it is necessary to create a data base that "matches" company records concerning service features with customer survey data describing customers' perceptions and assessments of their service. Records can be matched at the level of the organizational unit (e.g., retail outlet) or at the level of the individual customer. The goals of the study will determine whether cross-sectional or time series data are appropriate.

Ideally, company records should contain information at the individual customer level that is relevant to the customer's experiences. Internal measures are recorded for a variety of reasons—to satisfy government regulations, to evaluate employees, to facilitate production or accounting processes, and so forth—which may not be meaningfully related to customer concerns. In addition, the reporting period used in company records should match a customer's specific service encounters. In some service industries, such as financial services, the matching process is reasonably straightforward. In others, appropriate company records may not exist, or they may be virtually impossible to access.

The preceding discussion has assumed that operations affect customer assessments of services (attributes → assessments), but this causal flow can be reversed. Managers may respond to customer feedback by manipulating certain engineering or operational measures. For example, companies do not randomly allocate repair resources: they disproportionately allocate them to troubled areas. In this situation, conventional statistical analysis is inappropriate because the "natural" causal flow has been confounded by feedback effects (assessments → attributes). Simultaneous equation methods may be necessary to disentangle these reciprocal effects. Alternatively, *controlled* field experiments are a useful approach to investigating how internal measures are related to customer perceptions. An experimental manipulation of one or more features may be necessary when there is insufficient variation in the data or a confounding of service features.

Links Between Customer Assessments and Service Outcomes

Companies are interested in enhancing customer satisfaction and service quality because they are convinced that (in the long run) these activities will lead to increased revenues and profits. This conviction is supported by a small number of studies that show that higher levels of customer satisfaction and quality are associated with market success (e.g., Buzzell & Gale, 1987, p. 107; Lele & Sheth, 1987, pp. 35-36). For example, in a recent study that combined national customer satisfaction surveys with business performance data, Anderson, Fornell, and Lehmann (1992) found that customer satisfaction and perceived quality have a positive impact on market share and profitability. In addition, customer satisfaction is related to industry characteristics.

Surprisingly, there are very few studies that relate individual customers' assessments of services to behavioral outcomes. A stream of research with the CS/D literature examines how satisfaction and attitudes are related to customer complaining behavior and (ultimately) retention rates (e.g., Bearden & Teel, 1983; Fornell & Wernerfelt, 1987; Halstead & Droge, 1991; Singh, 1988). However, studies that relate customer assessments to actual purchase behavior are rare. In a study of grocery products, LaBarbera and Mazursky (1983) found it difficult to predict repurchase behavior from CS/D variables without incorporating consumers' prior experience with the brand. Because customer satisfaction had a weak effect on behavior, they speculated that situational variables, such as coupons and promotions, were affecting the purchase decisions. In a services marketing context, Rust and Zahorik (1992) applied a mathematical framework that links customer perceptions, satisfaction, retention rates, and market share in a study of banking customers.

Application Issues. There has been very little research that examines how individual customers' assessments are related to their behavior and (consequently) company revenues/profits. A variety of behavioral or market outcomes could be studied, including complaint behavior, purchase behavior, and customer loyalty. For example, it could be useful to investigate whether higher levels of perceived quality (as measured by customer survey data) are associated with savings because of decreases in rework and decreases in customers' invocations of guarantees and warranties. Because companies usually maintain purchase records, it should be possible to link internal measures of customer behaviors to external measures of CS/D and perceived quality using descriptive models. In addition, laboratory or field experiments—similar to the aforementioned studies linking service operations to customer assessments—could be used to study the relationship between customer assessments of services, customer behaviors, and company revenues. Unfortunately, services, unlike products, pose some unique problems. For example, many services, such as financial services and utilities, entail continuous relationships characterized by a variety of discrete service encounters.

Applications

Prior research has focused on the relationships *among* constructs that describe customer assessments of services, particularly CS/D, perceived service quality, and customer perceptions. This section describes three case studies of how customer assessments of services were linked to service operations or outcomes. All three examples concern services provided by GTE Telephone Operations—that is, local call provision, long distance access, operator services, customer services (e.g., installation, repair, and service changes), and billing services.

Case Study 1: A Model of Aggregate Customer Dissatisfaction

In the absence of a CS/D program, organizations can exploit company records to investigate how service operations affect customers' assessments of services. At a minimum, their investigation requires aggregate statistics based on internal measures of service attributes and outcomes. For example, the telephone company conducts physical tests of its lines and cables on a systematic basis. It records the percentage of lines passing/failing these tests each month in each geographic region. Due to public utilities commission requirements, it also records the number of trouble reports by customers each month in each region.

Using these data, it is possible to model customer dissatisfaction, described by an external measure, namely trouble reports, as a function of service features described by internal records of line tests. The structural model can be described algebraically as follows:

(1) DISSATISFACTION = f(FEATURES, GEOGRAPHY, TREND)

DISSATISFACTION is measured by TROUBLE reports per region per month. Service FEATURES are represented by a vector of two variables representing the percentage of telephone lines passing two different tests (TEST1 and TEST2). GEOGRAPHY differences are captured by dummy variables (STATE1 and STATE2), and any TREND over time is captured by an index variable that represents the month.

Using data describing trouble reports and telephone line tests for three states over a 24-month period (i.e., $N = 72$), the company operationalized Equation (1) as a linear additive model, estimated it with ordinary least squares and obtained the following results:

(2)   TROUBLE = 32.17 + 2.56 STATE1 + 0.31 STATE2 −
          26.92 TEST1 − 0.30 TEST2 − 0.04 TREND.

As expected for an aggregate level analysis, the explanatory power of this equation is reasonably good; the R^2 is 0.60. Each coefficient was different from zero and statistically significant ($p < .05$). The results indicate: (a) there are differences in the aggregate number of trouble reports across geographic regions, (b) trouble reports are substantially lower in states where telephone lines typically pass TEST1, (c) trouble reports are somewhat lower in where telephone lines typically pass TEST2, and (d) trouble reports decreased slightly over time. Note that the implications for organizational action are relatively straightforward. Because CS/D is strongly related to the percentage of lines passing TEST1, managers should focus on improvements to telephone lines so that they meet TEST1 standards.

Discussion. From a managerial perspective, this model is simple, yet powerful. Nevertheless, it provokes as many questions as it answers due to several limitations: (a) the dependent variable is a relatively narrow measure of DISSATISFACTION, namely complaint behavior; (b) the independent variables consist of a limited number of service features that are potential dissatisfiers, rather than satisfiers; (c) referring to Figure 8.2, it can be seen that Equation (1) is a reduced form model that omits the mediating role of cognitive variables, such as customer perceptions and disconfirmation (hence, the model can give little insight into customers' evaluative processes); (d) each construct (e.g., dissatisfaction, service features) is measured by a single indicator; (e) trouble reports can't be linked to outcome variables, such as revenues, so managers cannot conduct a cost-benefit analysis of potential telephone line improvements; and (f) despite the intriguing results shown above, aggregation may mask statistical relationships between constructs.

Case Study 2: A Model of the Customer's Perceptions of Quality

Models based on individual level data overcome some of the aforementioned shortcomings. The second case study illustrates how individual level data can be used to develop a model of the perceived quality of local telephone service. Based on Figure 8.2, the model describes customers' post-usage evaluation of the overall QUALITY of telephone service as a function of their DIS/SATISFACTION with recent telephone service and their PERCEPTIONS of performance, after controlling for INDIVIDUAL differences. Algebraically:

(3)   QUALITY = g(DIS/SATISFACTION,
            PERCEPTIONS, INDIVIDUAL)

The telephone company obtained the data to operationalize this model by matching customer records from three different sources. The telephone company routinely surveys a probability sample of its customers and asks them their perceptions of service attributes and their evaluation of overall quality. To operationalize Equation (3), it matched survey data from 293 customers contacted during February 1988 with billing records and repair records. The billing records described each subscriber's purchase history, including length of service, current and late or delinquent bill amounts, and so on. The repair records described each subscriber's service history, including the date and nature of any service problems.

The dependent variable in Equation (3), QUALITY, was measured with a question tracked by the survey questionnaire: "How would you rate the overall quality of services provided by your local telephone company? Would you say: poor . . . excellent?" The independent variables were operationalized by the measures shown in Table 8.1. Note that many of the measures originate from the customer, although they are stored in the company's billing and repair records. Then, Equation (3) was specified as a linear additive model and estimated with ordinary least squares. The R^2 is 0.27 and the coefficient estimates are displayed in the last column of Table 8.1. (If the dependent variable is treated as nominal rather than interval scaled and Equation (3) is estimated with logistic regression procedures, the results are substantially the same.)

TABLE 8.1   Operationalization of a Model of the Customer's Perceptions of Quality

Construct	Measures	Coefficient
DIS/SATISFACTION	REPORTED: Trouble reported by the customer within the past 90 days (Dichotomous variable, YES = 1)	−0.38***
	UNREPORTED: Trouble recalled, but not reported, by the customer within the past 90 days (Dichotomous variable, YES = 1)	-0.32***
	REPORTED90: Trouble reported by the customer more than 90 days ago (Dichotomous variable, YES = 1)	0.26**
PERCEPTIONS	LOCAL: Customer report of whether the telephone line was out of service (Dichotomous variable, NO = 1)	−0.42***
	LONG: Customer rating of long distance telephone service (POOR = 1, . . . , EXCELLENT = 4)	0.37***
	BILL: Customer rating of billing service (POOR = 1, EXCELLENT = 4)	0.20**
INDIVIDUAL	REVIEW: Customer report of whether he/she pays or reviews the bill (Dichotomous variable, YES = 1)	0.49**
	LENGTH: Indicator of whether customer has had service for more than 15 years (Dichotomous variable, YES = 1)	−0.10

***$p < .001$; **$p < .05$; *$p < .15$; intercept = 2.30.

Consistent with prior research, the results show that customers' post-usage evaluations of overall quality depend on their satisfaction with recent service and their perceptions of performance attributes. Although perceptions of performance account for a large percentage of the explained variance, customer dis/satisfaction also plays a significant role, accounting for 25% of the explained variance in perceived quality. Surprisingly, customers' perceptions of local service performance (LOCAL) seem to have a negative impact on perceived service quality. This result is explained by the fact that perceptions of local service were measured by an indicator variable that took on the value of one if the telephone line had *not* been reported out of service. Customers may not "blame" the telephone company for out-of-service trouble because the cause of the trouble is typically outside the company's control and the company is highly responsive to out-of-service problems; as a result, the customer evaluates the repair outcome positively. These notions are consistent with current theories about customer attributions concerning unexpected events. Interestingly, the impact of reported and unreported trouble on perceived service quality is about the same. Unreported problems (e.g., static on the line, call blockages) tend to be less disruptive than reported problems (e.g., line out of service), but they are more difficult for the organization to correct. Hence, this result implies that the telephone company should consider allocating more resources to these less disruptive, but highly dissatisfying, service problems. In addition, as suggested by Fornell and Wernerfelt (1987), the company could encourage complaint behavior so that such service problems can be resolved.

Discussion. This example illustrates some of the advantages of individual level models utilizing internal and external measures. First, the company gained considerable insights by estimating a structural model in which perceived quality depended on mediating cognitive variables, such as satisfaction and perceptions. As a result, it learned that customers seem to attach more weight to "minor" service problems than managers anticipated. Second, the results were considered actionable by managers because the cognitive variables were operationalized by attribute-specific measures. Customer dis/satisfaction was measured by trouble report records that managers could link directly to specific engineering or operational failures. Third, internal and external measures are useful complements, particularly when customers are unable to provide accurate information about certain aspects of the service delivery process, such as the nature of service problem.

There are also certain difficulties in developing individual models operationalized by internal and external measures. First, company records may not contain measures of certain constructs. In this example, billing records did not show itemized charges for specific services (e.g., local calls, custom calling services). Hence, it wasn't possible to model the link between purchase behavior and perceived service quality. Second, when external measures are required of key cognitive variables, surveys must be specially designed (or temporarily modified) to measure them. The survey questionnaire was primarily designed to measure customer perceptions and perceived service quality (suitable for a multi-attribute model), rather than the cognitive antecedents of CS/D with a specific encounter. Consequently, there was no information available about customer attributions concerning out-of-service problems. Third, internal measures may not exactly correspond with theoretical constructs. In this study, customer dis/satisfaction was measured with three dichotomous indicators reflecting complaint behavior rather than the external measures suggested in the CS/D literature. Fourth, like external measures, internal measures can be error prone. For example, repair center staff may code service problems incorrectly.

Case Study 3: A Model of the Customer's Satisfaction With a Repair Encounter

In this study, the telephone company created a very rich data base by matching external and internal measures that described a probability sample of repair service encounters in one operating region over a 13-month period (April 1990-April 1991). External measures were obtained from a survey of residential telephone customers who had called the repair office in the previous 30 days. These survey responses were matched with company records that described the repair problem (e.g., can't call out, can't hear), the cause (e.g., customer, company employee), and how it was resolved (e.g., repair to wall jack)—using over 50 specialized codes. The matching process yielded 1847 observations.

Based on Figure 8.2, customers' SATISFACTION with repair service is positively related to favorable perceptions of the company's performance of the repair, favorable subjective DISCONFIRMATION, and favorable ATTRIBUTIONS about events in the repair process. Research concerning service performance has focused on customers' perceptions of EMPLOYEE role performance, their perceptions of CONTROL and their perception of the company's personalization strategies. Hence, three types of perceptions of performance are represented separately in the structural model. Algebraically:

(4)   SATISFACTION = h(EMPLOYEE, CONTROL,
        PERSONALIZATION, DISCONFIRMATION, ATTRIBUTIONS)

where:

(5)   CONTROL = h_1(SERVICE ATTRIBUTES)

(6)   PERSONALIZATION = h_2(SERVICE ATTRIBUTES)

(7)   ATTRIBUTIONS = h_3(SERVICE ATTRIBUTES)

Although it is desirable to estimate the complete structural model (Equations 4-7), external measures of perceived control, perceived personalization, and attributions were not available. Hence, a reduced form model was obtained by substituting Equations (5)-(7) into Equation (4) as follows:

(8)   SATISFACTION = j(EMPLOYEE,
DISCONFIRMATION, SERVICE ATTRIBUTES)

The dependent variable in Equation (8), SATISFACTION, was measured with a question tracked by the repair survey: "Considering your repair service in total, that is, from the time the trouble was reported until now, how would you rate the way the repair was handled? Would you say: poor . . . excellent?" The independent variables were operationalized by the external and internal measures shown in Table 8.2. For example, the customer's perceptions of different employees' PERFORMANCE were directly measured by survey ratings (CALL-REP, CENTER-REP, and REPWORK). Dummy variables (CALL and CENTER) are used to capture differences between customer-employee encounters that took place over the telephone versus encounters that took place at a repair center.

Unfavorable DISCONFIRMATION concerning the company's response time is measured by the number of REPEAT calls to the repair center; favorable disconfirmation is measured by the customer's report of whether the repair was done when promised (DONEPROM).

The remaining independent variables in Equation (8) are selected by considering how perceived control, perceived personalization, and attributions are related to service features. Customers' satisfaction is positively related to higher levels of perceived control (Hui & Bateson, 1991). In this study, perceived control of the repair process is considered to decrease with the company's response time, where the effect varies depending on the nature of the problem. For example, perceived control is likely to be low when the telephone is "dead" (because the customer can't call out) and repair times are slow. Thus, the customer's perceived CONTROL is represented by two interaction terms describing service attributes; these terms are created by multiplying a dummy variable indicating the nature of the service disruption by the *actual* amount of time that elapsed between when the problem was reported and when it was resolved (i.e.,

TABLE 8.2   Operationalization of a Model of the Customer's Satisfaction With a Repair Encounter

Construct	Measure	Coefficient
EMPLOYEE	CALL: Customer's report of whether he/she telephoned the repair center (YES = 1).	−4.0134***
	CALL-REP: Customer's rating of the service received when he/she reported the problem over the telephone (POOR = 1, . . . , EXCELLENT = 4)	+1.1204***
	CENTER: Customer's report of whether he/she visited the repair center (YES = 1)	−5.6556***
	CENTER-REP: Customer's rating of the service received when he/she reported the problem at the repair center (POOR = 1, . . . , EXCELLENT = 4)	+1.6106**
	REPWORK: Customer's rating of the repair work that took place after he/she reported the problem (POOR = 1, . . . , EXCELLENT = 4)	+1.9661***
CONTROL	DEAD*TIME: Repair trouble code indicating that the telephone line was dead (YES = 1, multiplied by repair time (in hours)	−0.0113 **
	OTHER*TIME: Repair trouble code indicating any other problem, such as noise on the line (YES = 1, multiplied by repair time (in hours)	−0.0048

DEAD*TIME and OTHER*TIME). It is hypothesized that satisfaction levels will be negatively related to DEAD*TIME and OTHER*TIME. As discussed above, the absolute magnitude of the DEAD*TIME coefficient is likely to be larger than the other two coefficients.

Customer satisfaction has been found to be positively related to higher levels of customized personalization (Surprenant & Solomon, 1987). In this study, customer perceptions of the extent of customized personalization of the repair process were hypothesized to depend on whether a date/time was given when the trouble would be corrected and whether a repair person visited the premises. It was expected that perceived personalization would be higher when either of these attributes were present. These attributes were measured by customer reports (GIVETIME, VISIT), rather than internal

TABLE 8.2   Continued

Construct	Measure	Coefficient
PERSONALIZATION	GIVETIME: Customer report of whether he/she was told a date or time when the trouble would be corrected (Dichotomous variable, YES = 1)	−0.0760
	VISIT: Customer report of whether a repair person visited the premises (Dichotomous variable, YES = 1)	+0.3473***
DISCONFIRMATION	REPEAT: Company records of the number of times the customer contacted the repair office about the problem	−0.3266***
	DONEPROM: Customer report of whether the work was completed when promised (Dichotomous variable, YES = 1)	+0.5427***
ATTRIBUTION	CUSTOMER: Repair cause code indicating that the problem was due to the customer, such customer leaving the handset off the hook (YES = 1)	+0.6169*
	PHYSICAL: Repair trouble code indicating that the problem was physical and (consequently) might be observed by the customer (YES = 1)	+0.4550**

NOTES: ***p <.001; **p < .05; *p < .15; intercept = -6.7274.

measures. Hence, it is hypothesized that satisfaction will be positively related to GIVETIME and VISIT.

Last, customers' satisfaction has been shown to depend on their attributions about the locus of responsibility for the problem, whether the cause was perceived to be within the company's control, and whether the cause is likely to recur (e.g., Bitner, 1990). Satisfaction with the repair process is hypothesized to be higher when customers consider that they (rather than the company) are responsible for the problem (CUSTOMER). Unlike network or central office failures, physical equipment failures (e.g., customer premise equipment, jacks, telephone lines) are readily observable by the customer—with the possibility of external explanations for the failure (e.g., weather, construction work). Hence, customers are likely to attribute less control to the company and to believe that the problem is rare. Hence, it is hypothesized that satisfaction will be higher for PHYSICAL causes than for other causes.

For estimation purposes, the dependent variable was treated as nominally scaled by recoding it to take the value one when the customer rated service as excellent and zero otherwise. The functional form of Equation (8) was specified to be linear additive. Then, the model was estimated using logistic regression procedures (i.e., maximum likelihood estimation). The coefficient estimates are displayed in the last column of Table 8.2.

Managers can draw a rich set of implications from these results. As expected, satisfaction is positively related to perceptions about performance and disconfirmation. In fact, the impact of disconfirmation, as indicated by REPEAT calls to the repair office, is substantial. More notably, satisfaction decreases as repair time increases, where the magnitude of the effect depends on the nature of the repair problem. Graphs were used to illustrate this notion to managers (see Figure 8.3). For example, the percentage of customers giving excellent ratings is significantly lower when the telephone line is dead for an increasing period of time, probably due to lower levels of perceived control over the repair process. (As an aside, customers overestimate actual repair times when the actual time exceeds 24 hours.) Satisfaction levels are also significantly higher when the repair is completed when promised and when it entails a visit to customer premises, probably due to higher levels of perceived personalization of the repair process. Last, satisfaction levels vary depending on the locus of the responsibility for the problem and whether the problem was within the company's control (i.e., nonphysical problems). In general, these results suggest that the telephone company could consider reallocating resources depending on the nature of the service failure. For example, customization (e.g., making an appointment for the repair person's visit) might substitute for rapid response times when a visit to the customer's premises is required.

Discussion. The similarities and differences between Case Studies 2 and 3 illustrate some of the trade-offs researchers face in estimating individual level models with internal and external measures. First, in Case Study 2, the dependent variable is perceived quality of local telephone service, whereas in Case Study 3, the dependent variable is customer satisfaction with repair service. The differences between these two constructs lead to completely different model specifications and (consequently) inferences. Second, Case Study 3 utilized a reduced form model

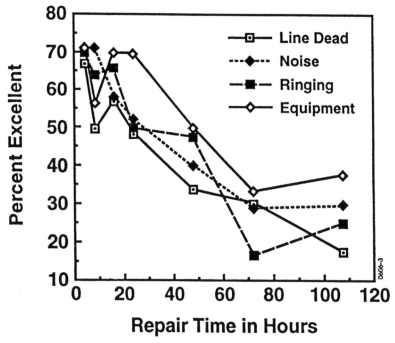

Figure 8.3. Satisfaction Ratings as a Function of the Nature of the Repair Problem and the Repair Time

primarily based on service features instead of a structural model based on cognitive variables. The results suggest that there are significant effects due to the cognitive variables—namely perceived control, perceived personalization, disconfirmation, attributions—under field conditions. Hence, it is clearly important to measure these mediating variables.

Third, organizations frequently fail to measure key cognitive variables, such as customer attributions concerning out-of-service problems. Surveys are usually designed to measure perceptions of performance and CS/D or service quality. Managers prefer perceptual ratings over other cognitive variables because these are useful in evaluating the effectiveness of organizational units and personnel (often a primary goal of quality programs). Specially designed (or temporarily modified) surveys may be necessary to obtain external measures of key cognitive variables. Fourth, because local telephone service is a continuously provided service in a regulated market, it is particularly difficult to identify suitable measures of market outcomes. Hence, the three case studies were unable to link customer assessments to behavior or revenues. As indicated by the paucity of prior research, the links between customer assessments, customer behavior, and revenues are difficult to investigate for many other services as well. Last, researchers are usually willing to assume that their measures have interval properties, but this assumption may not be appropriate. Although prior research has documented the existence of "satisfiers" and "dissatisfiers," few researchers have recognized the implications of this finding for statistical analyses—namely, that it may be necessary to use estimation procedures that do not require interval properties. Note that Case Study 3 did *not* assume that customer ratings of "excellent" and "poor" repair service are a function of the same set of service features, with coefficients of the same magnitude.

Concluding Remarks

Managers are interested in predicting the effect of service changes on customer satisfaction, revenues, and profits. Although market researchers have made substantial progress in understanding the theoretical relationships among customer assessments of services, other relationships are not well understood. For example, longitudinal—rather than cross-sectional—analyses are needed to examine the relationship between customer satisfaction, perceived service quality, and behavioral outcomes. Descriptive studies or field experiments are needed to investigate how service features are linked to customer perceptions and cognitive variables.

There are numerous practical issues associated with designing field studies, such as implementing service changes under controlled conditions, fielding customer surveys with an appropriate domain of questionnaire items, and matching customers' service experiences with appropriate company records describing the delivery process. In addition, as descriptive studies and field experiments address more sophisticated issues, the statistical issues become increasingly complex. Researchers have already begun to recognize the existence of simultaneous relationships among key constructs and to utilize multiple measures of key constructs. In the future, they will also have to account for the fact that internal and external measures may lack interval properties and that they are likely to be characterized by measurement error. However, it seems likely that design issues, rather than statistical issues, will prove more intractable.

There is also a critical need for *comprehensive* models of customer assessments, service operations, and outcomes, that is, models with multiple, structural equations that recognize potentially simultaneous relationships. By necessity, these models must be operationalized with measures of service operations and outcomes from within the organization. Unfortunately, many organizations do not systematically collect relevant internal measures. If they do, it can be very difficult to retrieve and match them at the individual level. Surprisingly, it can be equally difficult (but not infeasible) to measure certain cognitive variables within existing customer satisfaction or quality survey programs. As a result, special data collection efforts, possibly combined with the experimental manipulation of service features, are often required. As a result, field experiments are a particularly attractive approach to investigating how changes in service features affect customer assessments and market outcomes.

This chapter has described how company actions and outcomes are integral parts of a loop designed to improve customer satisfaction and perceived service quality. Many studies have explored isolated relations within this loop, but few, if any, have modeled the entire loop over one or more of its cycles. The description, monitoring, and modeling of the entire loop would be a major advance in the study of customer satisfaction/quality management for services.

References

Anderson, E. W., Fornell, C., & Lehmann, D. R., (1992). *Perceived quality, customer satisfaction, market share and profitability: Evidence from the Swedish National Satisfaction Barometer.* Working paper, University of Michigan.

Anderson, E. W., & Sullivan, M. (1993). The antecedents and consequences of customer satisfaction for firms. *Marketing Science, 12,* 125-143.

Assael, H., & Keon, J. (1982). Nonsampling vs. sampling errors in survey research. *Journal of Marketing, 45,* 114-123.

Barbeau, J. B. (1985). Predictive and normative expectations in consumer satisfaction: A utilization of adaption and comparison Levels in a unified framework. In H. K. Hunt & R. L. Day (Eds.), *Consumer satisfaction, dissatisfaction and complaining behavior* (pp. 27-32). Bloomington: Foundation for the School of Business, Indiana University.

Bearden, W. O., & Teel, J. E. (1983). Selected determinants of consumer satisfaction and complaint reports. *Journal of Marketing Research, 20,* 21-28.

Bitner, M. J. (1990). Evaluating service encounters: The effects of physical surrounding and employee responses. *Journal of Marketing, 54,* 69-82.

Bitner, M. J. (1992). Servicescapes: The impact of physical surroundings on customers and employees. *Journal of Marketing, 56,* 57-71.

Bitner, M. J., Booms, B. M., & Tetreault, M. S. (1990). The service encounter: Diagnosing favorable and unfavorable incidents. *Journal of Marketing, 54,* 71-84.

Bolton, R. N., & Drew, J. H. (1991a). A longitudinal analysis of the impact of service changes on customer attitudes. *Journal of Marketing, 55,* 1-9.

Bolton, R. N., & Drew, J. H. (1991b). A multi-stage model of customers' assessments of service quality and value. *Journal of Consumer Research, 17,* 375-384.

Bolton, R. N., & Drew, J. H. (1992). Mitigating the effect of service encounters. *Marketing Letters, 3,* 57-70.

Boulding, W., Kalra, A., Staelin, R., & Zeithaml, V. A. (1993). A dynamic model of service quality: From expectations to behavioral intentions. *Journal of Marketing Research, 30.* 7-27.

Brunswick, E. (1952). *The conceptual framework of psychology.* Chicago: University of Chicago Press.

Buzzell, R. D., & Gale, B. T. (1987). *The PIMS principles.* New York: Free Press.

Cardozo, R. (1965). An experimental study of customer effort, expectation and satisfaction. *Journal of Marketing Research, 2,* 244-249.

Chapman, R. G., & Jackson, R. (1987). *College choice of academically able students: The influence of no-need financial aid and other factors* (Research Monograph No. 10). New York: College Entrance Examination Board.

Churchill, G. A., Jr., & Surprenant, C. (1982). An investigation into the determinants of customer satisfaction. *Journal of Marketing Research, 19,* 491-504.

Clemmer, E. C., & Schneider, B. (1989). *Toward understanding and controlling customer dissatisfaction with waiting* (Working Paper 89-115). Cambridge, MA: Marketing Science Institute.

Cronin, J. J., Jr., & Taylor, S. A. (1992). Measuring service quality: A reexamination and extension. *Journal of Marketing, 56,* 55-68.

Crosby, L. A., & Stephens, N. J. (1987). Effects of relationship marketing on satisfaction, retention and prices in the life insurance industry. *Journal of Marketing Research, 24,* 404-411.

Drew, J. H., & Bolton, R. N. (1991). The structure of customer satisfaction: The effects of survey measurement. *Journal of Consumer Satisfaction, Dissatisfaction and Complaining Behavior, 4,* 21-31.

Folkes, V. S. (1984). Consumer reactions to product failure: An attributional approach. *Journal of Consumer Research, 10,* 498-509.

Fornell, C., & Bookstein, F. L. (1982). Two structural equation models: LISREL and PLS applied to consumer exit voice theory. *Journal of Marketing Research, 19,* 440-452.

Fornell, C., & Wernerfelt, B. (1987). Defensive marketing strategy by customer complaint management. *Journal of Marketing Research, 24,* 337-346.

Green, P. E., & Wind, Y. (1975). New way to measure consumers' judgments. *Harvard Business Review, 53,* 107-117.

Halstead, D., & Droge, C. (1991). Consumer attitudes toward complaining and the prediction of multiple complaint responses. In R. H. Holman & M. R. Solomon (Eds.), *Advances in consumer research* (Vol. 18, pp. 210-216). Provo, UT: Association for Consumer Research.

Hauser, J. R., & Clausing, D. (1988). The house of quality. *Harvard Business Review, 66,* 63-73.

Hauser, J. R., & Simmie, P. (1981). Profit maximizing perceptual positions: An integrated theory for the selection of product features and price. *Management Science, 27,* 33-56.

Holbrook, M. B. (1981). Integrating compositional and decompositional analyses to represent the intervening role of perceptions in evaluative judgments. *Journal of Marketing Research, 18,* 13-28.

Holbrook, M. B., & Corfman, K. P. (1985). Quality and value in the consumption experience: Phaedrus rides again. In J. Jacoby & J. Olson (Eds.), *Perceived quality* (pp. 31-57), Lexington, MA: Lexington.

Hui, M. K., & Bateson, J.E.G. (1991). Perceived control and the effects of crowding and consumer choice on the service experience. *Journal of Consumer Research, 18,* 174-184.

Hunt, H. K. (1977). CS/D—Overview and future research directions. In H. K. Hunt (Ed.), *Conceptualization and Measurement of Customer Satisfaction and Dissatisfaction* (pp. 455-488). Cambridge, MA: Marketing Science Institute.

Huppertz, J. W., Arenson, S. J., & Evans, R. H. (1978). An application of equity theory to buyer-seller exchange situations. *Journal of Marketing Research, 15,* 250-260.

Inman, J. J., & Dyer, J. S. (1992). *An extended paradigm of consumer satisfaction based on generalized utility theory.* Working paper, University of Southern California.

Johnston, J.(1972). *Econometric methods.* New York: McGraw-Hill.

LaBarbera, P. A., & Mazursky, D. (1983). A longitudinal assessment of consumer satisfaction/dissatisfaction: The dynamic aspect of the cognitive process. *Journal of Marketing Research, 20,* 393-404.

Lele, M. M., & Sheth, J. N. (1987). *The customer is key.* New York: John Wiley.

Louviere, J. J. (1988). *Analyzing decision making: Metric conjoint analysis* (Sage University Paper series on Quantitative Applications in the Social Sciences, 07-067). Newbury Park,CA: Sage.

Narasimhan, C., & Sen, S. (1990). *Linking engineering attributes to perceptual characteristics.* Working paper, Washington University at St. Louis.

Neslin, S. B. (1983). Designing new outpatient health services: Linking service features to subjective consumer perceptions. *Journal of Health Care Marketing, 3,* 8-21.

Oliver, R. L. (1977). Effect of expectation and disconfirmation on postexposure product evaluations: An alternative interpretation. *Journal of Applied Psychology, 62,* 480-486.

Oliver, R. L. (1980). A cognitive model of the antecedents and consequences of satisfaction decisions. *Journal of Marketing Research, 17,* 460-469.

Oliver, R. L. (1981). Measurement and evaluation of satisfaction processes in retail settings. *Journal of Retailing, 57,* 25-48.

Oliver, R. L. (1989). Processing of the satisfaction response in consumption: A suggested framework and research propositions. *Journal of Consumer Satisfaction, Dissatisfaction and Complaining Behavior, 2,* 1-16.

Oliver, R. L. (1993). A conceptual model of service quality and service satisfaction: Compatible goals, different concepts. In T. A. Swartz, D. E. Bowen, & S. W. Brown (Eds.), *Advances in services marketing and management: Research and practice* (Vol. 2, pp. 65-85). Greenwich, CT: JAI.

Oliver, R. L., & DeSarbo, W. S. (1988). Response determinants in satisfaction judgments. *Journal of Consumer Research, 14,* 495-507.

Oliver, R. L., & Swan, J. E. (1989a). Consumer perceptions of interpersonal equity and satisfaction in transactions: A field survey approach. *Journal of Marketing, 53,* 21-35.

Oliver, R. L., & Swan, J. E. (1989b). Equity and disconfirmation perceptions as influences on merchant and product satisfaction. *Journal of Consumer Research, 16,* 372-383.

Olshavsky, R. W. (1985). Perceived quality in consumer decision making: An integrated theoretical perspective. In J. Jacoby & J. Olson (Eds.), *Perceived quality* (pp. 3-29), Lexington, MA: Lexington.

Olshavsky, R. W., & Miller, J. A. (1972). Consumer expectations, product performance and perceived product quality. *Journal of Marketing Research, 9,* 19-21.

Olson, J. C., & Dover, P. (1976). Effects of expectation creation and disconfirmation on belief elements of cognitive structure. In B. B. Anderson (Ed.), *Advances in Consumer Research* (Vol. 3, pp. 168-175). Ann Arbor, MI: Association for Consumer Research.

Parasuraman, A., Zeithaml, V. A., & Berry, L. L. (1985). A conceptual model of service quality and its implications for future research. *Journal of Marketing, 49,* 41-50.

Parasuraman, A., Zeithaml, V. A., & Berry, L. L. (1988). SERVQUAL: A multiple item scale for measuring consumer perceptions of service quality. *Journal of Retailing, 64,* 12-37.

Ram, S., & Jung, H. S., (1991). How product usage influences customer satisfaction. *Marketing Letters, 2,* 403-411.

Rust, R. T., & Zahorik, A. J. (1992). *The value of customer satisfaction.* Working paper, Vanderbilt University.

Singh, J. (1988). Consumer complaint intentions and behavior: Definitional and taxonomical issues. *Journal of Marketing, 52,* 93-107.

Solomon, M. R., Surprenant, C., Czepiel, J. A., & Gutman, E. G. (1985). A role theory perspective on dyadic interactions: The service encounter. *Journal of Marketing, 49,* 99-111.

Surprenant, C. F., & Solomon, M. R. (1987). Predictability and personalization in the service encounter. *Journal of Marketing, 51,* 86-96.

Tse, D. K., & Wilton, P. C. (1988). Models of consumer satisfaction formation: An extension. *Journal of Marketing Research, 25,* 204-212.

Westbrook, R. A. (1980). A rating scale for measuring product/service satisfaction. *Journal of Marketing, 44,* 68-72.

Westbrook, R. A. (1987). Product/consumption-based affective responses and postpurchase processes. *Journal of Marketing Research, 24,* 258-270.

Westbrook, R. A., & Oliver, R. L. (1981). Developing better measures of consumer satisfaction: Some preliminary results. In K. B. Monroe (Ed.), *Advances in consumer research* (Vol. 8, pp. 94-99). Ann Arbor, MI: Association for Consumer Research.

Wilkie, W. L., & Pessemier, E. A. (1973). Issues in marketing's use of multi-attribute attitude models. *Journal of Marketing Research, 10,* 428-441.

Woodruff, R. B., Cadotte, E. R., & Jenkins, R. L. (1983). Modeling consumer satisfaction processes using experienced based norms. *Journal of Marketing Research, 20,* 296-304.

Zeithaml, V. A. (1988). Consumer perceptions of price, quality and value: A means-end model and synthesis of evidence. *Journal of Marketing, 52,* 2-22.

CHAPTER NINE

On the Measurement of Perceived Service Quality

A Conjoint Analysis Approach

WAYNE S. DeSARBO

LENARD HUFF

MARCELO M. ROLANDELLI

JUNGWHAN CHOI

School of Business Administration, University of Michigan

Parasuraman, Zeithaml, and Berry (1988) have proposed the use of a 22-item SERVQUAL instrument for the measurement of perceived service quality. Since their important work, several authors have criticized the use of this instrument in applied settings suggesting that the number and type of dimensions may vary by service category, that there are problems in attempting to use the same wording across different service categories and in dealing with services that provide multiple service functions (e.g., hospitals), that the analysis of difference scores between perceptions and expectations raises questions about the psychometric properties of such a scale, and that the SERVQUAL instrument confounds the measurement of service satisfaction with service quality. We present an alternative measurement scheme for the measurement of perceived service quality, based on conjoint analysis, that can be easily modified to any service category by expectancy confirmation/disconfirmation response. The advantages of the proposed procedure are, first, that we measure true perceptions, as opposed to perceptions confounded with expectations and satisfaction; second, that the number, type, and operationalization of the specific dimensions (vis-à-vis the wording) are completely flexible according to the specific usage scenario; third, that estimation can be performed in an efficient manner utilizing orthogonal designs and simple OLS; and last, that the proposed model can lead to interesting quality optimization models as well as models that explore segmentation. The proposed methodology is illustrated with service quality perceptions of banks and dental offices. We conclude by discussing directions for future research.

As firms seek a competitive advantage in an ever more hostile environment with trends toward deregulation, intense global competition, and more intelligent consumers, managers have rediscovered the importance of "quality." Marketing strategists have found that firms with comparatively higher levels of quality typically reap higher market share and return (Buzzell & Gale, 1987; Philips, Chang, & Buzzell, 1983). It has also been well documented that higher quality can lead to lower costs and thus higher profit margins (Crosby, 1979, 1984; Garvin, 1983, 1984). As noted by Parasuraman, Berry, and Zeithaml (1991), delivering high quality in the service industry has been recognized as the most effective means of ensuring that a company's offerings are uniquely positioned in a market filled with "look-alike" competitive offerings.

Much of the earlier efforts aimed at defining and measuring quality have come from the manufacturing sector and have been based on the traditional "conformance to standards" engineering paradigm (see Crosby, 1984; Garvin, 1983). More recently, a number of European marketing researchers (e.g., Edvardsson & Gustavsson, 1991; Grönroos, 1984, 1990; Gummesson, 1991) and a team of U.S. scholars (Parasuraman, Zeithaml, & Berry, 1985, 1988, 1991) have recognized the need to develop valid and distinct measures of service quality given the rise of services development in the past few decades. As Grönroos (1990) notes, statistical data published by GATT (General Agreement on Trade and Tariffs) show that the service sector accounted for 66% of the GNP in the United States and 58% in the EEC countries in 1984. According to Bateson (1989), the proportion of the population in the United States employed in the service sector increased from 30% in 1900 to 74% in 1984. Koepp (1987) documented that 85% of all new jobs created since 1982 have been in service industries (Cronin & Taylor, 1992). According to Lewis and Booms (1983), even for manufactured goods, service is important. A study published in 1983 by the Office of the U.S. Trade Representative showed that approximately three quarters of the total value added in the goods sector was created by service activities within the sector (Grönroos, 1990).

As Parasuraman et al. (1985) and Zeithaml, Parasuraman, and Berry (1990) aptly note (see also Berry, 1984; Berry & Parasuraman, 1991), knowledge about manufacturing quality is not sufficient to fully comprehend service quality because of four distinguishing characteristics of services: their intangibility, heterogeneity, inseparability, and perishability. To quote Parasuraman et al. (1991):

The intangibility of services implies that precise manufacturing specifications concerning uniform quality can rarely be set for services as they can for goods. This difficulty is compounded by the fact that services, especially those with a high labor content, are heterogeneous: their performance often varies from producer to producer, from customer to customer, and from day to day. As a result, uniform quality is difficult to ensure. . . . The inseparability of production and consumption of services implies that quality cannot be engineered and evaluated at the manufacturing plant prior to delivery to consumers. Perishability means that goods and services cannot be saved, and this can lead to unsynchronized supply and demand problems. Clearly, goods-quality principles are not directly pertinent to services. (p. 253)

In an effort to explain how customers perceive service quality, Grönroos (1984) introduced a model of service quality based on three essential points. First, functional quality, or how the service is performed and delivered, is as important as technical quality, or what the consumer receives. Second, because a consumer will be able to see the firm and its resources during the buyer-seller interactions, image is of utmost importance to most service firms. Third, the overall perception of quality is a function of the consumer's evaluation of the service and the difference between this evaluation and his or her expectations of the service. An illustration of Grönroos's (1984) model is displayed in Figure 9.1.

Borrowing conceptually from the Grönroos (1984) model, Parasuraman et al. (1985) have developed a "comprehensive" measurement instrument, known as SERVQUAL, originally devised to measure perceived service quality. In its current form (see Parasuraman et al., 1988), SERVQUAL contains 22 pairs of Likert-type items. One set of measures, containing one item from each pair, is utilized to measure customers' expected levels of service for a particular service industry as a way of calibrating expectations. The second set of measures, containing the remaining item from each pair, is intended to measure the level of service provided by a specific service company as experienced by the consumer as a way of calibrating perceptions. A measure of service quality is then formulated by calculating the difference scores between the corresponding set of items (i.e., perceptions minus expectations).

As will be shown, this SERVQUAL measurement has come under much criticism from several authors questioning both the conceptual foundation and empirical operationalization of SERVQUAL. This chapter is intended to provide an alternative methodology for operationalizing

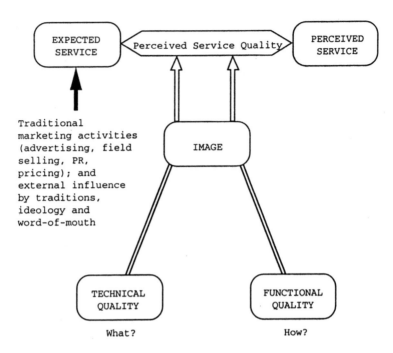

Figure 9.1. The Perceived Service Quality Model
SOURCE: Adapted from Grönroos (1984).

the conceptual basis of SERVQUAL in a conjoint measurement (Green & Rao, 1971) framework. In this manner, many of the shortcomings of SERVQUAL can be avoided, and a host of analytical models traditionally associated with conjoint analysis become gainfully available. In the next section, we review the SERVQUAL methodology in more depth, as well as the criticisms levied against its use in measuring perceived service quality. The following section presents an illustration of the proposed conjoint-based methodology, with perceptions of service quality collected for two different services. We conclude with suggestions for future research in the area, including a discussion of previous measurement models that could be applied to such data and the resulting insights managers could thus obtain.

The SERVQUAL Methodology

The early exploratory research of Parasuraman et al. (1985) revealed that the primary criteria utilized by consumers in assessing service quality could be described by 10 separate dimensions: (a) tangibles, (b) reliability, (c) responsiveness, (d) communication, (e) credibility, (f) security, (g) competence, (h) courtesy, (i) understanding/knowing the consumer, (j) access. These 10 dimensions were later combined and condensed to 5: tangibles, reliability, responsiveness, assurance (knowledge and courtesy of employees and their ability to inspire trust and confidence), and empathy (caring; individual attention the firm provides its customers). These last two constructs, assurance and empathy, contain items representing seven of the original dimensions—communication, credibility, security, competence, courtesy, understanding/knowing customers, and access—that did not remain distinct after sequential testing. The original SERVQUAL instrument, consisting of 22-item scale pairs (expectations-perceptions) is reported in Parasuraman et al. (1988, pp. 38-40). These authors claim that the instrument can be utilized in a wide array of services without modification, and that the SERVQUAL instrument has high reliability and validity.

Carman (1990) was among the first scholars to formally question and criticize the SERVQUAL methodology. In attempting to replicate the Parasuraman et al. (1985) findings across a number of different services, Carman found a need to add and expand on certain dimensions that were differentially important across different services. In settings in which multiple service functions are performed (e.g., a hospital), Carman recommended that SERVQUAL be administered for each function separately. His major concern, however, relates to the differencing of the perceptions-expectations terms in SERVQUAL, and he questions the psychometric properties of such differences in their use for subsequent analyses. Carman recommends the collection of (perception-expectation) differences directly in combined form rather than asking separate questions about each (see Oliver, 1977). In addition, he suggests collecting importances for each of the tested dimensions and explicitly embedding them in subsequent multiattribute models.

Babakus and Boller (1992) further confirmed some of Carman's suspicions in their more recent article criticizing SERVQUAL. They conducted a large empirical study with an electric and gas utility company using the SERVQUAL instrument. Exploratory factor analyses yielding a five-dimensional solution produced low discriminant and convergent validity. In fact, the interpretations of the dimensions were quite different than those suggested in Parasuraman et al. (1988) and confirmed by subsequent factor analyses, suggesting that the dimensionality of service quality may be a function of the type of service under study. Babakus and Boller also found significant effects due to the positive or negative wording of the items, with consistently larger variabilities associated with the negatively worded items. Finally, these authors questioned the separate use of perceptions and expectations batteries and performed analyses suggesting that the difference scores did not provide any additional information beyond that already contained in the perceptions component of the SERVQUAL scale. They agree with Carman's (1990) suggestion of combining perceptions and expectations into a single scale.

The final major criticism of SERVQUAL was levied by Cronin and Taylor (1992), questioning the conceptual basis of SERVQUAL with the claim that SERVQUAL confounds service satisfaction (see Oliver, 1980; Churchill & Surprenant, 1982) with service quality. Cronin and Taylor provide empirical and literature-based support suggesting that service quality should be measured as an attitude. Their SERVPERF scale recasts the 22-item SERVQUAL scale into performance-based items, and the authors' LISREL analyses support their contention that SERVPERF better explains service quality. Obviously, there are limitations to the performance-based SERVPERF approach, in that its use, like SERVQUAL, is limited to services in which the consumer has already had direct involvement.

The Proposed Conjoint Measurement-Based Methodology

Against this development, we propose an alternative measurement approach for perceived service quality calibration based on conjoint analysis (Green & Rao, 1971). Cattin and Wittink (1982) and Wittink and Cattin (1989) have documented the substantial use of conjoint analysis for commercial product/service design problems, as well as the popularity of the full-profile, metric rating, multiple regression combination to perform such studies (see also Green & Srinivasan, 1978, 1990). Neslin (1983) was the first to utilize a conjoint measurement approach for service quality measurement (for health care services), varying objectively defined health care service features according to some fractional factorial design in a paired-comparison data collection format. Later, Narasimhan and Sen (1992) proposed the use of conjoint analysis for the measurement of product quality perceptions collected from users of office copiers, examining the relationship between perceived quality and underlying engineering attributes.

In contrast, we specifically operationalize the original 10 dimensions of SERVQUAL as the "design" variables (not features or attributes) in a conjoint experimental design. Based on Carman's (1990) suggestion and Oliver's (1977, 1980, 1981) conceptual disconfirmation work, the levels of the variables are "worse than expected," "same as expected," and "better than expected." We applied this conjoint design approach to two different types of services, banks and dental clinics. Table 9.1 presents the specific variables used for assessing service quality perceptions for these two services, and how they relate to the SERVQUAL framework. Table 9.2 presents a hypothesized service description for a bank and a dental clinic, and the 7-point quality response scale (and binary consideration scale) to be used.

A few comments are in order at this point. One, as illustrated in Tables 9.1 and 9.2, the proposed conjoint measurement approach can be tailored to the specific service industry application desired by adding, dropping, or rewording factors, thus alleviating one of the major sets of concerns cited in Carman (1990) and Babakus and Boller (1992). Two, the full-profile descriptions illustrated in Table 9.2 describe hypothetical services. As such, direct experience with these hypothetical services is clearly impossible, thus ensuring no confounding of perceptions and satisfaction—a serious concern raised by Cronin and Taylor (1992). Third, as recommended by Carman (1990), expectations are directly worded into the collection of perceptions in the conjoint measurement methodology. There is no differencing of scores to be later analyzed via a multivariate technique. Fourth, each hypothesized service is processed as a gestalt, with full information on all relevant dimensions presented. As such, one could also validate the derived results by collecting prior expectations from these consumers, as well as overall evaluations of service quality on the consumer's presently utilized service establishment. In addition, predictive validation on holdout profiles is possible. Finally, importance weights are derived by the conjoint analysis estimation procedure and provide a basis for segmenting consumers as to differences in the importances they implicitly assign to the various SERVQUAL dimensions utilized in an application. The following illustration will help to clarify the details of application of the proposed methodology.

TABLE 9.1   SERVQUAL Factors Utilized in Conjoint Experiments

SERVQUAL Dimensions	Banks	Dental Service
Tangibles	A. Facility and equipment	A. Dentist's equipment
	B. Selection and quality of financial offerings	B. Appearance of clinic or office
Reliability	C. Accuracy and dependability	C. Consistency and dependability of service
Responsiveness	D. Speed of service	D. Waiting time
Communication	E. Communication with customers	E. Clear and understandable communication
Credibility	F. Reputation for honesty and integrity	F. Reputation for honesty and integrity
Security	G. Financial strength and security	G. Safe and sanitary treatment
Competence	H. Knowledge and competence of personnel	H. Knowledge and competence of personnel
Courtesy	I. Politeness and courtesy of personnel	I. Politeness and courtesy of personnel
Understanding	J. Understanding of individual customer needs	J. Providing personalized attention
Access	K. Convenience of location and operating hours	K. Convenience of location and operating hours

Methodology

Study Design

We chose to examine two rather different services for investigation in order to compare the estimated part-worths for the different SERVQUAL environments, banks and dental services. These two particular services were selected for the following reasons. First, the sample consisted of undergraduate and graduate students in a major Midwestern university, and most students have considerable familiarity with both banks and dental services. Second, these two services differ dramatically as to the degree of labor intensity and level of interaction and customization, and thus provide an interesting basis for contrast concerning the differential importance and relevance of the 10 SERVQUAL factors. Third, banks and dental services have been examined in previous service quality studies

TABLE 9.2   Illustrative Conjoint Profiles

BANK 2:

Selection and quality of financial offerings: **worse** than expected
Speed of service: **worse** than expected
Accuracy and dependability of service: **worse** than expected
Bank's facility and equipment: **worse** than expected
Reputation for honesty and integrity: about the **same** as expected
Knowledge and competence of personnel: about the **same** as expected
Financial strength and security: **better** than expected
Communication with its customers: about the **same** as expected
Politeness and courtesy of personnel: **better** than expected
Convenience of location and operating hours: **better** than expected
Understanding of individual customer needs: about the **same** as expected

Your evaluation of this bank's quality:

(Please circle one)

Poor   Excellent
1   2   3   4   5   6   7

Would you consider banking at this bank?
(Please circle one)   YES   NO

DENTAL SERVICE 9

Reputation for honesty and integrity: **better** than expected
Safe and sanitary treatment: about the **same** as expected
Knowledge and competence of personnel: about the **same** as expected
Clear and understandable communication: **better** than expected
Waiting time: about the **same** as expected
Providing personalized attention: about the **same** as expected
Appearance of clinic/office: **better** than expected
Politeness and courtesy of personnel: **worse** than expected
Dentist's equipment: **worse** than expected
Consistency and dependability of service: **better** than expected
Convenience of location and operating hours: **worse** than expected

Your evaluation of this dental clinic's quality:

(Please circle one)

Poor   Excellent
1   2   3   4   5   6   7

Would you consider going to this dental clinic?

(although detailed results are not available), and thus provide a basis for validation. Finally, both services can be provided in a heterogeneous manner in that different respondents will typically have experienced substantial variance in the quality of service rendered for these two services in the past.

Based on several in-depth interviews with students and an extensive literature review (e.g., Parasuraman et al., 1988, examined banks, and Carman, 1990, reports on a study of dental clinics), we tailored operationalizations of the original set of 10 SERVQUAL dimensions for banks and dental services as shown in Table 9.1. We chose to split the tangibles factor into two separate variables for each service due to the (a priori determined) importance and complexity of this factor, resulting in 11 conjoint factors. Note that we chose to deal with the original set of 10 SERVQUAL concrete dimensions rather than the condensed final set of 5 discussed earlier because the last two condensed dimensions (assurance and empathy) were excessively abstract, involving combinations of potentially important and more concrete constructs. In the absence of prior theory and to reduce respondent fatigue, a 3^{11} fractional factorial design was selected for main effects-only estimation (see Addelman, 1962). Note that this procedure is sufficiently flexible to accommodate more complex experimental designs (involving higher order interactions) if warranted.

The actual design matrix, converted to dummy variables, is shown in Table 9.3. Twenty-seven profiles were used for estimation, and the last three profiles for validation. Note that the levels of each factor are coded so that "same as expected" is always represented by (0, 0), whereas "worse than expected" is represented by (1, 0), and "better than expected" is represented by (0, 1). This was purposely done in order to directly estimate possible asymmetric effects between the positive and negative level states for each of the factors. The estimates for the intermediate or neutral level, "same as expected," for each factor are thus confounded with the intercept term.

After two rounds of pretesting, two separate questionnaires were developed (one for banks, the other for dental services). Respondents were first asked to list the attributes they thought were important to their use of the service in an open-ended framework. They were then asked to evaluate the importance of the 11 factors described in Table 9.1 on a 9-point scale. The conjoint task then followed, where the 30 profiles and the order of the factors were randomized. We then asked a battery of questions concerning the respondents' evaluations of their current bank

TABLE 9.3 3^{11} Fractional Factorial Design With Validation Profiles

	SERVQUAL Dimension/Factor																					
Profile	A		B		C		D		E		F		G		H		I		J		K	
1	1	0	1	0	1	0	1	0	1	0	1	0	1	0	1	0	1	0	1	0	1	0
2	1	0	1	0	1	0	1	0	0	0	0	0	0	1	0	0	0	1	0	0	0	1
3	1	0	1	0	1	0	1	0	0	1	0	1	0	0	0	1	0	0	0	1	0	0
4	1	0	0	0	0	0	0	1	1	0	1	0	1	0	0	0	0	0	0	0	0	0
5	1	0	0	0	0	0	0	1	0	0	0	0	0	1	0	1	1	0	0	1	1	0
6	1	0	0	0	0	0	0	1	0	1	0	1	0	0	1	0	0	1	1	0	0	1
7	1	0	0	1	0	1	0	0	1	0	1	0	1	0	0	1	0	1	0	1	0	1
8	1	0	0	1	0	1	0	0	0	0	0	0	0	1	1	0	0	0	1	0	0	0
9	1	0	0	1	0	1	0	0	0	1	0	1	0	0	0	0	1	0	0	0	1	0
10	0	0	1	0	0	0	0	0	1	0	0	0	0	0	1	0	1	0	0	0	0	0
11	0	0	1	0	0	0	0	0	0	0	0	1	1	0	0	0	0	1	0	1	1	0
12	0	0	1	0	0	0	0	0	0	1	1	0	0	1	0	1	0	0	1	0	0	1
13	0	0	0	0	0	1	1	0	1	0	0	0	0	0	0	0	0	0	0	1	0	1
14	0	0	0	0	0	1	1	0	0	0	0	1	1	0	0	1	1	0	1	0	0	0
15	0	0	0	0	0	1	1	0	0	1	1	0	0	1	1	0	0	1	0	0	1	0
16	0	0	0	1	1	0	0	1	1	0	0	0	0	0	0	1	0	1	1	0	1	0
17	0	0	0	1	1	0	0	1	0	0	0	1	1	0	1	0	0	0	0	0	0	1
18	0	0	0	1	1	0	0	1	0	1	1	0	0	1	0	0	1	0	0	1	0	0
19	0	1	1	0	0	1	0	1	1	0	0	1	0	1	1	0	1	0	0	1	0	1
20	0	1	1	0	0	1	0	1	0	0	1	0	0	0	0	0	0	1	1	0	0	0
21	0	1	1	0	0	1	0	1	0	1	0	0	1	0	0	1	0	0	0	0	1	0
22	0	1	0	0	1	0	0	0	1	0	0	1	0	1	0	0	0	0	1	0	1	0
23	0	1	0	0	1	0	0	0	0	0	1	0	0	0	0	1	1	0	0	0	0	1
24	0	1	0	0	1	0	0	0	0	1	0	0	1	0	1	0	0	1	0	1	0	0
25	0	1	0	1	0	0	1	0	1	0	0	1	0	1	0	1	0	1	0	0	0	0
26	0	1	0	1	0	0	1	0	0	0	1	0	0	0	1	0	0	0	0	1	1	0
27	0	1	0	1	0	0	1	0	0	1	0	0	1	0	0	0	1	0	1	0	0	1
28	0	0	1	0	0	1	0	0	0	0	1	0	0	1	1	0	0	0	1	0	1	0
29	0	1	1	0	0	0	0	0	0	0	0	0	0	0	1	0	0	1	0	1	0	1
30	1	0	0	0	0	1	0	1	0	1	1	0	1	0	0	1	0	1	0	1	0	1

or dental service, including an overall quality assessment, ratings of their bank's performance on these 11 factors based on their previous expectations, and usage and experience levels with the particular aspects of these services. Finally, demographic questions concerning age, marital status, gender, home ownership, and level of education were included in the survey. Fifty-three students completed the bank questionnaire, and a different fifty completed the dental service questionnaire. In each group, a mix of undergraduate, graduate, and (older) evening students were utilized. Respondents were paid $5 for completing the questionnaire, and their name was entered into a lottery for a portable TV set. The time taken for completing the questionnaires typically took 30-45 minutes.

Conjoint Model and OLS Results

As mentioned above, we will focus on a standard main-effects part-worth model estimated by ordinary least squares (OLS). The response of a given respondent to the jth profile is given by:

(1)
$$Y_j = \sum_{p=1}^{t} \sum_{q=1}^{q_p} B_{pq} X_{jpq} + U_j,$$

where:

Y_j = the perceived service quality judgment for the jth experimental profile ($j = 1, \ldots, 30$);

B_{pq} = the part-worth of the qth level of the pth SERVQUAL factor;

X_{jpq} = a dummy variable that has the value of 1 if profile j takes on the qth level of the pth SERVQUAL factor, and zero otherwise;

q_p = the number of levels of the pth SERVQUAL factor (here $q_p = 3$ for all p);

t = the number of SERVQUAL factors ($t = 11$); and,
U_j = an error term.

With N (= 30) profiles, the relationships in (1) for a given respondent can be summarized in matrix form via:

(2) $Y = XB + U,$

where:

$$Y' = (Y_1, Y_2, \ldots, Y_N);$$

$X =$ an $N \times K$ dummy variable matrix with a column of 1's and $q_p - 1$
columns to code a factor with q_p levels;

$$K = \sum_{p=1}^{t} q_p - t + 1;$$

$$B = (B_0, B_1, \ldots, B_{K-1})$$

$$U = (U_1, U_2, \ldots, U_N);$$

and the prime denotes transpose. The estimate of B' will be denoted $b = (b_0, b_1, \ldots, b_{K-1})$ and is equal to $(X'X)^{-1}X'Y$, where the negative one signifies a matrix inverse. In our application, X corresponds to an orthogonal fractional factorial design (e.g., Addelman, 1962). Note that Expressions (1) and (2) can be specified and estimated by respondent (individual-level analysis) or over the entire sample via an aggregate or pooled analysis (see Moore, 1980).

Table 9.4 presents the multiple regression results for the aggregate (over all subjects), pooled samples separately for banks and dental services. Figure 9.2 portrays the importances for each of the SERVQUAL dimensions graphically by service. (As in conjoint analysis, these importances were calculated on the basis of the range of the coefficients for the three levels within each SERVQUAL factor.) With very few exceptions, the absolute value of the coefficients in Table 9.4 for "worse than expected" levels are much greater than those for "better than expected" levels for both services across most SERVQUAL dimensions, reflecting an interesting asymmetry in the responses. This implies that the costs induced by not meeting customers' expectations (negative disconfirmation) may exceed the benefits of exceeding those expectations (positive disconfirmation)—a result also found by Oliver and DeSarbo (1988) and Anderson and Sullivan (1993) in a satisfaction context. Such results may also be explained through prospect theory (Kahneman & Tversky, 1979) via a risk aversion tendency on the part of the majority of respondents. For respondents who may be characterized as seeking minimal variance (deviation from expectation) and maximal mean net benefit (expected amount of net benefit), experiencing the negative factor level ("worse than expected") will both decrease the mean and increase the variance, whereas experiencing the positive factor level ("better than expected") will increase the mean while increasing the variance. This argument implies, therefore, that the "worse than expected" levels would have a much larger impact on responses than the "better than expected" levels, as witnessed in Table 9.4.

For banks, dependability and integrity are the most important SERVQUAL-based dimensions in assessing perceptions of service quality, followed by security and financial offerings. For dental services, safety/security dominates as the key factor, followed by competence and equipment. This dominant importance on safety may reflect patients' increasing concern for contracting AIDS or hepatitis from dentists—a worry frequently vocalized in our pretest sample. As seen as Figure 9.2, large differences in the derived SERVQUAL factor importances between the two services are witnessed with respect to equipment, dependability, integrity, security/safety, competence, and access. These findings corroborate Carman's (1990) argument that different numbers and types of dimensions are deemed as important or relevant for different types of services.

Table 9.4 also provides the basis for maximizing service quality perceptions. Given the compensatory linear model in Expressions (1) and (2), managers need to select the most positive significant level for each of the SERVQUAL factors. That is, a firm should attempt to exceed customer expectations on those SERVQUAL factors with the highest "better than expected" coefficients while ensuring that expectations are met on the other factors. For banks, exceeding expectations in the areas of equipment, financial offerings, dependability, communications, integrity, and access while meeting current expectation levels for the remaining dimensions (with the possible exception of understanding) would lead to significantly higher overall perceived service quality ratings. For dental services, exceeding expectations with respect to equipment, office appearance, dependability, integrity, safety, competence, and understanding while maintaining current expectations for the remaining dimensions would lead to significantly higher perceived service ratings. Operationally, these recommendations need to be conditioned with specific cost estimates for achieving the desired results, as well as a valid model to map managerial actions with changes in levels of expectations.

TABLE 9.4   Aggregate Conjoint Results for Banks and Dental Services

		Banks Coefficient	Factor Importance	Dental Services Coefficient	Factor Importance
Intercept		4.46***		4.57***	
A. Equipment	Worse	−0.13*	.32	−0.48***	.71
	Better	0.19**		0.23***	
B. Offering/Office	Worse	−0.44***	.60	−0.31***	.47
	Better	0.16**		0.16**	
C. Dependability	Worse	−0.60***	.85	−0.27***	.39
	Better	0.25***		0.12*	
D. Speed	Worse	−0.28***	.31	−0.21***	.31
	Better	0.03		0.10	
E. Communication	Worse	−0.01	.16	−0.08	.13
	Better	0.15**		0.05	
F. Integrity	Worse	−0.60**	.80	−0.27***	.43
	Better	0.20***		0.16**	
G. Security	Worse	−0.58***	.66	−1.12***	1.24
	Better	0.08		0.12*	
H. Competence	Worse	−0.28***	.28	−0.60***	.83
	Better	0.00		0.23***	
I. Courtesy	Worse	−0.27***	.36	−0.21***	.23
	Better	0.09		0.02	
J. Understanding	Worse	−0.09	.13	−0.08	.20
	Better	0.04		0.12*	
K. Access	Worse	−0.30***	.48	−0.12*	.14
	Better	0.18***		0.02	
R^2		0.29		0.40	
F		26.06***		39.84***	

$*p \leq .10; **p \leq .05; ***p \leq .01$

Additionally, a combined, total sample ($N = 100$) analysis was conducted across both samples (because a common design matrix was used for both samples) and a Chow F-test was performed to examine this one regression model result versus the two separate regression models reported in Table 9.4. This was done in order to formally test the hypothesis that perceptions of service quality are the same across the two services.

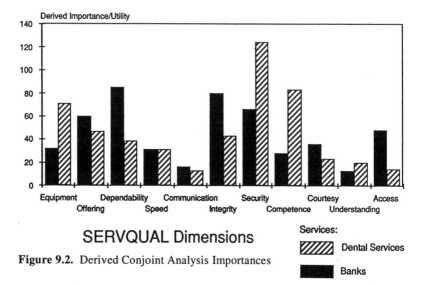

Figure 9.2. Derived Conjoint Analysis Importances

The hypothesis of a common regression equation was rejected ($F = 5.72$, $p < .01$) in favor of the two separate service equation system, lending further support for Carman's (1990) service heterogeneity claim.

Summary results for the individual-level analyses conducted for each of the 100 respondents (not shown) provide a mean R^2 for the bank and dentist samples of 0.934 and 0.947, respectively (0.573 and 0.655 mean adjusted R^2, respectively). A number of points can be gleaned from these findings. First, based on a cursory inspection of the F-statistics, there seems to be a sizable number of subjects in each sample who are not particularly well fit by this main-effects model. This fit problem is particularly prevalent in the bank sample. Perhaps a more complicated experimental design incorporating higher order interactions may be necessary for these individuals. Or perhaps a noncompensatory evaluation scheme was utilized by these subjects. Second, there also seems to be substantial individual heterogeneity with respect to the estimated coefficients for these SERVQUAL-derived factors. Third, within subjects, there is still evidence of the dominance of the absolute magnitude of the typically negative coefficient for the "worse than expected" level over the typically positive "better than expected" level, as witnessed earlier in the aggregate analyses. Finally, it is possible to cluster analyze these individual-level coefficients to form benefit segments (Green, 1977; Oliver & DeSarbo, 1988) whose members share similar SERVQUAL-factor importances. Or one could apply recently developed latent structure models as developed by DeSarbo and Cron (1988) and DeSarbo, Wedel, Vriens, and Ramaswamy (1992) to simultaneously estimate segments and segment level part-worths.

Validation

Table 9.5 presents in the top panel a statistical summary of the predictive validation results in comparing the actual versus predicted responses for the three holdout conjoint profiles. All the correlations are significantly greater than zero ($p < .01$). A more pronounced improvement in predictive accuracy is witnessed with respect to all three measures in moving from the aggregate model to the individual-level model for the bank sample. However, that is clearly not the case with respect to two of the three measures involving the dental services sample. At first glance, this seems contradictory to the average adjusted R^2 computed for both samples over individuals reported earlier. It may be that Hagerty's (1985) conjecture concerning overparameterized (in this case, individual-level models) conjoint models fitting better but predicting worse may be in evidence here.

We also performed a predictive validation test with respect to the collected dimension expectation evaluations and overall perceived service quality perceptions generated for each subject's own bank or dental service. Here, we constructed a binary vector corresponding to the subject's SERVQUAL expectation evaluation (worse, same as, or better than expected) for their present service based on their prior experiences and created predicted overall perceived service quality ratings by applying the aggregate and individual-level part-worth coefficients. These predictions were then compared with their elicited overall response. Table 9.5 reports in the bottom panel the various goodness-of-fit statistics for banks and dental service. Again, all correlations are significantly greater than zero ($p < .01$). However, one immediately notices an appreciable worsening in most measures in moving from the aggregate to the individual-level models, especially with the dentist sample. This result again lends support to the findings by Hagerty (1985) where overparameterized (i.e., here, individual-level) conjoint models calibrated with fewer degrees of freedom tended to perform significantly worse in predictive validation tests than simpler and more parsimonious (i.e., here, aggregate) models. What is particularly interesting in Table 9.5 is the fact that the predictive validation statistics tend to be better for the dental services sample with the use of the aggregate models, yet somewhat better for banks with use

TABLE 9.5   Individual-Level Versus Aggregate Model Validation

	Banks	Dental Services
	Holdout Profiles	
Aggregate Model Results		
Root-Mean-Square	1.32	1.06
Correlation	0.51	0.40
Sums-of-Squares Accounted for	0.92	0.93
Individual Model Results		
Root-Mean-Square	1.20	1.11
Correlation	0.65	0.52
Sums-of-Squares Accounted for	0.93	0.92
	Subjects' Own Services	
Aggregate Model Results		
Root-Mean-Square	1.15	0.96
Correlation	0.33	0.52
Sums-of-Squares Accounted for	0.97	0.98
Individual Model Results		
Root-Mean-Square	1.24	1.35
Correlation	0.47	0.19
Sums-of-Squares Accounted for	0.95	0.95

of the individual-level models. This may be indicative of the need for more disaggregate level models for the banking sample to account for respondent heterogeneity. This issue will be addressed in the next section concerning future research suggestions.

Discussion

We have presented a description and critique of the SERVQUAL approach to measuring perceived service quality. A conjoint analysis based methodology that operationalizes the 10 basic SERVQUAL dimensions has been presented with a small-scale illustration. We have demonstrated how the proposed methodology can be tailored to particular services by rewording or adding or dropping relevant factors/dimensions. The problem of separate measurement of expectations and perceptions has been overcome with the suggested use of experimental designs that embed disconfirmation levels as the designated factor/dimension levels (Oliver 1981). Thus, no differences are taken, and there seems to be less of a problem of confounding perceived service quality with satisfaction. The response tasks involve hypothetical service description for which actual experience is not possible or necessary, helping to ensure that perceptions, not satisfactions, are in fact measured.

Factor importances are derived in aggregate form or by individual and are explicitly part of the multiattribute, compensatory model structure. Finally, the flexibility to validate the model on either holdout or actual services is accommodated in a traditional conjoint analysis fashion. As noted, "optimal service designs," which designate which particular SERVQUAL dimensions need to be adjusted, can be devised with subsequent predictions in associated changes in perceived service quality.

Concerning limitations, as witnessed in the illustration provided, for some respondents, main-effect designs may not be sufficient in truly capturing perceptions of service quality. More complicated designs involving interaction terms may have to be employed, increasing the response burden. In addition, more complicated, noncompensatory models may better describe these evaluations for some subjects. Finally, the small degrees of freedom available for individual-level estimation are troublesome from a statistical perspective. Manifestations of this are displayed in the mixed results at the individual level of the predictive validation.

Future research should therefore occur on a number of fronts. One, the use of hybrid conjoint models (Green, 1984) employing more efficient experimental designs for the estimation of both aggregate and individual-level parameters should be explored to accommodate more sophisticated response models and to increase the degrees of freedom for estimation (over individual-level models). Second, the use of choice models and associated designs (Louviere, 1988) can also be explored in this context. Third, as mentioned earlier, latent structure approaches such as that of DeSarbo et al. (1992) should be explored as another alternative to resolve individual-level overparameterized models (see also DeSarbo, Oliver, & Rangaswami, 1989; Hagerty, 1985; Kamakura, 1988; Ogawa, 1987; Wedel & Kistemaker, 1989; Wedel & Steenkamp, 1989, 1991) and examine segmentation via these estimated coefficients (Green, 1977). Subsequent validation studies akin to Green and Helson (1989) could contrast predictive validation at the individual, segment, and aggregate levels. Fourth, choice simulators (Green & Krieger, 1991) employed in traditional conjoint settings can be applied in the perceived service quality context to investigate the impact of competitive reactions. Finally, the proposed conjoint-based methodology needs to be applied to a variety of commercial scenarios in which objective tests of performance and validation can be established.

References

Addelman, S. (1962). Orthogonal main-effect plans for asymmetrical factorial experiments. *Technometrics, 4,* 21-46.

Anderson, E. W., & Sullivan, M. W. (1993). The antecedents and consequences of customer satisfaction for firms. *Marketing Science, 12,* 125-143.

Babakus, E., & Boller, G. W. (1992). An empirical assessment of the SERVQUAL scale. *Journal of Business Research, 24,* 253-268.

Bateson, J. E. (1989). *Managing services marketing.* London: Dryden.

Berry, L. L. (1984). Services marketing is different. In C. Lovelock (Ed.), *Services marketing* (pp. 29-37). Englewood Cliffs, NJ: Prentice-Hall.

Berry, L. L., & Parasuraman, A. (1991). *Marketing services: Competing through quality.* New York: Free Press.

Buzzell, R. D., & Gale, B. T. (1987). *The PIMS principles: Linking strategy to performance.* New York: Free Press.

Carman, J. M. (1990). Consumer perceptions of service quality: An assessment of the SERVQUAL dimensions. *Journal of Retailing, 66,* 33-55.

Cattin, P., & Wittink, D. R. (1982). Commercial use of conjoint analysis: A survey. *Journal of Marketing, 44,* 44-53.

Churchill, G. A., Jr., & Surprenant, C. (1982). An investigation into the determinants of customer satisfaction. *Journal of Marketing Research, 19,* 491-504.

Cronin, J. J., & Taylor, S. A. (1992). Measuring service quality: A reexamination and extension. *Journal of Marketing, 56,* 55-68.

Crosby, P. B. (1979). *Quality is free: The art of making quality certain.* New York: New American Library.

Crosby, P. B. (1984). *Quality without tears.* New York: McGraw-Hill.

DeSarbo, W. S., & Cron, W. L. (1988). Maximum likelihood methodology for clusterwise linear regression. *Journal of Classification, 5,* 249-282.

DeSarbo, W. S., Oliver, R. L., & Rangaswami, A. (1989). A simulated annealing methodology for clusterwise linear regression. *Psychometrika, 54,* 707-736.

DeSarbo, W. S., Wedel, M., Vriens, M., & Ramaswamy, V. (1992). Latent class metric conjoint analysis. *Marketing Letters, 3,* 273-288.

Edvardsson, B., & Gustavsson, B. (1991). Quality in service and quality in service organizations: A model for quality assessment. In S. W. Brown, E. Gummesson, B. Edvardsson, & B. Gustavsson (Eds.), *Service quality: Multidisciplinary and multinational perspectives* (pp. 319-340). Lexington, MA: Lexington.

Garvin, D. A. (1983). Quality on the line. *Harvard Business Review, 61,* 65-73.

Garvin, D. A. (1984). What does product quality really mean? *Sloan Management Review, 26,* 25-43.

Green, P. E. (1977). A new approach to market segmentation. *Business Horizons, 20,* 61-73.

Green, P. E. (1984). Hybrid models for conjoint analysis: An expository review. *Journal of Marketing Research, 11,* 155-169.

Green, P. E., & Helsen, K. (1989). Cross-validation assessment of alternatives to individual-level conjoint analysis: A case study. *Journal of Marketing Research, 26,* 346-350.

Green, P. E., & Krieger, A. (1991). Segmenting markets with conjoint analysis. *Journal of Marketing, 55,* 20-31.

Green, P. E., & Rao, V. R. (1971). Conjoint measurement for quantifying judgmental data. *Journal of Marketing Research, 8,* 355-363.

Green, P. E., & Srinivasan, V. (1978). Conjoint analysis in consumer research: Issues and outlook. *Journal of Consumer Research, 5,* 103-123.

Green, P. E., & Srinivasan, V. (1990). Conjoint analysis in marketing research: New developments and directions. *Journal of Marketing, 54,* 3-19.

Grönroos, C. (1984). A service quality model and its marketing implications. *European Journal of Marketing, 18,* 36-44.

Grönroos, C. (1990). *Service management and marketing: Managing the moments of truth in service competition.* Lexington, MA: Lexington.

Gummesson, E. (1991). Service quality, A holistic view. In S. W. Brown, E. Gummesson, B. Edvardsson, & B. Gustavsson (Eds.), *Service quality: Multidisciplinary and multinational perspectives* (pp. 3-22). Lexington, MA: Lexington.

Hagerty, M. R. (1985). Improving the predictive power of conjoint analysis: The use of factor analysis and cluster analysis. *Journal of Marketing Research, 22,* 168-184.

Kahneman, D., & Tversky, A. (1979). Intuitive prediction: Biases and corrective procedures. *TIMS Studies in Management Science, 12,* 313-327.

Kamakura, W. A. (1988). A least squares procedure for benefit segmentation with conjoint experiments. *Journal of Marketing Research, 25,* 157-167.

Koepp, S. (1987, February 2). Pul-eeze! Will somebody help me? *Time,* pp. 28-34.

Lewis, R. C., & Booms, B. H. (1983). The marketing aspects of service quality. In L. Berry, G. Shostack, & G. Upah (Eds.), *Emerging perspectives on services marketing* (pp. 99-107). Chicago: American Marketing Association.

Louviere, J. J. (1988). *Analyzing decision making: Metric conjoint analysis.* Newbury Park, CA: Sage.

Moore, W. L. (1980). Levels of aggregation in conjoint analysis: An empirical comparison. *Journal of Marketing Research, 17,* 516-523.

Narasimhan, C., & Sen, S. (1992). Measuring quality perceptions. *Marketing Letters, 3,* 147-156.

Neslin, S. A. (1983). Designing new outpatient health services: Linking service features to subjective consumer perceptions. *Journal of Health Care Marketing, 3,* 8-21.

Ogawa, K. (1987). An approach to simultaneous estimation and segmentation in conjoint analysis. *Marketing Science, 6,* 66-81.

Oliver, R. L. (1977). Effect of expectation and disconfirmation on postexposure product evaluations: An alternative interpretation. *Journal of Applied Psychology, 62,* 480-486.

Oliver, R. L. (1980). A cognitive model of the antecedents and consequences of satisfaction decisions. *Journal of Marketing Research, 17,* 460-469.

Oliver, R. L. (1981). Measurement and evaluation of satisfaction processes in retail settings. *Journal of Retailing, 57,* 25-48.

Oliver, R. L., & DeSarbo, W. S. (1988). Response determinants in satisfaction judgments. *Journal of Consumer Research, 14,* 495-507.

Parasuraman, A., Berry, L. L., & Zeithaml, V. A. (1991). Understanding, measuring, and improving service quality. In S. W. Brown, E. Gummesson, B. Edvardsson, & B. Gustavsson (Eds.), *Service quality: Multidisciplinary and multinational perspectives* (pp. 253-268). Lexington, MA: Lexington.

Parasuraman, A., Zeithaml, V. A., & Berry, L. L. (1985). A conceptual model of service quality and its implications for future research. *Journal of Marketing, 49,* 41-50.

Parasuraman, A., Zeithaml, V. A., & Berry, L. L. (1988). SERVQUAL: A multiple-item scale for measuring consumer perceptions of service quality. *Journal of Retailing, 64,* 12-40.

Parasuraman, A., Zeithaml, V. A., & Berry, L. L. (1991). Refinement and reassessment of the SERVQUAL scale. *Journal of Retailing, 67,* 420-450.

Phillips, L. W., Chang, D. R., & Buzzell, R. D. (1983). Product quality, cost position and business performance: A test of some key hypotheses. *Journal of Marketing, 47,* 26-43.

Wedel, M., & Kistemaker, C. (1989). Consumer benefit segmentation using clusterwise linear regression. *International Journal of Research in Marketing, 6,* 45-59.

Wedel, M., & Steenkamp, J.B.E.M. (1989). Fuzzy clusterwise regression approach to benefit segmentation. *International Journal of Research in Marketing, 6,* 241-258.

Wedel, M., & Steenkamp, J.B.E.M. (1991). A clusterwise regression method for simultaneous fuzzy market structuring and benefit segmentation. *Journal of Marketing Research, 28,* 385-396.

Wittink, D. R., & Cattin, P. (1989). Commercial use of conjoint analysis: An update. *Journal of Marketing, 53,* 91-96.

Zeithaml, V. A., Parasuraman, A., & Berry, L. L. (1990). *Delivering quality service: Balancing customer perceptions and expectations.* New York: Free Press.

CHAPTER TEN

Explanations for the Growth of Services

STEVEN M. SHUGAN

College of Business Administration, University of Florida

Service growth in the United States has been remarkable. Even when expressed as a percentage of all employment, service employment growth shows no sign of slowing. The U.S. government defines this sector as all nongoods-producing industries. Given that definition, the service sector accounts for nearly three of every four jobs and that number will continue to increase. Despite these facts, no one explanation for service growth emerges. Moreover, competing explanations provide diverse implications. This chapter examines many possible traditional explanations for service growth, including increasing levels of income, nonproductivity of services, urbanization, deregulation, women in the work force, demographic shifts, growth of government, environmentalism, general growth in GNP, and changes in the demand composition. Recent research raises doubt about the sufficiency of these explanations. After discussing these older explanations, we turn to recent explanations with more credibility, including specialization of labor and international competition. The chapter concludes that specialization has two effects. Specialists do many of the functions previously done within a manufacturing operation. As the role of knowledge-based specialists grow, functions move from manufacturing to the service sector. Second, specialists perform their specialties more efficiently than nonspecialists. As the scale economies allow use of specialists, efficiency increases and costs decrease. As costs decrease, prices decrease and the demand for services increases. This explanation has many implications for organizational structure and the definition of organizations.

AUTHOR'S NOTE: The author wishes to thank Sarita Bhagwat for her substantial help in preparing this chapter.

Service Stature

Noble Services

For many years, marketing academics and practitioners have debated the definitions and roles of services and goods. Usually services take the role of the ignoble. Some argue that service production is immaterial. Others argue that service production detracts resources from more valuable activities. Indeed, the debate starts with the classification of output as either "services" or "goods." This classification seems to imply that services are somehow "nongoods" or "bads."

Recent research is rapidly changing that view. We now know that all advanced economies move toward service production (Riddle, 1986). Achieving service production is, in fact, a trait of a truly advanced economy. Services are the fuel of a truly advanced economy. Productive manufacturing and agricultural operations cannot exist without critical infrastructure services. Without financing, distribution of raw materials, distribution of replacement parts, maintenance, repair services, electricity and water, a modern farm or factory would cease to operate.

Indeed, most highly educated workers find employment in the service sector (e.g., as financial analysts, health care professionals, attorneys, consultants, researchers). Even the modern manufacturing company might consist entirely of services. The company could have substantial funding in research and development. This department designs safe, effective, high-quality, and economical products. This department also develops efficient production techniques using minimal energy and producing minimal waste. Finally, the department develops production scheduling and shipping procedures.

Assembly might be subcontracted or performed in another country. After assembly occurs, the modern manufacturing company directs distribution of the finished goods, provides advertising and marketing support, arranges for financing, and performs all other distribution services. Indeed, the modern manufacturer might become a service provider.

A New Focus on Services

The service sector now receives more respect and attention from both academics and practitioners. Practitioners are helping the service sector become more marketing oriented as the sector faces rising competition and deregulation. The academic marketing literature now recognizes services marketing as a legitimate field of study. Many major universities have started teaching courses on services marketing. An increasing number of academic journals are publishing articles on services marketing.

The predominant factor causing both academics and practitioners to recognize services is the extraordinary growth of the service sector. In this chapter, we first examine that growth. Then we consider some of the possible explanations for service growth.

Service Growth

Economists have observed and made various comments on the growth of services in terms of gross national product, labor or employment statistics, and trade statistics.The services sector includes business services, retailing, wholesaling, financial services, insurance, real estate, communications, utilities, transportation, government, and many personal services. Although some U.S. government publications use the term "services" only for personal services, most U.S. government publications use the term to refer to all services, that is, all products not manufactured or extracted. We use the term "service sector" to refer to all service categories.

The service sector is overwhelmingly important to the U.S. economy. According to data from the U.S. Bureau of Labor Statistics, the service sector accounts for nearly three of every four jobs. According to *Fortune* magazine, that fraction will continue to increase. Over 80 million U.S. citizens work in services-producing industries. The service sector exports over $60 billion in services each year. It is one of few areas in which U.S. exports exceed U.S. imports.

Figure 10.1 shows the steady growth of nongoods production in the United States. In 1959, nongoods accounted for about 56% of all production. By 1995, projections show that 67% of all production will be nongoods. Service output continues to grow as a major component of the U.S. economy.

Not only are services currently important, service economies are a vision of the future. Growth in the service sector continues throughout the world in nearly every developed and developing country. Figure 10.2 shows the steady growth of services employment in the U.S. economy. In 1990, employment in nongoods-producing industries accounted for over 74% of all jobs. By 1995, projections expect nongoods employment to account for over 77% of all jobs. The service sector will create 9 out of every 10 new jobs (Personick, 1985) in the period of 1984 through 1995.

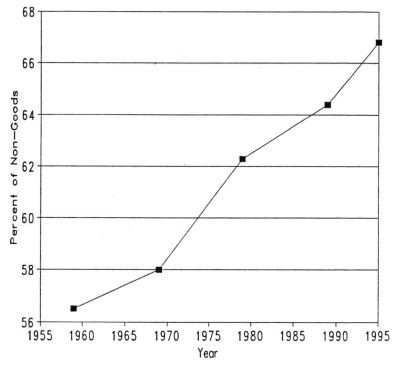

Figure 10.1. Percent of Gross National Product

From 1982 to 1987, annual receipts from services increased by 76.2%. Business services, the fastest growing of the service industries, had an increase of 102.9% in annual receipts.

Explanations

Miscellaneous Explanations for Service Growth

Economic data suggest the importance of services in the world economy and the high level of service growth. To fully understand the nature of the service economy, we now examine some reasons for that growth. We start with some older explanations: increasing levels of income, nonproductivity of services, urbanization, deregulation, women in the

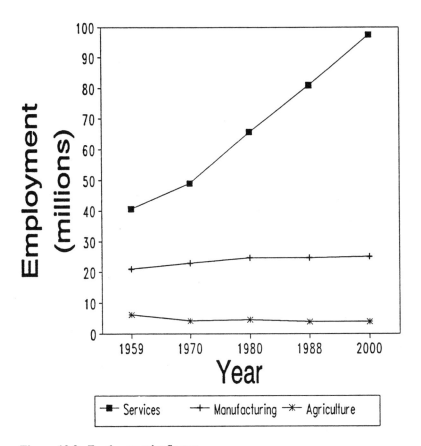

Figure 10.2. Employment by Sector

work force, demographic shifts, growth of government, environmentalism, general growth in GNP, and changes in the demand composition. Recent research raises doubts about the sufficiency of these explanations.

After discussing these older explanations, we progress to some recent explanations that have more credibility, including specialization of labor and international competition.

Increasing Levels of Income. Several books (e.g., Bell, 1973; Kuznets, 1971) have studied the hypothesis that consumers buy more services as average income levels increase. This hypothesis assumes a causal relationship between income and services. Certainly, service economies thrive in developed countries and developed countries have greater average income. But the relationship between the consumption of services and income levels is complex. Service growth often leads to enhanced productivity in other sectors and enhanced incomes. Service growth precedes or accompanies increased income. As income increases, the use of many infrastructure services increases. The use of other services remains constant or declines. Occasionally, increasing incomes lead to higher prices for services. The higher prices often equalize demand. The cost of hiring a cook or a baby-sitter in India, for example, is far less than the cost in the United States.

The relationship between income and service consumption (Riddle, 1986) depends on the degree of development of the country. It appears that as income increases, consumers spend less on agricultural products and more on either services or manufactured products only during certain phases of development. The prices of services dictate where consumers spend. As the prices of personal services escalate, even wealthy individuals substitute quality durables. Also, the increased income theory is only applicable to personal services. However, business services are the fastest growing part of the service sector. In fact producer services that include business services (SIC 73), legal services (SIC 81), and miscellaneous professional services (SIC 89) have observed the most rapid growth. This does not fit the increased income assumption about service growth. Our explanation in a later section fits better with this growth in producer services.

Nonproductivity of Services. Productivity measures the resources required to generate output. Consider a worker who assembles 10 units per hour. If that worker could assemble 11 units per hour, that worker's productivity would increase by 10%. However, if that worker's compensation increased by 20%, productivity would fall because input increased at a faster rate than output.

Measuring productivity in manufacturing can be difficult when higher quality causes higher costs. Fortunately, we can often observe higher quality. Manufacturing a superior car, for example, leads to many virtually identical high-quality cars. We can drive any one car and observe objective enhancement in fuel efficiency, comfort of the interior, smooth pickup, and likely additions such as air bags, antilock brakes, power steering, power windows, and so on. Mass production and durability help us measure quality for manufactured products.

Measuring productivity for services is more complicated. Suppose a beautician's wages increase with no corresponding increase in the number of haircuts performed. The beautician's productivity appears lower. This observation can be deceptive. Although the beautician performs the same number of haircuts, his/her intangible output may increase. The beautician may be more accurate or imaginative or spend more time with the customer to help him/her choose the right haircut. He/she may even use computerized images to make the decision easier for the customer and ultimately build up a relationship between the service organization and the customer. Enhancements in service productivity are often invisible because we do not observe many quality improvements. This invisibility and a historic belief in the unproductivity of the service sector combine to make service productivity appear weak.

From the early theories of Allan Fisher and Colin Clark, many researchers questioned the idea of enhancing service productivity. At that time, most researchers believed that services are, by definition, labor intensive. Personal services such as haircuts, taxicab rides, shoe shines, and domestic work all require a human worker. The human worker is difficult to remove and therefore it is difficult to increase the output per worker. This argument suggests that employment in the service sector should increase as other sectors become more productive. Services are doomed to be labor intensive and should eventually employ most workers.

Later researchers better understand the complexity of the service sector. As we have seen, services are diverse, and personal services are only a modest part of the entire service sector. Most of the output in the service sector comes from other services such as business services, transportation services, retailing, social services, and so on. It is important to consider productivity by service type. Personal services are not representative of the service sector.

Another complexity involves interpretation of service prices. Sometimes higher prices reflect lower productivity, whereas at other times increased prices reflect better output. The price-quality relationship for services is even more complex than that for products. For example, suppose you stay in a hotel for one night and it costs you $30. The next year, you stay at the same hotel and the hotel charges you $40. Your purchase of a service, a one-night stay in a hotel, has many experience-based attributes attached to it. This makes it difficult to interpret the price increase. Perhaps productivity increased because the hotel provided better rooms and furniture. Or it could be because it hired more efficient and more highly trained staff. It is not very easy for a consumer to interpret the price increase by saying that he/she paid $10 more than the last time because the person at the register was more polite. It is difficult to put a price tag on the enhancement in quality of a service. Perhaps productivity decreased because the hotel offered exactly the same quality of service at a higher price; that is, inflation of over $10. Perhaps productivity increased by more than $10 because the service had really improved and the consumer only paid $10 more for the additional quality.

Considering different types of services and carefully choosing output measures allows us to examine service productivity. Service productivity depends on the service industry (Mark, 1988). Like manufacturing, productivity varies widely across industries. Gasoline stations, air transportation, telephone communications, apparel retailing, and railroads show large gains in productivity. Retail food stores, public utilities, and commercial banking show poor gains in productivity. The goods-producing sector may show fewer productivity gains than the service sector.

Additional research (Riddle, 1986) concludes that productivity in the service sector is higher than most researchers previously believed. It also shows that service sector productivity is higher than for the economy as a whole. An additional worker to many service operations often provides a greater increase in output than an additional worker to a manufacturing operation.

Urbanization. A third hypothesis (Singelmann, 1978) puts urbanization as the cause of service growth. This hypothesis is consistent with the requirement of service proximity. Service providers and suppliers sometimes require direct contact. Urban areas facilitate that contact. In addition, urbanization promotes the growth of government and nonprofit services.

Although this hypothesis might explain the service growth in the United States to a certain extent, it fails to explain the growth in developing countries like India where, with the exception of five or six major cities, the population is rural. Moreover, the hypothesis does not explain the growth of many national and international services such as banking and insurance.

Deregulation. Deregulation of several U.S. industries in the 1980s resulted in net employment gains and growth of the deregulated services. These industries include trucking, busing, air transportation, communications, financial services, and cable television. The gains in employment, unfortunately, were often accompanied by lower wages and disruptive relocation. In addition, loss of government subsidies has sometimes slowed growth. However, deregulation led to increased competition and enhanced performance in these industries in the United States. This, in turn, contributed to service growth in the United States.

Women in the Work Force. In the United States, the value of time changes as women enter the work force. According to the U.S. Bureau of Labor Statistics, 33.3% of U.S. workers in 1960 were women. By 1990, that percent increased to 45.3%. In 1975, only 13.1% of economists were women; today 43.8% are. In 1975, only 7.1% of lawyers were women; today 20.8% are. In 1975, only 14.8% of computer systems analysts were women; today 34.5% are.

Participation of women in the work force results in their departure from household activities. But the tasks they used to perform in the households still exist. The house still needs to be cleaned, food needs to be bought and cooked, and babies and children to be looked after (Bellante & Foster, 1984). These services are not included in any of the three manufacturing, extractive, or service sectors, although there is a definite value attached to each of these services. As such, the government does not include these services in output statistics. However, once women stop performing these services around the house, someone else has to step in and perform the services for the household; hence the growth enjoyed by restaurants, cleaning services, baby-sitters, and day care centers. There is also a cost associated with producing these services. Households, usually women, invest many hours in production of household services. Women entering the work force make time more precious and increase the cost of producing these services. When a woman can earn $12 an hour, for example, the cost of her spending 2 hours producing a meal is $24. This figure would be larger if we included the cost associated with lost leisure time. As women's wages increase, the cost of spending time on household tasks increases and the cost of preparing a meal eventually exceeds the cost of buying a prepared meal at a restaurant.

When professional day care centers, cleaning services, and restaurants come into existence, they become part of national output. The service sector grows.

Demographic Shifts. The population of the United States is aging. In 1960, only 29.2% of the population was over 44 years of age. By 2020, 44.1% of the population will be over 44 years of age. As the population ages and life expectancy increases, demand for many services increases because the elderly consume a disproportionate share of services. These include recreation, financial planning, and retirement services. Health care may be the biggest beneficiary of this aging process. The fastest growing occupations are medical assistants, home health aides, radiologic technologists, and medical secretaries.

Growth of Government. In 1920, government activities represented less than 9% of GNP. Today, government is more than 20% of GNP. The government is a major supplier of services, producing both social services and defense services. Government growth is certainly a factor contributing to the growth of the service sector in the United States and other countries. Japan also is steadily increasing its government expenditures. Japan, nevertheless, is still spending far less than the United States on government as percent of GNP.

Environmentalism. Both manufacturing and extraction activities can cause damage to the environment, such as air, water, or noise pollution and destruction or depletion of natural resources. The service sector, however, generates fewer complaints. The nonpolluting nature of many services is now an important impetus to the growth of services. For these reasons, many communities encourage the development of clean services with the use of tax incentives and zoning accommodations.

GNP Growth. Expansion of the total economy is one reasonable explanation for growth in the service industry. GNP growth, however, explains only about 40% of the growth in producer services, which is one of the largest parts of the service sector. Moreover, growth in GNP explains only about 50% of the communication industry's growth and 65% of media services growth. It does explain 90% of the growth in the eating and drinking industry, however.

Changes in Demand Composition. Economists argue that the composition of people's demand for goods and services changes over time. This could mean that people's preferences have merely shifted toward services. It is now, for example, more socially acceptable to leave children in day care, have others cater your parties, and lease your automobile. Tschetter (1987), however, demonstrates that this changing demand composition explains less than 2% of the growth in producer services.

Better Explanations for Service Growth

We first presented three older explanations for services growth. Empirical studies make these explanations questionable. We subsequently presented some slightly more relevant and acceptable explanations of service growth. However, none of these explanations are completely satisfactory in explaining the pattern of service growth that we observe throughout the world. We now present two more credible reasons for the growth of services in nearly all countries. As shown in Table 10.1, both reasons relate to the specialization of service functions.

National Specialization. As the world becomes more complex, knowledge generation enjoys an exponential growth. Years ago, a physician could have a good understanding of the different areas of medicine. "General" practitioners were sufficient. Today, physicians are lucky to keep abreast with new technologies in their own specialties. In just the area of diagnosis, physicians must be familiar with the areas of computerized axial tomography, digital subtraction angiography, magnetic resonance imaging, positron-emission tomography, single photo emission computer tomography, thermographic imaging and ultrasound imaging (Shugan, in press). Health care, like almost every other field, is becoming more complex. It is not surprising that the fastest growing occupations in the United States are medical assistants, home health aides, radiologic technologists, and medical secretaries. Advances in information technology are also resulting in increases in activities such as processing, manipulation, and utilization of information in all three sectors. In fact electronic information service is the fastest growing service industry.

One way of coping with enhanced knowledge, innovations, and technological advances is increasing task specialization (Shugan, in press). Specialization causes service growth in two different ways. First, there is a change in accounting. Activities previously performed in the extractive and manufacturing sectors move to the service sector. Second, there is an increase in productivity that causes growth in both the service and manufacturing/extractive sectors.

Let us first consider the change in accounting. When manufacturing of a product requires more knowledge-based expertise, it does not always justify permanent employment. Patent law, for example, is continuing to become more complex. As complexity increases, a firm's legal department

TABLE 10.1 Reasons for Service Growth

Older Explanations for Service Growth	• Increased Income
	• Lack of Productivity
	• Urbanization
	• Deregulation
	• Women in the Workforce
	• Demographic Shifts
	• Growth of Government
	• Environmentalism
	• GNP Growth
	• Changes in the Demand Composition
Better Explanations	• National Spcialization
	• International Specialization

may find it more efficient to out-source the services of a patent attorney from a legal service rather than permanently employ more attorneys. The need for specialized services causes many businesses to purchase these specialized or knowledge-based services rather than employ additional generalists.

As more firms from extractive and manufacturing sectors purchase specialized services, more of the tasks performed within manufacturing or extractive sectors get performed in the service sector. This causes a change in accounting as activities of the manufacturing or extractive sectors shift to the service sector. What was counted as manufacturing activity in national accounting now becomes service activity. This results in service sector growth.

We can illustrate this accounting effect for software development. Consider a manufacturing firm that has its own team of computer professionals who design software for tasks such as scheduling jobs, releasing jobs from a backlog to the shop floor, and sequencing jobs at different work stations within the shop.

Suppose a manufacturing firm spends $100,000 on software development and generates $300,000 in shipments. When the manufacturing firm spends money on software development, the government considers this to be part of the manufacturing sector. The $300,000 is the output of the manufacturing sector. There is no service sector output (see the column labeled In-source in Table 10.2).

TABLE 10.2 Using a Software Vendor: Accounting Effect
(same output but different sector)

	In-Source *No Software Supplier*	*Out-Source* *External Software Supplier*
Software Spending	$100,000	$100,000
Shipments	$300,000	$300,000
Service Sector Output	**$0**	**$100,000**
Gross Mfr. Output		$300,000
Less Expenses		−$100,000
Manufacturing Sector Output	**$300,000**	**$200,000**
Service Sector Output	$0	$100,000
Manufacturing Output	+$300,000	+$200,000
Total Output	**$300,000**	**$300,000**

Now suppose the manufacturing firm out-sources software development. Here, the activity of software development, which accounts for $100,000 in output, shifts from the manufacturing sector to the service sector (see the column labeled Out-source in Table 10.2). Total output remains at $300,000. There is merely a shift in activity from the manufacturing sector to the service sector. An accounting transaction causes the growth in the service sector.

We should remember, however, that the manufacturing firm would not out-source the software development unless it was more productive to do so. We would, therefore, expect GNP to be greater with out-sourcing than without out-sourcing simply because out-sourcing occurs. The sophisticated software helps the manufacturing company increase productivity. The manufacturing firm, consequently, lowers production costs. That enables the firm to lower prices and boost shipments.

Table 10.3 illustrates this effect. The first column in Table 10.3 matches the second column in Table 10.2, reflecting the accounting shift caused by mere out-sourcing. The second column in Table 10.3, however, illustrates the increased productivity caused by the sophisticated software. In the column labeled Out-source With Growth, shipments increase from $300,000 to $400,000. Although shipments increase, manufacturing sector output remains constant. Total shipments increase from $300,000 to $400,000, but the manufacturing sector loses $100,000 to the service

TABLE 10.3 Using Software Vendor: Productivity Effect
(out-sourcing increasing output)

	Out-Source No Growth External Software Supplier	Out-Source With Growth External Software Supplier
Software Spending	$100,000	$100,000
Shipments	$300,000	$400,000
Service Sector Output	**$100,000**	**$100,000**
Gross Mfr. Output	$300,000	$400,000
Less Expenses	−$100,000	−$100,000
Manufactoring Sector Output	**$200,000**	**$300,000**
Service Sector Output	$100,000	$100,000
Manufactoring Output	+$200,000	+$300,000
Total Output	**$300,000**	**$400,000**

sector. Hence, total manufacturing output remains at $300,000. The accounting effect moves the productivity gain of $100,000 to the service sector. Total output enjoys an increase of $100,000, but the national accounting shows that increase in the service sector.

The service sector grows as business services enhance the productivity of the manufacturing and extractive sectors. Accounting effects exaggerate service sector growth, but growth is still real.

Figure 10.3 illustrates how national accounting causes growth in the service sector. The pie on the left represents a manufacturing firm. The firm does manufacturing and many services functions including inventorying, accounting, finance, marketing, management. As functions become specialized, the manufacturing firm subcontracts or spins off many of the service functions. As a consequence, these same functions move from the manufacturing sector to the service sector without any change in either input or output. Economists call this the "unbundling" phenomenon. However, if this is the only explanation for growth in the service sector, we should observe a decline in the manufacturing output. Also, there should not be an increase in the volume of total service activity, only a change of location.

Without an increase in the total pie, the dollar growth in the service sector is merely a change in national accounting: a change in where the

M = Manufacturing Function

S = Service Function

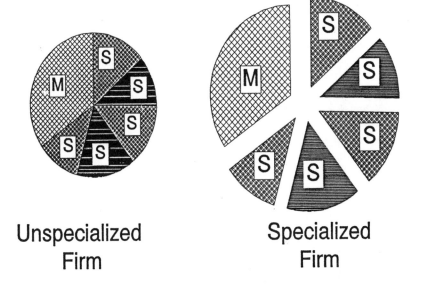

Unspecialized
Firm

Specialized
Firm

Figure 10.3. Spin-off of Services Causes Growth in Services

government records the $100,000. The government could assign the expenses to a services account (e.g., business services) or to a manufacturing account (e.g., auto manufacturing). But the change should involve more than just national accounting. Specialization can actually increase both service and manufacturing output (see Table 10.2).

Service specialization causes producer services to be more effective. This allows manufacturer output to improve. Hence, services growth and manufacturing growth can occur together.

International Specialization. In the previous section, we discussed how specialization of knowledge-based functions leads to the separation of service functions from the manufacturing and extractive sectors within a nation. Service providers develop and perform many services previously performed within manufacturing and extraction. When this event occurs within one country's economy, it causes both service sector growth and growth in the national economy.

When this event occurs across countries, specialization causes international trade. Countries that have a relative or comparative advantage at some function tend to specialize in that function. Consider the creation of a video camera. The design function might take place at a university in the United States. A Korean steel firm might provide the raw materials. A Swiss bank might provide the financing. A Mexican assembly plant might construct the device, and a Japanese firm might provide distribution.

Many researchers believe that services are the relative or comparative advantages of advanced countries. Less developed countries often have very low wage rates. These low wages provide them with an advantage in labor-intensive manufacturing not enjoyed by more developed or advanced countries.

Advanced countries, in contrast, have great advantages in infrastructure, information, education, communications, transportation, and other services. A truly advanced company manufacturing computers might entirely become a service business. The company might do market research and demand analysis. The company might develop new technologies with faster processing speeds, memory, storage capacity, and so on. The company might also develop superior manufacturing techniques, including flexible computer integrated manufacturing and intelligent manufacturing equipment.

Actual assembly might occur in another country. A foreign company might do the assembly, or assembly could occur at a foreign subsidiary. The complex part of the assembly process would require advanced equipment. The simple parts of the assembly process would require relatively unskilled labor.

The assembler ships the final assembled products back to the original company for distribution. The company provides financing, distribution, advertising, market research, maintenance, repairs, and other pre- and postsale service activities. The company in the advanced country effectively imports manufacturing and exports services. From these arguments, we might expect developed countries to focus on service exports. We would also predict increased international trade of services. But the area of international trade is controversial. Some researchers emphasize the significance of barriers and tariffs that countries impose on pure trade. These obstacles inhibit the trade of both manufactured products and services. Exporters of transportation services, for example, must consider many regulations and restrictions. Despite these problems, international service trade continues to grow.

For good or bad, governments cannot continuously inhibit strong market forces. For example, despite great expense governments have had great difficulties eliminating the illegal drug trade. Regulations do impose costs, but persistence and creativity can overcome many regulatory barriers. Toys-Я-Us, for example, collaborated with local lobbyists to change Japanese law so that Toys-Я-Us could locate its retailing services in Japan.

Creativity and advanced technology create difficulties for regulators. A consultant or accountant working in a foreign country can get remote access to computers, data bases, staff, and software. Advances in technology allow information, software, and images to flow over telephone lines. Restrictions on export and import of knowledge and other intangibles are more difficult to administer than restrictions on the physical transfer of manufactured products.

We have provided two important reasons for the growth of services. The first reason is the need for specialization created by increasing complexity. This creates a demand for the services of specialists who often provide services to multiple customers. The second reason is the consequence of business globalization. Here, specialization and the comparative advantage of developed countries lead to the increased trade of services.

The Likely Consequences of Specialization

As we saw earlier, specialization leads to spin-offs or out-sourcing of activities by manufacturing firms. This is likely to have a considerable impact on organizational structures. Researchers predict that future organizations are likely to be vertically disaggregated, with many of their functions performed by a network of specialized organizations (Miles & Snow, 1984).

Organizations will go beyond just operating from a global base to becoming a "quasicorporation" participating in a global partnership of skills and resources (Achrol, 1991). The Scoupe car is a very apt example of such activities with its body designed by Ital Design of Italy, suspension by Lotus of England, and manufacturing by Hundai of Korea. Flatter organizations will also lead to changes in hierarchies within organizations and place more emphasis on teamwork. The traditional roles of all the functions in a firm will undergo changes.

Summary

The service sector is the fastest growing sector of the economy. Advancement in technology and information leading to specializations at national and international levels is the chief reason for this growth. Older explanations for service growth are questionable. Researchers no longer believe that increased income results in service growth. Also questionable is the belief that lack of productivity is the explanation. Many service providers are very productive. Finally, urbanization does not explain service growth.

There are two effects of specialization. Specialists do many of the functions previously done within a manufacturing operation. As the role of knowledge-based specialists grow, functions move from manufacturing to the service sector. There is a change in national accounting that leads to the growth of the service sector.

Specialization has a second effect on service growth. Specialists perform their specialties more efficiently than nonspecialists. As the scale economies allow the use of specialists, efficiency increases and costs decrease. As costs decrease, prices decrease and the demand for services increases. Specialization leads to out-sourcing, which has an effect on organizational structures and hierarchies within the organizations.

References

Achrol, R. S. (1991). Evolution of the marketing organization: New forms for turbulent environments. *Journal of Marketing, 55*, 77-93.

Bell, D. (1973). *The coming of the post-industrial society: A venture in social forecasting.* New York: Basic Books.

Bellante, D., & Foster, A. C. (1984). Working wives and expenditure on services. *Journal of Consumer Research, 11*, 700-707.

Kuznets, S. (1971). *Economic growth of nations: Total output and production structure.* Cambridge, MA: Harvard University Press.

Mark, J. A. (1988). Productivity in service industries. In W. Candilis (Ed.), *United States service industries handbook* (pp. 45-55). New York: Praeger.

Miles, R. E., & Snow, C. C. (1984). Fit, failure and the hall of fame. *California Management Review, 26*, 10-28.

Personick, V. A. (1985). A second look at industry output and employment trends through 1995. *Monthly Labor Review, 108*, 26-41.

Riddle, D. (1986). *Service-led growth.* New York: Praeger.

Shugan, S. M. (in press). *Marketing and managing services: A context specific approach.* Homewood, IL: Richard D. Irwin.

Singelmann, J. (1978). *From agriculture to services: The transformation of industrial employment.* Beverly Hills, CA: Sage.

Tschetter, J. (1987). Producer services industries: Why are they growing so rapidly? *Monthly Labor Review, 110*, 31-40.

CHAPTER ELEVEN

A Customer Satisfaction Research Prospectus

EUGENE W. ANDERSON

CLAES FORNELL

School of Business Administration, University of Michigan

Customer satisfaction drives future profitability. It is a vital measure of performance for firms, industries, and national economies. However, although there has been extensive investigation of customer satisfaction at the level of the individual, there has been relatively little research addressing the role of customer satisfaction at the microeconomic or macroeconomic level. This chapter provides a prospectus for future customer satisfaction research by discussing theoretical, empirical, and methodological issues arising at both the microeconomic and macroeconomic levels, as well as identifying similar, unaddressed issues at the individual level. In addition, several high-priority directions for future research are identified.

What drives future profitability? If customers are the ultimate source of all revenue, then efficiency in acquiring and retaining customers is the key to long-term financial health. Moreover, given that customers are more costly to acquire than to retain, customer retention should be one of the highest priorities of any business enterprise.

What drives customer retention? Whether or not a customer remains loyal depends critically on the overall level of satisfaction with the current supplier and the availability of alternatives. Hence, to a large extent, customer satisfaction drives future profitability. As such, it is an

AUTHORS' NOTE: The authors wish to thank the Office for Customer Satisfaction Research at the University of Michigan for supporting this research.

important measure of a firm's past and current performance, as well as its future financial health.

Customer satisfaction is also an important performance measure at the macroeconomic level. Macroeconomic satisfaction provides valuable information regarding past and current economic performance. In addition, macroeconomic satisfaction may potentially be a leading indicator of future economic performance. It is an important measure of the value of the goods and services produced and an important gauge of the future financial prospects of industries and nations. As such, understanding macroeconomic satisfaction could be critical to improving a nation's economic performance, global competitiveness, and quality of life.

Why is satisfaction increasing in importance? First, customers are an increasingly scarce resource pursued by an increasingly large number of aggressive suppliers. This is because firms in most developed countries face slowing growth, mature markets, and increasing foreign competition. Moreover, cost structures make price competition difficult for these firms. Quality competition is therefore becoming an increasingly attractive alternative. Providing quality that satisfies customers provides an important source of competitive advantage by reducing price elasticities and retaining current customers. Second, there is a growing need for focusing on long-term relationships between customers and their suppliers. Continued growth in services means that more business transactions involve long-term relationships. Moreover, in a competitive environment in which it is increasingly difficult to compete on technology alone, there is increased interest in customer service as a means of product differentiation. In addition, increasingly complex technologies and the increasing emphasis on strategic alliances between buyers and suppliers require a close relationship between buyer and supplier. An ability to deliver superior levels of customer satisfaction is a key source of competitive advantage in building and maintaining such ties.

This means that customer satisfaction is not just another management fad or "flavor of the month" that is likely to disappear in the wake of the next "big idea." Customer satisfaction is central to assessing past performance and predicting future financial success. Firms that treat customer satisfaction as a fad—and do not respond to the need for restructuring, reorganizing, reallocating resources, and redesigning incentive plans to genuinely pursue customer satisfaction—will fall behind in the competition for tomorrow's customers. There is an urgent need to transcend old ways of doing business and find new ways to efficiently acquire and retain customers.

However, despite the increasing importance of customer satisfaction, the vast majority of research and practice focuses on customer acquisition rather than customer retention—on offensive rather than defensive strategy. The purpose of this chapter is to provide a prospectus for future research on customer satisfaction. The body of the chapter is devoted to an overview of theoretical, empirical, and methodological issues arising at both the microeconomic and macroeconomic levels. Table 11.1 provides a summary of the topics to be discussed. The chapter's organization follows the first row of the table. We discuss, in turn, each of the theoretical issues listed at each level of analysis, as well as pertinent measurement and estimation issues. Important empirical and methodological issues are discussed as they arise. Hence, the next section discusses issues regarding the definition, antecedents, consequences, measurement, and estimation of customer satisfaction at the individual level. The following section addresses issues arising at the microeconomic or firm level, including the role of satisfaction in corporate accounting; the antecedents and consequences of satisfaction at the firm level; the implications of satisfaction for resource allocation, employee compensation, and competitive strategy; the role of switching costs; and the measurement and estimation of firm-level or microeconomic satisfaction. Finally, we discuss macroeconomic level issues such as the role of satisfaction in national accounting, quality and productivity as antecedents of macroeconomic satisfaction, the complementary roles of satisfaction and price indices, industrial organization, differences in satisfaction across cultures, implications for public policy and overall subjective well-being, and the measurement of macroeconomic satisfaction. The chapter concludes by identifying some high priority directions for future research.

Customer Satisfaction at the Customer Level

The majority of existing research on customer satisfaction focuses on the individual or customer level (e.g., Churchill & Surprenant, 1982; Oliver, 1980; Oliver & DeSarbo, 1988; Westbrook & Oliver, 1991). An excellent review of this stream of research is provided by Yi (1991). Rather than provide an additional review, we identify key issues that have

TABLE 11.1 Summary Of Customer Satisfaction Research Issues

| | Level of Analysis | | |
Issue	Customer	Microeconomic	Macroeconomic
Theoretical	Definition Antecedents Consequences	Corporate Accounting Antecedents Consequences Resource Allocation and Compensation Employee and Customer Satisfaction Competitive Strategy Switching Costs	National Accounting Quality and Productivity Satisfaction and Price Indices Industrial Organization Cultural Differences Public Policy Subjective Well-Being
Empirical	Construct Validity Importance of Antecedents Inferred vs. Subjective Gap Repurchase Intentions Reliability Segmentation Moderating Effects and Interactions	Relative Importance of Offense and Defense Relative Costs of Offense and Defense Value of Current Customers Compensation Measures Effects of Index on Firm Value Reservation Prices	Relative Impact of Quality and Productivity Accounting for Industry Differences Effects of Changes in Public Policy Value of Change in the Index Switching Costs
Methodological	Monadic vs. Comparative Instruments Measurability Comparability Additivity Multicollinearity Nonnormality	Aggregating Multicollinearity Nonnormality Unobservables Cross-Section Time Series Quality *Elasticity* of Demand	Aggregation Productivity Measurement

either gone unresolved or have recently been brought into question. As shown in Table 11.1 this section begins by discussing the definition of satisfaction and how satisfaction differs from quality. Next, the antecedents of satisfaction—disconfirmation, expectations, and perceived quality—and the consequences of satisfaction are discussed. Finally, several important measurement and estimation issues are raised.

What Is Customer Satisfaction?

Perhaps the most basic issue that needs to be addressed is the definition of satisfaction itself. Two quite different conceptualizations of the satisfaction construct can be distinguished: transaction specific and brand specific. From a transaction-specific perspective, satisfaction is viewed as a postchoice evaluative judgment of a specific purchase occasion. Most behavioral research can be interpreted as focusing on this conceptualization of satisfaction (e.g., Oliver, 1980; Oliver & DeSarbo, 1988). However, recent research has focused more on satisfaction as brand specific. From a brand-specific perspective, satisfaction is an overall evaluation based on many transient experiences with a good or service over time (e.g., Anderson, Fornell, & Lehmann, 1992; Fornell, 1992; Johnson & Fornell, 1991; Westbrook & Oliver, 1991). Hence, satisfaction is an ongoing evaluation of the brand's ability to deliver the benefits a customer is seeking. This is an important distinction from the transaction-specific conceptualization, because it is a customer's overall evaluation of the brand that is of interest to management. Clearly, however, satisfaction may be measured with regard to a specific transaction, specific product or service attributes, a particular brand or product, or even a particular company. In general, satisfaction judgments may pertain to any object or idea and the context will determine the appropriate scope of analysis and the types of measures employed. However, future researchers need to look more closely at the question of which conceptualization of satisfaction is more appropriate under different conditions, as well as the validity of the construct and the reliability of measures.

An important and related issue is how to distinguish between satisfaction and quality. Different conceptualizations of quality also exist in the literature. In marketing, quality has most often been viewed as the levels of a product's attributes (e.g., Hauser & Shugan, 1983). In operations management (e.g., Juran, 1988), quality is defined as having two important meanings: (a) fitness for use—does the product possess features that meet the needs of customers and thereby provide product satisfaction? and (b) reliability—is the product free from deficiencies? Hence, in marketing as well as other fields—such as the total quality management movement—quality is viewed as a potential of product attributes to provide satisfaction. Perceived quality is then dependent on an individual's utility function for the level of quality provided.

Satisfaction is a postconsumption evaluation of perceived quality relative to expected quality. This perspective on the relation between the perceived quality or utility provided by a good or service and satisfaction dates back at least to the philosopher-economist Jeremy Bentham (1789, 1802), who distinguished between utility and satisfaction by viewing the former as a property inherent in a product that creates the latter. However, recent research in marketing has focused on quality as a cumulative construct or overall assessment of a firm's service delivery system (e.g., Parasuraman, Zeithaml, & Berry, 1985). This approach, embodied by the SERVQUAL measurement scale, appears to be similar in spirit to the overall-evaluation conceptualization of satisfaction. Hence, there appears to be a need for resolving the distinction between quality and satisfaction, as well as whether satisfaction is a "local" or "global" assessment of product experience. Oliver (1993) provides a promising theoretical attempt to address this issue; his approach, however, will require empirical testing.

More generally, there is a need for clearer definition of the underlying phenomena of interest. Practitioners are clearly more interested in the customer's overall evaluation of their offering (e.g., brand, product, service). However, there are several areas of research in marketing that seem to overlap in this area. For example, research on brand equity, brand loyalty, brand inertia, carryover effects of brand experience, attitude toward the brand, brand reputation, and so on all have significant intersections with customer satisfaction, as well as customer retention and the valuation of customer assets. Future researchers may wish to reassess this proliferation of approaches.

What Are the Antecedents of Customer Satisfaction?

What is the appropriate set of antecedents (and relations) for satisfaction at the individual level? Understanding how satisfaction is generated has important implications for management (e.g., product design, service delivery, marketing mix allocations). Whether local or global in nature, satisfaction has almost always been viewed as an evaluation based on past experience. This evaluation process has been characterized in several ways, but the key elements are the perceived quality, performance, or utility actually experienced and a comparison standard such as expectations. As shown in Figure 11.1, these antecedents influence both satisfaction, and subsequently, the likelihood of repurchase. Beginning with Oliver (1977, 1980), research concerned with the antecedents of satisfaction focuses primarily on the expectancy-disconfirmation paradigm. Drawing on adaptation level theory, Oliver (1980, 1981) posits expectations as an

Figure 11.1. The Antecedents and Consequences of Satisfaction at the Customer Level

adapted standard that provides a frame of reference for buyers' evaluative judgments. Accordingly, expectations provide a baseline or anchor for a customer's level of satisfaction. If disconfirmation—a difference between perceived and expected performance—is perceived to have occurred, then customer satisfaction increases or decreases from this baseline level created by expectations.

Disconfirmation has received widespread support as an important antecedent of satisfaction at the individual level (Oliver & DeSarbo, 1988; Yi, 1991). However, there is some question as to whether disconfirmation should be inferred from the mathematical difference between perceived quality and expectations or whether individuals' subjective disconfirmation should be measured directly. Based on work by Oliver and Bearden (1985) and Swan and Trawick (1981), Yi (1991) points out several reasons for preferring the latter measure. For example, a ceiling or floor effect on ratings of perceived quality and expectations might occur with the inferred method. The subjective method allows disconfirmation to be measured in such an event. In addition, reliability decreases as the correlation between two measures increase. Given the high correlation between expectations and perceived quality, the reliability of the inferred method will be quite low compared to the subjective method. Moreover, there is an overspecification problem when using inferred disconfirmation in addition to expectations or perceived quality as predictors of satisfaction. Future researchers may wish to pursue further investigation of this important issue.

Although disconfirmation is widely accepted as an antecedent of individual satisfaction, there is mixed empirical evidence as to whether expectations directly affect satisfaction. For example, Churchill and Surprenant (1982) find that perceived performance rather than expectations directly affects satisfaction for a VCR used in their study. Oliver and DeSarbo (1988) find disconfirmation and perceived performance have a stronger impact on satisfaction than expectations. Anderson and Sullivan (1993) introduce a theoretical framework in which satisfaction is a function of perceived quality and disconfirmation when disconfirmation occurs, and a function of expectations when disconfirmation does not occur. They find the proposed specification is better supported by their data than the expectancy-disconfirmation model. In addition, they find that the direct impact of perceived quality on satisfaction is greater than the impact of disconfirmation, and negative disconfirmation has a greater effect on satisfaction than positive disconfirmation.

However, future researchers need to further investigate the antecedents of satisfaction, their relations, possible moderating factors, and the relative impact of each on satisfaction. These are important issues because current models at the individual level typically explain 40% to 60% of the variation in satisfaction (Anderson & Sullivan, 1993; Fornell, 1992). Although this figure is higher at the organizational level (e.g., Fornell & Robinson, 1983), the economic importance of satisfaction suggests that even incremental improvement in the explanatory power of satisfaction models is desirable.

Identifying additional antecedents of satisfaction is an important direction for future research. For example, customers have expectations not only about the brand, but also about the category, and more generally, their ideal product. Understanding the different types of comparison standards that can affect satisfaction, and how marketing variables might affect these comparison standards, would appear to be a potential area for future research. Another possible antecedent to consider is a halo or reputational effect that influences customer satisfaction and its consequences from period to period, such as the influence of prior attitude in Oliver (1980). Not accounting for a halo effect that carries over from period to period may lead to overestimation of the impact of current product and service attributes on satisfaction.

There are also opportunities in specifying the system of relations between the antecedents and satisfaction. Identifying additional antecedents of satisfaction will lead to further refinement of the specification. In addition, interactions between the antecedents might exist (e.g., Oliver & DeSarbo, 1988). For example, does having high expectations increase the impact of disconfirmation on satisfaction? Finally, relations between the antecedents are often modeled as linear. What nonlinearities should be expected? Are there diminishing returns to the effects of the assorted antecedents on satisfaction?

What factors might moderate the effects of the antecedents on satisfaction? For example, disconfirmation is found to be greater when ease of evaluating quality is high (Anderson & Sullivan, 1993). Additionally, disconfirmation is driven more by perceived quality and less by expectations when ease of evaluating quality, frequency of usage, and difficulty of standardization are high (Anderson, 1992). Future researchers may wish to further investigate how factors such as the level of buyer involvement, buyer uncertainty, or variance in supply might moderate the effects of satisfaction's antecedents.

How might the importance of antecedents vary across individuals? Little work has been done showing how satisfaction and response to antecedents varies across individuals. Most studies of satisfaction are cross-sectional and therefore aggregate individual satisfactions without controlling for differences. However, accounting for different segments may offer further improvements in explanatory power, as well as enhanced diagnostic information for practitioners. For example, customers with greater expertise or involvement may be more likely to experience disconfirmation, and satisfaction may be more sensitive to perceived quality and disconfirmation for these individuals (Anderson, 1992). Conversely, satisfaction for customers who do not experience disconfirmation may appear to be driven more by expectations than by perceived quality and disconfirmation (Oliver, 1989). Moreover, the responsiveness of very dissatisfied customers to changes in quality may be different from those of satisfied customers. Understanding when it is worth investing in trying to respond to dissatisfied customers is an important avenue for future research. In the absence of segmentation variables, a latent class approach may be useful in approaching these issues.

What Are the Consequences of Customer Satisfaction?

What is the appropriate set of consequences (and relations) for satisfaction at the individual level? How does customer satisfaction influence repurchase behavior, willingness to pay or reservation prices, firm reputation and brand equity, and attitude toward the brand? Understanding the cognitive and behavioral consequences of satisfaction also has important implications for management (e.g., customer recovery, complaint management).

Individual customer satisfaction has been linked to repurchase intentions (Anderson & Sullivan, 1993; Fornell, 1992; Oliver, 1980; Oliver & Swan, 1989). However, it is not well understood how predictive repurchase intentions are of actual purchase behavior (Morrison, 1979). Understanding the conditions under which repurchase intentions are reliable or unreliable in predicting actual behavior might be an important question for future research. For example, how might product category characteristics such as frequency of use affect the reliability of repurchase intentions? How rapidly does satisfaction or the effect of satisfaction on repurchase intentions decay (cf. Oliver, 1981)? There is a need for empirical work addressing these questions.

Several researchers have looked at the implications of satisfaction for exit/voice behavior, where exit and voice are analogous to switching and complaining behavior (Andreasen, 1985; Hirschman, 1970). One key objective of management in understanding exit/voice behavior is improved efficiency in customer recovery. That is, when a customer is dissatisfied, how can he or she be retained? Fornell and Wernerfelt (1987, 1988) examine the strategic implications of exit/voice behavior for customer satisfaction. They discuss the importance of defensive marketing efforts to reduce the likelihood of switching. Their results suggest that firms should first encourage dissatisfied customers to complain and then manage those complaints in order to retain customers. One example would be the use of 800 numbers to reduce the cost of complaining.

Further understanding of customer recovery could improve the allocation of marketing resources by the firm. For example, segmenting customers by their response to dissatisfaction experiences may lead to improved targeting of customer recovery efforts. Similarly, if groups of customers differ in their likelihood of being dissatisfied, then marketing effort needs to be targeted appropriately. In addition, it is important to understand the responsiveness of customers to recovery efforts. Recovering dissatisfied customers may be too costly in some instances.

In general, future researchers might find it fruitful to investigate both cognitive and behavioral responses to satisfaction. What types of cognitive changes occur as a result of a satisfactory or dissatisfaction experience? For example, does satisfaction influence attitude toward the brand? Similarly, what types of behavioral responses exist? For example, how does the level of satisfaction carry over to influence future purchases? What are the implications of different types of switching and complaining behavior? What determines whether a customer will switch or complain? How much should switching be discouraged and complaining encouraged?

Measuring Individual Satisfaction

An important issue in the measurement of satisfaction is whether the measuring instrument should be monadic or comparative. For example, is it sufficient to measure satisfaction with a customer's current product or service choice? Or should satisfaction be evaluated with respect to competing products as when assessing utility in paired comparison approaches? There may be conditions under which one approach or the other may be more appropriate. For example, in many product and service categories, a customer may not be very familiar with a competitor's product and service delivery attributes (e.g., in banking services, legal services, and automobiles). In such categories, a monadic approach may be reasonable. However, this may not be the case in a packaged goods category such as paper towels or toilet tissue where a customer has greater familiarity with competitors. Future researchers may wish to look more closely at the issues surrounding this question. For example, under what conditions is a monadic approach appropriate? What biases may result when the monadic approach is used under other conditions?

Other potential problems in measuring satisfaction exist. For example, economists have long expressed reservations about whether individuals' satisfaction or utility can be measured, compared, or aggregated (Hicks, 1939, 1943, 1981; Pareto, 1906; Ricardo, 1817; Samuelson, 1947). Early economists who believed it was possible to produce a "cardinal" measure of utility (Bentham, 1802; Marshall, 1891), have been replaced by or-dinalist economists who argue that the structure and implications of utility-maximizing economics can be retained while relaxing the cardinal assumption. However, cardinal or direct measurement of such judgments and evaluations is common in other fields. For example, in marketing, conjoint analysis is used to measure individual utilities (Green & Srinivasan, 1978, 1990; Green & Tull, 1975).

Given that measurement of satisfaction has such important implications, it seems reasonable to identify means of overcoming, or at least minimizing, the measurement difficulties involved (Anderson, in press). For example, Johnson and Fornell (1991) argue that although satisfaction is an inherently unobservable construct, a latent variable methodology provides a means of taking measurement error into account. Fornell (1992) uses partial least squares to estimate satisfaction for Swedish firms. A possible direction for future research would be to investigate whether the resulting indices can be treated as interval scaled. It is possible that a hedonic approach would provide significant benefits by addressing this issue (Anderson, 1993).

Estimation Problems at the Customer Level

Estimating customer satisfaction models at the individual level poses several difficulties, particularly when there are many attributes that may affect perceived quality, and subsequently, satisfaction. Multicollinearity can be a significant problem in these types of models. In addition, responses to the types of survey instruments common in satisfaction research may lead to highly skewed or otherwise nonnormal distributions. Such data may also be noisy due to missing or unobservable factors. Many of these technical difficulties can be overcome through the use of second-generation multivariate techniques (Fornell, 1982). Moreover, such techniques theoretically provide a better estimate of unobservable satisfaction by treating satisfaction as part of a system composed of both the antecedents and consequences.

Whether data is collected cross-sectionally or over time may also present problems for the analyst. For example, what are the trade-offs in using a cross-section of customers versus tracking individuals over time? How useful are techniques developed for handling short cross-sectional time series in such situations? What are the trade-offs involved in tracking customer satisfaction over time using a new, randomly selected cross-section in each period rather than an ongoing panel? It may be important for future research to further investigate such problems in estimating satisfaction models in order to better understand how they should be resolved.

Customer Satisfaction at the Microeconomic Level

The second column of Table 11.1 summarizes the key issues arising at the microeconomic or firm level. In this section, we begin by highlighting the importance of satisfaction for corporate accounting. Next, we discuss the antecedents of satisfaction, paying particular attention to differences between the microeconomic and individual level. In addition, the consequences of satisfaction for business performance are discussed. This leads to a discussion of issues arising with regard to resource allocation, employee compensation, and competitive strategy. Finally, we discuss the measurement and estimation of firm-level or microeconomic satisfaction.

Microeconomic Satisfaction and Corporate Accounting

What drives future profitability? Corporate accounting provides information on what drives costs, but it is also important to account for what drives revenue. The goal of measuring satisfaction at the firm level is to obtain information about the firm's financial prospects by gaining insight into the sources of future revenue. Higher customer satisfaction should indicate increased life expectancy for current customers, reduced price elasticities, insulation of current customers from competitors' efforts, lower costs of future transactions, lower costs of attracting new customers, and an enhanced reputation for the firm. Hence, customer satisfaction should reflect the value of customers as an asset. Such information could allow for the value of this asset to be included on corporate balance sheets and marketing costs accounted for as an investment in that asset. Moreover, given that it is based on customer perceptions, such a measure should not be subject to many of the problems associated with traditional accounting measures of performance (e.g., changes in accounting practices, seasonality).

What Are the Antecedents of Microeconomic Satisfaction?

What is the appropriate set of antecedents (and relations) for satisfaction at the firm level? For individual customers, satisfaction is widely viewed as involving both perceived quality and expectations. However, firm-level antecedents may exist at a different level of analysis.

Recent research indicates that perceived quality is an important antecedent of satisfaction at the customer level (Anderson & Sullivan, 1993); no reason exists not to expect satisfaction to also be largely dependent on the level of perceived quality at the microeconomic level. However, is disconfirmation likely to be an important antecedent at the firm level? Psychological phenomena such as disconfirmation and assimilation are unlikely to be appropriate at a microeconomic level of analysis (Johnson, Anderson, & Fornell, 1992). At this level, customers as a group should have expectations that are rational. Hence, expectations should reflect actual quality, particularly in mature industries. Any deviations at the individual level leading to disconfirmation should cancel each other out where the group's levels of perceived quality, expectations, and satisfaction are considered. Hence, satisfaction should be almost wholly a function of perceived quality as summarized in Figure 11.2. In fact, Johnson et al. (1992) investigate the relations between firm-level measures of perceived

Figure 11.2. The Antecedents and Consequences of Satisfaction at the Micro-economic Level

quality, expectations, and satisfaction and find perceived quality to have a large positive impact on satisfaction whereas expectations have a positive, but very small, impact on satisfaction. Future researchers may wish to look more closely at the topic of aggregating individual customer satisfaction to the firm level.

Future researchers may also wish to look more closely at how specific firm actions, such as marketing mix variables, influence satisfaction. A wide variety of product features, service delivery attributes, and firm actions make up perceived quality, and subsequently, affect satisfaction (e.g., price, variety, availability, customer service, salesperson support, delivery). Understanding the relations between specific firm actions and satisfaction will allow for more accurate accounting of resource expenditures. For example, how does advertising influence satisfaction? How does price affect perceived quality or value? Under what conditions should we expect different marketing actions to be more important than others? How do different types of attributes affect perceived quality and satisfaction (e.g., functional, aesthetic)? Accounting for expenditures in advertising as an investment in a revenue-generating customer asset may radically alter how management views marketing effort.

What Are the Consequences of Microeconomic Satisfaction?

Customer satisfaction should indicate increased life expectancy for current customers, reduced price elasticities, insulation of current customers from competitors' efforts, lower costs of future transactions, lower costs of attracting new customers, and an enhanced reputation for the firm. Hence, customer satisfaction provides important information about the value of current customers. Moreover, by linking customer satisfaction to specific firm actions, firms can begin to view marketing expenditures as an investment in customer assets.

Anderson et al. (1992) have taken the first steps in linking microeconomic measures of satisfaction to business performance. They find substantiating evidence for the intuitive positive flow from perceived quality to satisfaction to profitability. Moreover, they find the economic consequences of increases in microeconomic customer satisfaction to be substantial. Interestingly, the findings also indicate that satisfaction may actually fall as market share increases. This occurs because share increases may come from customers with different preferences than those who are the primary target (Fornell, 1992). Hence, there appears to be an inherent trade-off between market share and customer satisfaction goals. For example, market share and satisfaction objectives may be incompatible in an industry that is highly differentiated, but satisfaction will lead to higher market share when there is less differentiation. Moreover, market share or volume goals may be incompatible with achieving high perceived quality and customer satisfaction.

In general, productivity and satisfaction should move in the same direction only under certain conditions. For example, although increases in *reliability* may lead to lower costs and fewer defects and consequently to higher productivity and satisfaction, increases in the *level* of quality provided should lead to higher costs, lower productivity, and higher satisfaction. Future researchers need to look more closely at the relations between the goals of different "generic strategies," such as "quality," "satisfaction," or "market share" in terms of their ultimate implications for long-term profitability.

There are a variety of opportunities for future research regarding the consequences of microeconomic satisfaction and how they are linked to firm actions. For example, how does the impact of firm actions on satisfaction and profitability vary across firms or categories? What is the impact of satisfaction on retention relative to that of switching costs? What is the impact of satisfaction on the price elasticity of demand? What is the value of encouraging complaining behavior? What is the loss incurred when customers defect? How can changes in customer assets best be traced to specific investments in marketing activity (e.g., product features, service delivery attributes, advertising)? How will treating marketing expenditures as an investment change current marketing practice? How does microeconomic satisfaction vary over time? Does a firm's customers' satisfaction level lead its stock price?

Resource Allocation

An improved understanding of the antecedents and consequences of satisfaction can have important implications for resource allocation. Allocating firm resources to develop or maintain customer assets should have a serious impact on strategy and tactics involved in marketing programs, as well as on compensation. At the most general level, there is a need for investigating how offensive and defensive marketing efforts affect satisfaction, and ultimately, profitability. What is an offensive marketing effort? What is a defensive effort? What kind of response curve best captures the impact of defensive marketing efforts? For example, there is substantial support in the marketing literature for an S-shaped response curve for offensive marketing efforts. Is this likely to hold true for defensive efforts? The response curve for defensive marketing efforts may be one of strictly diminishing returns. This is an important question for future research.

There is also a need for investigating the relative impact of offensive and defensive marketing efforts on satisfaction and profitability. If firms are overspending on offensive activity, then the findings could have a dramatic impact on both research and practice. For example, price promotions might be curtailed in favor of loyalty-building promotions such as contests, sweepstakes, and "frequent flyer" programs. Advertising dollars might need to be shifted away from providing price, product, and location information to building market power via image advertising or even to more targeted communications channels, such as direct mail. In general, if profitability is shown to be more sensitive to defensive efforts, then there should be a shift of resources from attracting new customers to defending current customers.

Determining what drives profitability is critical to achieving a better allocation of resources. For example, understanding how changes in service delivery attributes affect future revenue and taking into account the costs associated with each attribute can provide guidance in adjusting the level of service delivery attributes. Hence, as an indicator of the value of customer assets, customer satisfaction allows firms to determine how different dimensions of quality affect satisfaction, and consequently, long-term profitability. This can allow for better allocation of resources by identifying high-priority areas for improvement, as well as areas in which the firm is performing sufficiently well. Achieving a better understanding of what drives future revenue will also lead to more effective planning and evaluation of potential changes in strategy and tactics.

How should satisfaction affect employee compensation? What are the trade-offs between customer satisfaction and employee satisfaction? Many firms now use customer satisfaction as a criterion for diagnosing product or service performance and tie this information to compensation for top executives, middle management, and line employees. In rewarding top management, tying compensation to satisfaction brings a long-term focus to the organization. In rewarding middle management and line employees, determining which activities of the firm increase satisfaction can lead to incentive systems designed to enhance the future health of the firm. Hence, satisfaction can help bring a firm's organizational incentives in line with its long-run strategy. Moreover, it can help an organization provide an appropriate balance between offensive and defensive efforts of employees. What is the appropriate balance of offensive performance measures (e.g., productivity, volume) and defensive performance measures (e.g., customer satisfaction)? Future researchers need to look more closely at the role of customer satisfaction in compensation at all levels of the organization, as well as the interactions between customer satisfaction, employee satisfaction, and other components of organizational structure.

Competitive Strategy

What is the competitive intelligence value of one's own and competitors' customer satisfaction? How can knowledge of customer satisfaction levels be of aid to competitive strategy? Satisfaction provides a systematic benchmark for future improvement; competitive comparisons would provide a means of benchmarking firm performance against the competition. Moreover, satisfaction can be useful in analyzing weaknesses in the strategy of the firm or its competitors. For example, declining satisfaction should be symptomatic of deeper problems facing the firm. Satisfaction provides the firm with a measure of the effectiveness with which it is defending current customers. Customers of firms with low satisfaction are particularly vulnerable and provide expansion opportunities for more competent organizations. Given the large proportion of future business that comes from repeat customers and the higher cost of attracting new customers relative to maintaining old ones, understanding the effectiveness of defensive strategy should be of high priority.

There is a need to understand the role of satisfaction in retaining customers for modeling efforts in the area of competitive strategy as well. For example, most models of competitive promotional activity take the proportion of customers who are "loyals" or "switchers" to be given.

However, the conclusions of such models may be misguiding to practitioners if marketing effort only attracts new customers and does not affect loyalty. In general, the marketing mix implications of the carryover effect of past product experience on future purchase behavior needs to be looked at more closely.

Measuring Microeconomic Satisfaction

Perhaps the most basic issue at the microeconomic level is whether to aggregate individual satisfaction or estimate microeconomic satisfaction directly. However, in many industries, it is unlikely to be feasible to perform a census of all customers and aggregate their separate satisfactions. Given the goal of a unique measure representative of the firm's customers' level of satisfaction, information concerning how well satisfied a firm's customers are as a whole is obtainable by sampling users and estimating microeconomic satisfaction directly.

Fornell (1992) measures satisfaction directly at the firm level. A structural model is used to estimate a satisfaction index based on a cross-section of customers of a single product of the firm. The estimation procedure employed, partial least squares (Fornell, 1982), overcomes many of the technical difficulties discussed previously. As at the customer level, future researchers may wish to investigate refinements in the specification used in this study.

Another interesting problem for future research is how to measure firm-level satisfaction for multiproduct, multiservice firms. For example, should separate product indices be estimated and aggregated based on value of sales? If the firm has too many lines to make such a census feasible, then how should a sample of lines be chosen? How might the resulting sample then be aggregated? In such a situation, how might satisfaction be tied directly to individual or organizational responsibility? Analogously, when multiple suppliers are responsible for delivering the benefits sought by a customer, how can contributions to satisfaction by different channel members be determined? Examples include car dealers versus car makers versus automotive suppliers.

Estimating Microeconomic Satisfaction

As at the customer level, estimation at the microeconomic level poses technical difficulties such as multicollinearity and nonnormal distributions. In addition, there is the difficulty of dealing with cross-sectional time series data. To account for heterogeneity in a cross-section of industries (e.g., due to accounting practices or IO considerations) and other unobservable effects (e.g., firm strategy, pioneering advantage), state-dependent formulations can be employed (Boulding, 1990; Jacobson, 1990). Other methods, such as latent class analysis of time series data, may also prove useful in addressing these issues.

Customer Satisfaction and Macroeconomics

The last column of Table 11.1 summarizes the important issues arising at the macroeconomic level. Accordingly, this section begins by discussing the role of satisfaction in national accounting. In the process, the importance of quality and productivity as antecedents of macroeconomic satisfaction is discussed, as well as the potential complementary roles of satisfaction and price indices. Next, we turn to a discussion of industrial organization issues regarding satisfaction. This leads naturally into a discussion of differences in satisfaction across cultures. Finally, we discuss the implications for public policy and subjective well-being, as well as measurement issues.

Macroeconomic Satisfaction and National Accounting

How might measuring macroeconomic satisfaction complement current methods of assessing economic conditions? What is the potential role for satisfaction in evaluating the economic performance of nations? Macroeconomic satisfaction is reflective of the value of goods and services in a society, as well as a leading indicator of future financial performance. Even as understanding microeconomic satisfaction should aid individual firms in allocating resources, understanding macroeconomic satisfaction will help government act in ways that better allocate resources to enhance economic performance.

As an indicator of the nation's economic health, macroeconomic satisfaction would provide valuable information complementary to that provided by traditional indices of factors such as productivity and price. It is not enough for a nation to produce efficiently, it must also produce that which is highly valued as indicated by Figure 11.3. The value produced is what is important. Are customers better off with an increase in productivity or an increase in quality/satisfaction? The OECD Productivity Index indicates that Japan and Germany are below the average productivity level for developed countries, yet these countries have a positive balance of trade, strong economies, and a reputation for quality products (Fornell, 1992). Given the pervasive tendency to compare U.S. economic performance with that of these two nations, why isn't there a methodical evaluation of relative performance with respect to quality as well as productivity? Future researchers need to look more closely at how satisfaction and productivity affect macroeconomic performance, as suggested by Figure 11.3.

A national satisfaction barometer would provide a useful complement to current price indices. In general, price indices fail to provide quality information. Traditional price indices assume that the quality of goods is constant over time and consider only changes in price and quantity. For a measure such as the Consumer Price Index, the qualities inherent in the bundle of goods and services on which it is based change dramatically over time. Moreover, quality does not remain constant over time for most individual goods and services. For example, the quality of medical care has undoubtedly improved dramatically in the last 20 years. However, a traditional price index does not account for changes in quality. For example, a traditional price index does an injustice to a product for which the price index has remained steady while the satisfaction index has increased. The *value* provided by the product has increased, but this is not reflected in the price index. Future researchers may find it interesting to compare relative price indices for goods and services and their satisfaction scores. One possible alternative is to combine economic welfare and productivity information in a single "value" index. This would entail viewing the level of a hedonic customer satisfaction index as a benefit and price as a cost (Anderson, 1993).

In addition to improving national competitiveness and accounting, a satisfaction barometer would provide benefits in making policy decisions in both the domestic and trade arenas. Domestically, a satisfaction barometer would allow analysis of the effects of price ceilings, floors, and supports; taxes; subsidies; quotas; and so on. In the international arena, a satisfaction barometer would allow the welfare of the citizenry to be considered directly. In trade decisions, if one country has higher prices for a product than another, then free trade implies producers in the high-priced country will lose and consumers will gain. A satisfaction barometer would allow the size of these trade-offs to be measured and perhaps indicate a level of compensation to an injured party. It would also provide evidence as to which industries are most vulnerable to competitive encroachment under conditions of free trade.

Figure 11.3. The Antecedents and Consequences of Satisfaction at the Macroeconomic Level

Finally, it would allow for more accurate comparisons of the "wealth of nations." It would provide a benchmark for each nation to use as a reference point for future performance. Moreover, such an index should be a leading indicator of future economic performance.

Industrial Organization and Macroeconomic Satisfaction

How do market structure characteristics affect satisfaction in different industries? Systematic variation in satisfaction across industries may come from several sources. First, customer satisfaction is likely to be higher in industries where goods are differentiated (Fornell, 1992). In fact, using expert measures of the level of differentiation and customer heterogeneity in a market, Anderson and Fornell (1991) find that satisfaction increases with the ratio of differentiation with respect to heterogeneity.

There are a variety of industry characteristics that might lead to the industry differences observed. First, one might expect the overall importance of the good or service to lead to greater sensitivity to satisfaction. Second, the existence of switching barriers should have an influence on how sensitive retention is in a given industry. In addition, industries in which there are few alternatives are likely to have lower sensitivity to satisfaction. Other industry characteristics may influence the difficulty of offering a standardized good to all consumers. Sources of difficulty of standardization might be production- or consumption-oriented in nature. For example, on the production side, one would expect services to be more difficult to standardize. Complexity in products (e.g., automobiles, PCs) might also serve to increase the difficulty of standardizing and to explain greater observed sensitivity to satisfaction in such industries. On the consumption side, disconfirmation should be lower in industries where consumers are more uncertain in evaluating quality in a particular category.

For example, Anderson (1992) finds that disconfirmation is found to be greater when ease of evaluating quality, frequency of usage, and difficulty of standardization are high. Also, under these conditions, satisfaction is found to be driven more by perceived quality and disconfirmation and less by expectations. Finally, satisfaction is found to increase with the category's importance, competitiveness, and degree of product differentiation.

Although these findings are an important beginning, a comprehensive theoretical and empirical study of the effects of such industry characteristics might be an interesting possible direction for future research. Clearly, understanding whether differences in satisfaction across categories are structural in nature or attributable to firm effort will have important implications for policy decisions, as well as for the monitoring of product and employee performance. In order to understand whether industries (or firms) are performing well, we need to know what is possible. For example, given that other attributes of two categories are similar, satisfaction for a service that is difficult to standardize should not be compared with a service that is not difficult to standardize.

Differences Across Nations

Investigation of systematic variation in satisfaction across nations may also prove fruitful. For example, how does culture affect the level of satisfaction? A cultural trait that leads to greater criticism in evaluating quality might lead to lower satisfaction. This would have important implications for how firms might allocate resources in different parts of the global economy. In addition, future researchers may wish to look at the effects of other national characteristics such as economic organization, infrastructure, and orientation. It will be important to take such differences into account when comparing nations or aggregating macroeconomic satisfaction.

There are several difficulties to overcome in making cross-cultural comparisons. For example, such an approach must address the argument that satisfaction may be artificially high due to a culture's lack of knowledge of alternatives. Hence, comparisons across cultures may be difficult. In addition, it may be very difficult to obtain measures of such cultural characteristics.

Public Policy

As at the firm level, industry-level satisfaction measures provide a means of benchmarking performance over time. This requires not only measurement, but also an understanding of how industry differences might affect satisfaction as discussed earlier. Measures of industry-level satisfaction should encourage better quality and allow for public policy decisions to address industries that are not performing up to their potential.

Several general types of public policy decision rules have been suggested. To utilitarian economists, such as Bentham (1789, 1802), the objective is the greatest sum total of the happiness of all individuals in a society. This suggests that the objective of public policy should be to maximize the aggregate satisfaction of all individuals. However, economists of the Paretian school object to this straightforward criteria. Pareto (1896) attacks the direct aggregation of individual utilities because this implies trading off different individuals' welfare. Instead, he proposes what has come to be known as the Pareto Principle, namely that societal welfare is improved only when some persons are better off and no one is worse off. A Pareto Optimum is said to occur when there is no policy change that will move society in a Pareto direction (make at least one person better off while not making anyone else worse off). A satisfaction barometer would provide the measurement for whether more or less of a particular service would leave everyone at least as well off. Hence, a satisfaction barometer will help policy makers make Pareto decisions.

However, the Pareto Principle has been criticized as strongly favoring those with a high initial wealth position (Thurow, 1980). A weakening of Pareto's Principle is the Kaldor-Hicks Compensation Test, namely that a policy change is preferred if all individuals in a social system *could* be made better off. For example, if a policy change will benefit all but a few individuals, then a satisfaction barometer will enable direct estimation of the compensation due the group hurt by the change. However, like the Pareto Principle, Kaldor-Hicks Compensation strongly favors those with a high initial wealth position. For example, if taken to an extreme, the Pareto Principle would suggest that a ruling totalitarian government or aristocracy should not institute open elections. Ultimately, the choice of an aggregation method for social welfare would appear to be an ethical one (Little, 1950).

A third group of welfare economists, referred to as "contractarian," proposes a different approach. Contractarians recommend balancing basic liberties and rights versus social welfare and fairness. For example, an initial social contract, such as the Constitution of the United States, should provide for basic liberties and rights. All individual choices to maximize personal welfare must then be made subject to the social contract. In other words, citizens are free to choose the means of increasing their satisfaction as long as they do not violate the social contract. Under this system, each individual knows what is "good," and the role of social institutions is not to maximize the "good," but to allow individuals to pursue "good" without interference—given the limits of the social contract (Rawls, 1971). This would suggest that policy decisions, made on the basis of economic welfare as captured in a satisfaction barometer, should maximize aggregate satisfaction of the citizenry subject to the legal and social system in which all citizens participate. Further research into the role of macroeconomic satisfaction in public policy is needed. For example, can a change in policy be shown to have an effect on an appropriate satisfaction barometer? What is the value of that change in satisfaction to customers?

Subjective Well-Being

National satisfaction measures should lead to an improved standard of living. Such measures would provide product information and encourage quality competition. In a monopoly situation, satisfaction measurement would effectively "police" the goods and services being provided. In competitive situations, an objective satisfaction barometer will improve the substantive quality of the goods and services provided.

Moreover, as discussed above, public policy decisions could be designed to increase individuals' overall sense of subjective well-being. Although satisfaction is generally associated with economic life, satisfaction with other aspects of life can be measured as well. Hence, a satisfaction barometer should not only provide an accounting of the economic welfare of its citizens, but a means of controlling and improving overall satisfaction with "quality of life" as well.

Measurement

The central question in ascertaining macroeconomic satisfaction is how to aggregate microeconomic satisfaction. To obtain a measure at the national level, firms must be aggregated to the industry level, industries aggregated into sectors, and sectors to a national level. In an era when regional trading blocs are becoming more important, aggregating beyond the national level to the regional or trading bloc level will be essential. Finally, global measures of satisfaction might also be useful.

The problem is analogous in many respects to that of determining satisfaction for a multiproduct firm. A census of all firms in each of a nation's industries is unlikely to be feasible. Such a census at the trading bloc or even global level is even less likely. Perhaps the most direct approach is to select a sample of industries representative of each industrial sector and a sample of firms within each industry representative of a large proportion of end-user sales. Aggregation could be based on the dollar value of consumption that generates the measured levels of satisfaction. Hence, an industry leader with a high satisfaction level would have a relatively large weight in an industry. Similarly, a large industry may contribute more to sector indices. Aggregating from the sector to the national level and beyond would then be relatively straightforward. However, future researchers need to look at this issue much more closely.

Some Priorities for Future Research

This chapter has offered a broad overview of research problems in the area of customer satisfaction. Table 11.1 summarizes many of the important directions for future research that were discussed. In summary, we believe the following issues should be categorized as high priority:

Definition of Satisfaction:

> Is it transaction specific or brand specific?
> Is it distinct from quality?
> How can convergent and discriminant validity of the defined constructs be tested?

*Antecedents and Consequences of Satisfaction
at the Microeconomic Level:*

> What are the appropriate antecedents and their relations?
> Do expectations have a direct effect on satisfaction?
> Is there a halo effect for brand reputation?
> What is the impact of satisfaction on business performance?
> How does this vary across firms and categories?

Offense Versus Defense:

> How do marketing mix variables affect offensive and defensive strategy?
> What is the relative impact of offense and defense on business performance?

What are the relative costs of offense and defense?

What are the implications for resource allocation?

How does this vary across firms and categories?

Employee Compensation:

What influences the optimal mix of incentives for acquiring and retaining customers?

What is the relationship between firm productivity, employee satisfaction, customer satisfaction, and business performance?

Quality, Productivity, and Macroeconomic Satisfaction:

How do quality and productivity interact to produce macroeconomic satisfaction?

What is the relative impact of macroeconomic quality and productivity?

How does macroeconomic satisfaction relate to economic performance?

Industry and Cultural Differences in Satisfaction:

How can measures of category and cultural characteristics be obtained?

Can a latent class approach be useful in identifying groups?

How can "deflated" indices be constructed and aggregated?

Is a hedonic approach useful?

Public Policy and Macroeconomic Satisfaction:

What is the value of a change in public policy?

What decision rules are appropriate?

Quality of Life:

How can a value index be constructed to complement or replace the price index?

What is the overall impact of economic satisfaction on general quality of life?

References

Anderson, E. W. (1992). *Category differences in the impact of perceived quality, expectations, and disconfirmation on customer satisfaction.* Working paper, University of Michigan.

Anderson, E. W. (1993). Firm, industry, and national indices of customer satisfaction: Implications for services. In T. A. Swartz, S. W. Brown, & D. E. Bowen (Eds.), *Advances in services marketing management: Research and practice* (pp. 87-108). Greenwich, CT: JAI.

Anderson, E. W., & Fornell, C. (1991). *The impact of product performance on customer satisfaction: An investigation of industry differences.* Working paper, University of Michigan.

Anderson, E. W., Fornell, C., & Lehmann, D. (1992). *Perceived quality, customer satisfaction, market share, and profitability.* Working paper, University of Michigan.

Anderson, E. W., & Sullivan, M. (1993). The antecedents and consequences of customer satisfaction for firms. *Marketing Science, 12,* 125-143.

Andreasen, A. R. (1985). Consumer responses to dissatisfaction in loose monopolies. *Journal of Consumer Research, 12,* 135-141.

Bentham, J. (1789). *An introduction to the principles and morals of legislation.* London: T. Payne.

Bentham, J. (1802). *Principes de legislation et d'economie politique.* Paris: Guillaumin.

Boulding, W. (1990, Winter). Unobservable effects and business performance: Do fixed effects matter? *Marketing Science, 9*(1), 88-91.

Churchill, G. A., & Surprenant, C. (1982). An investigation into the determinants of customer satisfaction. *Journal of Marketing Research, 19,* 491-504.

Fornell, C. (1982). *A second generation of multivariate analysis.* New York: Praeger.

Fornell, C. (1992). A national customer satisfaction barometer: The swedish experience. *Journal of Marketing, 56,* 1-18.

Fornell, C., & Robinson, W. (1983). Industrial organization and consumer satisfaction/dissatisfaction. *Journal of Consumer Research, 9,* 403-412.

Fornell, C., & Wernerfelt, B. (1987). Defensive marketing strategy by customer complaint management: A theoretical analysis. *Journal of Marketing Research, 24,* 337-346.

Fornell, C., & Wernerfelt, B. (1988). A model for customer complaint management. *Marketing Science, 7,* 287-298.

Green, P. E., & Srinivasan, V. (1978). Conjoint analysis in consumer research: Issues and outlook. *Journal of Consumer Research, 5,* 103-123.

Green, P. E., & Srinivasan, V. (1990). Conjoint analysis in marketing research: New developments and directions. *Journal of Marketing, 54,* 3-19.

Green, P. E., & Tull, D. S. (1975). *Research for marketing decisions* (3rd ed.). Englewood Cliffs, NJ: Prentice-Hall.

Hauser, J. R., & Shugan, S. M. (1983). Defensive marketing strategies. *Marketing Science, 2,* 319-360.

Hicks, J. R. (1939). *Value and capital.* Oxford: Clarendon.

Hicks, J. R. (1943). The foundations of welfare economics. *Review of Economic Studies, 11,* 31-41.

Hicks, J.R. (1981). *Wealth and welfare.* Cambridge, MA: Harvard University Press.

Hirschman, A. O. (1970). *Exit, voice, and loyalty: Responses to decline in firms, organizations, and states.* Cambridge, MA: Harvard University Press.

Jacobson, R. (1990, Winter). Unobservable effects and business performance. *Marketing Science, 9*(1), 74-85.

Johnson, M. D., Anderson, E. W., & Fornell, C. (1992). *Micro- and macro-antecedents of customer satisfaction.* Working paper, University of Michigan.

Johnson, M. D., & Fornell, C. (1991). A framework for comparing customer satisfaction across individuals and product categories. *Journal of Economic Psychology, 12,* 267-286.

Juran, J. M. (1988). *Juran's quality control handbook* (4th ed.). New York: McGraw-Hill.

Little, I.M.D. (1950). *A critique of welfare economics.* Oxford, UK: Clarendon.

Marshall, A. (1891). *Principles of economics.* London: Macmillan.

Morrison, D. G. (1979). Purchase intentions and purchase behavior. *Journal of Marketing, 43,* 65-74.

Oliver, R. L. (1977). Effect of expectation and disconfirmation on postexposure product evaluations: An alternative Interpretation. *Journal of Applied Psychology, 62,* 480-486.

Oliver, R. L. (1980). A cognitive model of the antecedents and consequences of satisfaction decisions. *Journal of Marketing Research, 17,* 460-469.

Oliver, R. L. (1981). Measurement and evaluation of satisfaction processes in retail settings. *Journal of Retailing, 57,* 25-48.

Oliver, R. L. (1989). Processing of the satisfaction response in consumption: A suggested framework and research propositions. *Journal of Consumer Satisfaction, Dissatisfaction and Complaining Behavior, 2,* 1-16.

Oliver, R. L. (1993). A conceptual model of service quality and service satisfaction: Compatible goals, different concepts. In T. A. Swartz, D. E. Bowen, & S. W. Brown (Eds.), *Advances in services marketing and management: Research and practice,* (Vol. 2, pp. 65-85). Greenwich, CT: JAI.

Oliver, R. L., & Bearden, W. O. (1985). Disconfirmation processes and consumer evaluations in product usage. *Journal of Business Research, 13,* 235-246.

Oliver, R. L., & DeSarbo, W. S. (1988). Response determinants in satisfaction judgments. *Journal of Consumer Research, 14,* 495-507.

Oliver, R. L., & Swan, J. E. (1989). Consumer perceptions of interpersonal equity and satisfaction in transactions: A field survey approach. *Journal of Marketing, 53,* 21-35.

Parasuraman, A., Zeithaml, V. A., & Berry, L. L. (1985). SERVQUAL: A multiple-item scale for measuring consumer perceptions of service. *Journal of Retailing, 64,* 12-40.

Pareto, V. (1896). *Cours d'economie politique* (Vol. 2). Lausanne: G. Einaudi.

Pareto, V. (1906). *Manuel d'economie politique.* Paris: M. Girard.

Rawls, J. (1971). *A theory of justice.* Cambridge, MA: Harvard University Press.

Ricardo, D. (1817). *On the principles of political economy and taxation.* London: John Murray.

Samuelson, P. A. (1947). *Foundations of economic analysis.* Cambridge, MA: Harvard University Press.

Swan, J. E., & Trawick, I. F. (1981). Disconfirmation of expectations and satisfaction with a retail service. *Journal of Retailing, 57,* 49-67.

Thurow, L. C. (1980). *The zero-sum society: Distribution and the possibilities for economic change.* New York: Basic Books.

Westbrook, R. A., & Oliver, R. L. (1991). The dimensionality of consumption emotion patterns and consumer satisfaction. *Journal of Consumer Research, 18,* 84-91.

Yi, Y. (1991). A critical review of consumer satisfaction. In V. A. Zeithaml (Ed.), *Review of marketing 1990* (pp. 68-123). Chicago: American Marketing Association.

Author Index

Subject Index

About the Contributors

Mara B. Adelman (Ph.D., University of Washington) is Assistant Professor in the Department of Communication at Northwestern University where she teaches organizational communication and social support systems. Her research interests include "taking superficial relationships seriously"—the study of nonintimate relationships in sustaining social and community life. On a more intimate note, she has written extensively on the role of eroticism, play, and humor for safe-sex encounters and co-authored several papers with Aaron Ahuvia on social introduction services. She is co-author of *Communicating Social Support* (1987) and *Beyond Language: Cross-Cultural Communication* (1993) and has written in the areas of social support in community settings, business encounters, and cross-cultural adaptation. She recently produced a documentary film, *The Pilgrim Must Embark* (1991), on community life in a residential facility for persons with AIDS.

Aaron Ahuvia (Ph.D., Northwestern University) is Assistant Professor of Marketing in the Department of Marketing at the University of Michigan School of Business Administration. His research focuses on applying theories from interpersonal psychology to problems in marketing and consumer behavior. In addition to the current work on social support and services marketing, he has pursued two main areas of research. The first has looked at the effects of the increasing number of singles on services marketing. The second has applied theories of love to understanding people's love of products and consumption activities.

Eugene W. Anderson (Ph.D., University of Chicago) is Assistant Professor of Marketing at the University of Michigan School of Business Administration. He holds B.Sc. and M.B.A. degrees from the University of Illinois at Champaign-Urbana and a doctorate in marketing and statistics from the University of Chicago. His research has appeared in the *Journal of Consumer Research* and *Marketing Science.* His current research focuses on customer satisfaction and its implications for business performance, resource allocation, employee compensation, public policy, and national competitiveness.

Mary Jo Bitner (Ph.D., University of Washington) is Associate Professor of Marketing at Arizona State University, where she is actively involved in teaching and research on services marketing topics. Her research on customer satisfaction in service encounters and the management of service encounters has been published in the *Journal of Marketing, Journal of Retailing, Journal of Business Research,* and numerous books and conference proceedings. She has developed and taught courses on services marketing at both the undergraduate and M.B.A. levels and is a frequent presenter at executive education programs on service management. She served as the program director for the American Marketing Association and First Interstate Center for Services Marketing's annual Services Marketing Institute and Chair of the AMA 1993 Faculty Consortium on Services Marketing. She also serves on the Board of the International Service Quality Association.

Ruth N. Bolton (Ph.D., Carnegie-Mellon University) is a principal member of the technical staff in the Network Applications Department of GTE Laboratories. Her primary work at GTE involves the design and management of customer satisfaction programs. She has also worked on new service design and pricing issues. Her publications include articles in leading journals, including the *Journal of Consumer Research, Journal of Marketing, Journal of Marketing Research, Marketing Science, Management Science,* and *Marketing Letters.* She previously taught at the universities of Alberta and British Columbia and at Carnegie-Mellon University. She holds a doctorate in industrial administration from Carnegie-Mellon University.

Jungwhan Choi (Ph.D., Economics, University of Michigan) is presently a Ph.D. candidate in marketing at the University of Michigan and is developing a latent class double-hurdle model for his marketing dissertation, in which consumers are modeled to make two separate search decisions sequentially in a search process. His research interests lie in marketing decision models, choice models, new product (or service) development, quantitative models with qualitative or limited dependent variables, and econometric modeling of marketing issues such as dynamic or intertemporal choice behavior and consumer expectations under uncertainty.

John Deighton is Associate Professor of Marketing at the Graduate School of Business, University of Chicago. He studied marketing at the Wharton School and taught at Dartmouth College before moving to Chicago. His research is published in the *Journal of Marketing, Journal of Consumer Research, Organizational Behavior and Human Decision Processes, Sloan Management Review, Psychology and Marketing,* and in various books and conference proceedings. He teaches in Chicago's M.B.A. program in the areas of marketing management and services marketing, in the university's executive education programs in financial services marketing, and for service firms such as Citicorp, Sears, Roebuck & Co., Harris Bank, and BancOne.

Wayne S. DeSarbo (Ph.D., University of Pennsylvania) is the Sebastian S. Kresge Distinguished Professor of Marketing and Statistics at the Graduate School of Business of the University of Michigan in Ann Arbor. He received his B.S. degree in economics from the Wharton School of the University of Pennsylvania. He has M.A. degrees in sociology, administrative science/operations research, and marketing from Yale University and the University of Pennsylvania. He obtained his doctorate in marketing and statistics from the University of Pennsylvania and completed postdoctorate work in operations research and econometrics there. He has published more than 100 articles in such journals as the *Journal of Marketing Research, Psychometrika, Journal of Consumer Research, Journal of Mathematical Psychology, Marketing Science, Journal of Classification, Journal of Marketing, Management Science,* and *Decision Sciences.* His methodological interests lie in multidimensional scaling, classification, and multivariate statistics, especially as they pertain to substantive marketing problems in positioning, market structure, consumer choice, market segmentation, and competitive strategy. He was awarded the 1988 Raymond B. Cattell Award for his outstanding research contributions in mathematical psychology and nominated as president of the Psychometric Society. He was the chair of the Statistics in Marketing Section of the American Statistical Society. He is a member of AMA, ORSA/TIMS, Psychometric Society, ASA, RSS, Classification Society, INSNA, IMS, Econometric Society, ACR, DSI, and APA. He serves on the review boards of *Marketing Science,* the *Journal of Consumer Research, Marketing Letters,* the *Journal of Classification,* and the *Journal of Marketing Research.* He has been a consultant for such diverse firms as AMERITECH, AT&T, Ad Audit, Pfizer Drug, SENMED, Pacific Bell, Ethicon, General Motors, and Merck Pharmaceuticals.

James H. Drew (Ph.D., Iowa State University) is a principal member of technical staff in the Network Applications Department of GTE Laboratories. His current responsibilities include the technical design and analysis of GTE customer satisfaction surveys, other measurement instruments for telephone operations performance measurement, and the introduction of technical tools for total quality management in various GTE divisions. He holds a diploma in mathematical statistics from Cambridge University and a doctorate in statistics from Iowa State University. His publications include work in statistics, market science, and customer satisfaction.

Valerie S. Folkes (Ph.D., UCLA) is Associate Professor of Marketing at the School of Business of the University of Southern California. She received her doctorate in social psychology and a postdoctorate in marketing from the University of California, Los Angeles. She has published articles on customer satisfaction in a variety of journals, including the *Journal of Consumer Research* and the *Journal of Marketing.* She serves on the editorial board and the policy board of the *Journal of Consumer Research.* Her contributions have earned her the status of Fellow of the Consumer Psychology Division of the American Psychological Association and the American Psychological Society. She has also been elected treasurer of the Association for Consumer Research.

Claes Fornell (Ekon. Dr., University of Lund, Sweden) is the Donald C. Cook Professor of Business Administration and the Director of the Office for Customer Satisfaction Research at the University of Michigan. He has also been on the faculty of Northwestern University and Duke University. As a doctoral student, he was also a Fulbright fellow at the University of California, Berkeley. In 1987 he was a visiting professor at INSEAD, France, and at the Stockholm School of Economics, Sweden. He is one of the world's leading experts on customer satisfaction measurement and analysis. He has developed a system that makes it possible for a firm to identify those specific aspects of quality that have the largest impact on customer satisfaction as well as revenue. He has also designed an annual customer satisfaction index for Swedish industry that served as a prototype for the forthcoming U.S. National Quality Index (NQI) for which he is project director. He has been a consultant to several U.S. and European companies including General Motors, Ford, GTE, IBM, Stroh, Gould, Lorillard, Unilever (UK), Wehkamp (Holland), and PK Banken (Sweden). He has written more than 50 published articles and two books. He serves on the editorial board of the *Journal of Marketing Research, Marketing Letters, Marketing Science, Journal of Marketing,* and the *Journal of International Consumer Marketing.* He is also a member of the board of the Services Steering Group at Marketing Science Institute at Harvard.

Cathy Goodwin (Ph.D., University of California, Berkeley) is Associate Professor of Marketing at the University of Manitoba. She has studied role relationships in the service encounter, particularly with reference to satisfaction and complaining behavior. She has also published in the areas of consumption symbolism and consumer privacy. Her research has appeared in the *Journal of Public Policy and Marketing, Journal of Business Research, Journal of Consumer Psychology,* and the *Journal of Economic Psychology,* as well as numerous conference proceedings and presentations.

Donna L. Hoffman (Ph.D., University of North Carolina) is Associate Professor of Marketing at the Owen Graduate School of Management at Vanderbilt University. She received her doctorate from the L. L. Thurstone Psychometric Laboratory at the University of North Carolina at Chapel Hill. She has published in the *Journal of Marketing Research, Journal of Consumer Research, Multivariate Behavioral Research, Marketing Letters, Applied Psychological Measurement, American Statistician, Journal of Advertising Research,* and other journals and has written chapters on marketing and quality and various aspects of perceptual mapping techniques. She serves as frequent reviewer to the major marketing and psychometric journals and is a member of the editorial boards of *Marketing Science* and *Marketing Letters.* Her current research interests involve developing measurement models of service quality and investigating the relationships among perceived quality and customer satisfaction. She is the recipient of the 1991 William O'Dell Award for her 1986 *Journal of Marketing Research* article on correspondence analysis.

Morris B. Holbrook (Ph.D., Columbia University) is the W. T. Dillard Professor of Marketing in the Graduate School of Business at Columbia University. He graduated from Harvard College with a B.A. degree in English and received his M.B.A. and doctorate in marketing from Columbia University. Since 1975, he has taught courses at the Columbia Business School in such areas as marketing strategy, sales management, research methods, consumer behavior, and commercial communication in the culture of consumption. His research has covered a wide variety of topics in marketing and consumer behavior with a special focus on issues related to communication in general and to aesthetics, semiotics, art, and entertainment in particular. His hobbies include playing the piano, attending jazz and classical concerts, going to movies and the theater, and collecting musical recordings.

Amy R. Hubbert (M.S., Colorado State University) is a Ph.D. candidate at Arizona State University in the field of marketing. Her primary research interests include consumer satisfaction along with its antecedents and various services marketing topics.

Lenard Huff (M.B.A., Harvard University) is a Ph.D. candidate in marketing at the University of Michigan. He received a B.A. in economics from Brigham Young University. He has worked in the financial services, real estate, consulting, and consumer goods industries. His research interests lie primarily in perceived quality and customer satisfaction from both behavioral and managerial perspectives.

Richard L. Oliver (Ph.D., University of Wisconsin-Madison) is Professor of Marketing at Vanderbilt University's Owen Graduate School of Management where he teaches buyer behavior and service quality measurement and is a recent recipient of the Webb Award for Excellence in Teaching. His research interests include consumer and salesperson psychology with a special focus on customer satisfaction, service quality, and salesperson and sales manager behavior. He holds the position of Fellow of the American Psychological Association for his extensive writings on the topics of the psychology of the satisfaction response or "consumption processing," related cognitive processes such as equity/inequity, consumer affect and attitude theory, and the sales topics of motivation, negotiation, and sales control systems. His articles have appeared in the *Journal of Consumer Research, Journal of Marketing Research, Journal of Marketing, Journal of Retailing, Journal of Personal Selling & Sales*

Management, Journal of Consumer Satisfaction/Dissatisfaction & Complaining Behavior, Journal of Economic Psychology, Journal of Consumer Affairs, Journal of Applied Psychology, Psychometrika, and others. He has served on a number of editorial boards and has consulted for a variety of organizations on both consumer and sales projects. He previously taught at the Wharton School, University of Pennsylvania, and Washington University, St. Louis.

Marcelo M. Rolandelli (M.B.A., University of Kentucky) received a B.E./M.S. degree in industrial engineering from the Buenos Aires Institute of Technology and is a second year Ph.D. student in marketing at the University of Michigan. Upon finishing his engineering studies, he joined the IBM Corporation in Argentina where he was involved in planning of new products that were later exported to Canada, Japan, Australia, and Latin America. In 1988, he was transferred to IBM Corporation, Lexington (KY) Lab, where he worked as International Liaison in the development and announcement phases of new products and completed his M.B.A. His research interests include customer satisfaction and quantitative modeling of consumer choice and segmentation.

Roland T. Rust (Ph.D., University of North Carolina at Chapel Hill) is Professor and head of the marketing area at the Owen Graduate School of Management at Vanderbilt University, where he teaches one of the nation's few M.B.A. courses in customer service. As Director of the Owen School Center for Services Marketing, he works with leading businesses and nonprofit organizations to establish and evaluate their service quality and customer satisfaction programs. He has consulted, conducted training programs, and supervised research studies for such companies as AT&T, Procter & Gamble, Hampton Inns, Embassy Suites, Promus Companies, Humana, HCA, Northern Telecom, Marathon Oil, Consumers Union, Sierra Club, the Concord Group, and NationsBank. He is the author of numerous publications in marketing, advertising, and related fields, and serves on the editorial review boards of six journals, including the *Journal of Marketing Research, Marketing Science,* and the *Journal of Retailing.* He is the co-chair of the Frontiers in Services conference, cosponsored by the American Marketing Association and Vanderbilt Center for Services Marketing; was twice the co-chair of TIMS conferences on Service Quality, Customer Satisfaction, and Services Marketing; and served on the organizing committee for the First

Congress on Customer Satisfaction. He is a member of the Services Marketing Council of the American Marketing Association and the Services Steering Group of the Marketing Science Institute. His current research centers on the financial impact of quality improvement programs.

Steven M. Shugan (Ph.D., Northwestern University) is the Russ Berrie Eminent Scholar Chair and Professor of Marketing at the University of Florida. After receiving his doctorate in managerial economics and decision sciences in 1977, he taught at the University of Rochester for 2 years and at the University of Chicago for 13 years before joining the faculty at the University of Florida. He has been co-editor for the *Journal of Business* and has served on the editorial boards of the *Journal of Marketing Research, Management Science, Marketing Science, Journal of Direct Marketing,* and the *Journal of Consumer Research.* His published works include books, chapters, and many articles in the professional journals including the *Journal of Consumer Research, Journal of Marketing Research, Journal of Business, Management Science, Marketing Science,* and *Operations Research.* He has presented numerous papers in the United States and many other countries including France, Japan, Great Britain, Denmark, Switzerland, Canada, and Cyprus. He was the keynote speaker at the 1990 Albert Haring Symposium and has presented at several doctoral consortiums. He has chaired over 20 sessions at conferences and chaired the 1984 ORSA/TIMS Marketing Science Conference. His consulting includes work in services, durables, packaged goods, and nonprofit organizations. His research interests include models of competition, service policy, channels of distribution, and industrial marketing.

Jan-Benedict E. M. Steenkamp (Ph.D., Wageningen University, the Netherlands) is Associate Professor of Marketing at the Catholic University of Leuven, Belgium, and AGB Professor of Marketing Research at Wageningen University. His articles have appeared in the *Journal of Marketing Research, Journal of Consumer Research, International Journal of Research in Marketing, Journal of Retailing, Journal of Business Research,* and other journals. He has written three books, including a monograph on product quality. He is on the editorial boards of the *Journal of Consumer Research, International Journal of Research in Marketing,* and the *Journal of Business Research.* His current research interests include exploratory consumer behavior, quality, market segmentation, and international marketing.